University of Florida
1853

Chetham Society:

ESTABLISHED M.DCCC.XLIII., FOR THE PUBLICATION OF HISTORICAL AND LITERARY REMAINS CONNECTED WITH THE PALATINE COUNTIES OF

Lancaster and Chester.

COUNCIL FOR THE YEAR 1902-1903.

President.

ADOLPHUS W. WARD, LITT.D., LL.D., MASTER OF PETERHOUSE, CAMBRIDGE.

Vice-President.

LIEUT.-COLONEL HENRY FISHWICK, F.S.A.

Council.

HENRY BRIERLEY, ESQ., B.A.
HENRY THOMAS CROFTON, ESQ.
G. H. HANKINSON, ESQ.
JOHN HOWARD NODAL, ESQ.
FRANK RENAUD, ESQ., M.D., F.S.A.
WILLIAM O. ROPER, ESQ., F.S.A.
J. PAUL RYLANDS, ESQ., F.S.A.
REV. CANON J. H. STANNING, M.A.
PROF. JAMES TAIT, M.A.
PROF. T. NORTHCOTE TOLLER, M.A.

Treasurer.

J. JOSEPH JORDAN, ESQ., Warwick House, Heaton Norris, Stockport.

Honorary Secretary.

CHARLES W. SUTTON, Esq., M.A., Free Reference Library, King Street, Manchester.

FORMER OFFICERS OF THE SOCIETY.

Presidents.

EDWARD HOLME, M.D. (1843-47).
JAMES CROSSLEY, F.S.A. (1847-83).
RICHARD COPLEY CHRISTIE, M.A., LL.D. (1883-91).

Vice-Presidents.

Rev. RICHARD PARKINSON, D.D., Canon of Manchester (1843-58).
Rev. F. R. RAINES, M.A., F.S.A., Hon. Canon of Manchester (1858-78).
WILLIAM BEAMONT (1879-82).
R. C. CHRISTIE, M.A., LL.D. (1882).
Right Rev. WILLIAM STUBBS, D.D. Bishop successively of Chester and Oxford (1884-1901).

Vol. 25. Cardinal Allen's Defence of Sir William Stanley's Surrender of Deventer. Edited by THOMAS HEYWOOD.

Vols. 26, 27. The Autobiography of Henry Newcome, M.A. Edited by REV. RD. PARKINSON. 2 vols.

Vol. 28. The Jacobite Trials at Manchester in 1694. Edited by WILLIAM BEAMONT.

Vol. 29. The Stanley Papers, Part I. The Earls of Derby and the Verse Writers and Poets of the sixteenth and seventeenth centuries. By THOMAS HEYWOOD.

Vol. 30. Documents relating to the Priory of Penwortham, and other possessions in Lancashire of the Abbey of Evesham. Edited by W. A. HULTON.

Vol. 31. The Stanley Papers, Part II. The Derby Household Books, comprising an account of the Household Regulations and Expenses of Edward and Henry, third and fourth Earls of Derby; together with a Diary, containing the names of the guests who visited the latter Earl at his houses in Lancashire: by William Farrington, Esq., the Comptroller. Edited by the REV. F. R. RAINES.

Vols. 32, 34, 40, 44, The Private Journal and Literary Remains of John Byrom. Edited by REV. RICHARD PARKINSON. 4 vols.

Vols. 33, 51, 54. Lancashire and Cheshire Wills and Inventories from the Ecclesiastical Court, Chester. Edited by the REV. G. J. PICCOPE. 3 vols.

Vols. 35, 41, 43, 46. The House and Farm Accounts of the Shuttleworths of Gawthorpe Hall. Edited by JOHN HARLAND. 4 vols.

Vol. 37. Chetham Miscellanies, Vol. II. Edited by WILLIAM LANGTON: containing

- The Rights and Jurisdiction of the County Palatine of Chester, the Earls Palatine, the Chamberlain, and other Officers. Edited by JOSEPH BROOKS YATES.
- The Scottish Field (A Poem on the Battle of Flodden). Edited by JOHN ROBSON.
- Examynatyons towcheynge Cokeye More, Temp. Hen. VIII. in a dispute between the Lords of the Manors of Middleton and Radclyffe. Communicated by the REV. F. R. RAINES.
- A History of the Ancient Chapel of Denton, in Manchester Parish. By the REV. JOHN BOOKER.
- A Letter from John Bradshawe of Gray's Inn to Sir Peter Legh of Lyme. Edited by WILLIAM LANGTON.

Vol. 38. Bibliographical Notices of the Church Libraries of Turton and Gorton bequeathed by Humphrey Chetham. Edited by GILBERT J. FRENCH.

Vol. 39. The Farington Papers. Edited by MISS FFARINGTON.

Vol. 42. A History of the Ancient Chapels of Didsbury and Chorlton, in Manchester Parish, including Sketches of the Townships of Didsbury, Withington, Burnage, Heaton Norris, Reddish, Levenshulme, and Chorlton-cum-Hardy. By the REV. JOHN BOOKER.

Vol. 45. Miscellanies: being a selection from the Poems and Correspondence of the Rev. Thomas Wilson, B.D., of Clitheroe. With Memoirs of his Life. By the REV. CANON RAINES.

Vol. 47. A History of the Ancient Chapel of Birch, in Manchester Parish, including a Sketch of the Township of Rusholme. By the REV. JOHN BOOKER.

Vols. 48, 64. A Catalogue of the Collection of Tracts for and against Popery (published in or about the reign of James II.) in the Manchester Library founded by Humphrey Chetham. Edited by THOMAS JONES. 2 vols.

Vols. 49, 50. The Lancashire Lieutenancy under the Tudors and Stuarts. The Civil and Military Government of the County, as illustrated by a series of Royal and other Letters; Orders of the Privy Council, the Lord Lieutenant, and other Authorities, &c. Edited by JOHN HARLAND. 2 parts.

Vols. 52, 55, 71, 77, 91, 100, 101, 102, 106, 108, 111. Collectanea Anglo-Poetica: or, A Bibliographical and Descriptive Catalogue of a portion of a Collection of Early English Poetry, with occasional Extracts and Remarks Biographical and Critical. By the REV. THOMAS CORSER. 11 parts.

Vols. 53, 56, 58. Mamecestre: being Chapters from the early recorded History of the Barony, the Lordship or Manor, the Vill Borough or Town, of Manchester. Edited by JOHN HARLAND. 3 vols.

Vol. 57. Chetham Miscellanies. Vol. III. Edited by WILLIAM LANGTON. Containing:
On the South Lancashire Dialect, with Biographical Notices of John Collier, the author of *Tim Bobbin*. By THOS. HEYWOOD.
Rentale de Cokersand: being the Bursar's Rent Roll of the Abbey of Cokersand for the year 1501. Edited by the REV. F. R. RAINES.
The Names of all the Gentlemen of the best callinge w^thin the countye of Lancastre, whereof choyse ys to be made of a c'ten number to lend vnto her Ma^tye moneye vpon privie seals in Janvarye 1588. From a manuscript in the possession of the REV. F. R. RAINES.
Some Instructions given by William Booth Esquire to his stewards John Carington and William Rowcrofte, upon the purchase of Warrington by Sir George Booth Baronet and William Booth his son, A.D. MDCXVIII. Communicated by WILLIAM BEAMONT.
Letter from Sir John Seton, Manchester ye 25 M'ch, 1643. Edited by THOMAS HEYWOOD.
The Names of eight hundred inhabitants of Manchester who took the oath of allegiance to Charles II. in April, 1679. Communicated by JOHN HARLAND.
The Pole Booke of Manchester, May ye 22^d 1690. Edited by WILLIAM LANGTON.

Vols. 59, 60. A History of the Chantries within the County Palatine of Lancaster: being the Reports of the Royal Commissioners of Henry VIII., Edward VI., and Queen Mary. Edited by the REV. F. R. RAINES. 2 vols.

Vol. 61. I. Abbott's Journal. II. An Account of the Tryalls, &c., in Manchester in 1694. Edited by RT. REV. ALEXANDER GOSS.

Vol. 62. Discourse of the Warr in Lancashire. Edited by WILLIAM BEAMONT.

Vols. 63, 65. Court Leet Records of the Manor of Manchester in the Sixteenth Century. Edited by JOHN HARLAND. 2 vols.

Vols. 66, 67, 70. The Stanley Papers. Part III. Private Devotions and Miscellanies of James seventh earl of Derby, K.G., with a Prefatory Memoir and Appendix of Documents. Edited by REV. CANON RAINES. 3 vols.

Vols. 68, 72. Collectanea relating to Manchester and its Neigbourhood, at various periods. Edited by JOHN HARLAND. 2 vols.

Vols. 69, 73, 93, 94. The Admission Register of the Manchester School, with some Notices of the more distinguished Scholars. Edited by the REV. JEREMIAH FINCH SMITH. 3 vols., in 4 parts.

Vol. 74. Three Lancashire Documents of the Fourteenth and Fifteenth Centuries, namely: I. The Great De Lacy Inquisition, Feb. 16, 1311. II. Survey of 1320–1346. III. Custom Roll and Rental of the manor of Ashton-under-Lyne, 1421. Edited by JOHN HARLAND.

Vol. 75. Lancashire Funeral Certificates. Edited by THOMAS WILLIAM KING. With additions by the REV. F. R. RAINES.

Vol. 76. Observations and Instructions divine and Morall. In Verse. By Robert Heywood of Heywood, Lancashire. Edited by JAMES CROSSLEY.

Vols. 78, 79, 80. Tracts written in the Controversy respecting the Legitimacy of Amicia, daughter of Hugh Cyveliok, earl of Chester. A.D. 1673–1679. By sir Peter Leycester, bart., and sir Thomas Mainwaring, bart. Edited by WILLIAM BEAMONT. 3 parts.

Vol. 81. The Visitation of the County Palatine of Lancaster, made in the year 1567, by William Flower. Edited by the REV. F. R. RAINES.

Vol. 82. The Visitation of the County Palatine of Lancaster, made in the year 1613, by Richard St. George. Edited by the REV. F. R. RAINES.

Vol. 83. Chetham Miscellanies, vol. IV., containing:
Some Account of General Robert Venables, of Antrobus and Wincham, Cheshire; with an engraving from his Portrait at Wincham, together with the Autobiographical Memoranda or Diary of his Widow, Elizabeth Venables.
A Forme of Confession grounded vpon the Ancient Catholique and Apostolique Faith. By Lady Bridget Egerton. A.D. 1636.

A Kalender conteyning the Names of all such Gent. and others as upon her Maty's Pryvye Seales have paid there Money to the handes of Sir Hugh Cholmondley Knyghte Collect[r] of Her Hyghnes Loane with[in] the Countie of Chester, together wth the severall Somes and Daies of Receipt. A.D. 1597.

History of Warrington Friary. Edited by WILLIAM BEAMONT.

Vols. 84, 85, 88. The Visitation of the County Palatine of Lancaster, made in the year 1664–5, by Sir William Dugdale. Edited by REV. F. R. RAINES. 3 parts.

Vols. 86, 87. Annals of the Lords of Warrington for the first five centuries after the conquest. With historical notices of the place and neighbourhood. Edited by WILLIAM BEAMONT. 2 vols., 2 parts.

Vols. 89, 90. The Dr. Farmer Chetham MS., being a commonplace-book in the Chetham Library, temp. Elizabeth, James I. and Charles I., consisting of verse and prose, mostly hitherto unpublished. Edited by the REV. ALEXANDER B. GROSART. 2 parts.

Vol. 92. The History of the Parish of Kirkham. By HENRY FISHWICK.

Vols. 95, 99. Abstracts of Inquisitions post Mortem, made by Christopher Towneley and Roger Dodsworth. Extracted from Manuscripts at Towneley. Edited by WILLIAM LANGTON. 2 vols.

Vol. 96. Chetham Miscellanies. Vol. V. Edited by the REV. CANON RAINES.

A Description of the State, Civil and Ecclesiastical, of the County of Lancaster, about the year 1590, by some of the Clergy of the Diocese of Chester.

A Visitation of the Diocese of Chester, by John, Archbishop of York, held in the Chapter House of the Collegiate and Parish Church of Manchester, 1590, with the Archbishop's Correspondence with the Clergy.

Letters on the Claims of the College of Arms in Lancashire, in the time of James the First; by Leonard Smethley and Randle Holme, Deputy Heralds.

The Easter Rolls of Whalley in the years 1552 and 1553.

Vol. 97. Contributions towards a History of the Ancient Parish of Prestbury in Cheshire. By FRANK RENAUD.

Vols. 98, 110. The Visitation of Lancashire and a Part of Cheshire, A.D. 1533, by special commission of Thomas Benalt. Edited by WILLIAM LANGTON. 2 parts.

Vol. 103. Chetham Miscellanies. Vol. VI. Edited by the REV. CANON RAINES.

The Rent Roll of Sir John Towneley of Towneley, Knight, for Burnley, Ightenhill, &c., 1535-6.

The Autobiography of Mr. Langley of Prestwich.

A Close Catalogue of the Rectors of Prestwich, from 1316 to 1632.

Vols. 104, 105. The History of the Parish of Garstang. Edited by HENRY FISHWICK. 2 parts.

Vols. 107, 113. Inventories of Goods in the Churches and Chapels in Lancashire, taken in the year A.D. 1552. Edited by JOHN EGLINGTON BAILEY. 2 parts.

Vol. 109. Correspondence of Nathan Walworth and Peter Seddon of Outwood, and other Documents relating to the Building of Ringley Chapel. Edited by JOHN SAMUEL FLETCHER.

Vol. 112. Two Compoti of the Lancashire and Cheshire Manors of Henry de Lacy, Earl of Lincoln, A.D. 1294-6, 1304-5. Edited by the REV. P. A. LYONS. With an Introduction by JOHN EGLINGTON BAILEY.

General Index to vols. 1-114. 2 vols.

NEW SERIES.

Vols. 1, 2. The Vicars of Rochdale. By the late Rev. Canon Raines. Edited by SIR HENRY H. HOWORTH. 2 parts.

Vol. 3. Lancashire and Cheshire Wills and Inventories at Chester, with an Appendix of Abstracts of Wills now Lost or Destroyed. Transcribed by the late REV. G. J. PICCOPE. Edited by J. P. EARWAKER.

Vol. 4. The *Catechisme, or a Christian Doctrine necessary for Children and Ignorant people*, of Lawrence Vaux, 1574, sometime Warden of the Collegiate Church, Manchester. Edited by T. G. LAW.

Vols. 5, 6. The Rectors of Manchester, and the Wardens of the Collegiate Church of that Town. By the late Rev. F. R. RAINES. Edited by J. E. BAILEY. 2 parts.

Vol. 7. The Old Church and School Libraries of Lancashire. With Bibliographical and other Illustrations. By RICHARD COPLEY CHRISTIE.

Vol. 8. The History of the Parish of Poulton-le-Fylde. By HENRY FISHWICK.

Vols. 9, 11, 14. The Coucher Book of Furness Abbey. Edited by the Rev. J. C. ATKINSON. 3 parts.

Vol. 10. The History of the Parish of Bispham. By HENRY FISHWICK.

Vol. 12. The Crosby Records. Edited by the REV. T. E. GIBSON and the late Bishop Goss.

Vol. 13. A Bibliography of the Works Written and Edited by Dr. Worthington. By R. C. CHRISTIE.

Vols. 15, 16, 17, 18. The History of the Church and Manor of Wigan. By the Hon. and REV. CANON BRIDGEMAN. 4 parts.

Vol. 19. Correspondence of Edward, Third Earl of Derby, during the years 24 to 31 Henry VIII. Edited by T. NORTHCOTE TOLLER.

Vols. 20, 22, 24. The Minutes of the Manchester Presbyterian Classis, 1646–1660. Edited by DR. WM A. SHAW. 3 parts.

Vols. 21, 23. Lives of the Fellows of the College of Manchester. By the late F. R. Raines. Edited by FRANK RENAUD. 2 parts.

Vol 25. The History of the Parish of St. Michaels-on-Wyre. By HENRY FISHWICK.

Vols. 26, 31. Materials for the History of the Church of Lancaster. Edited by W. O. ROPER. Parts 1 and 2.

Vol. 27. Notes on the Churches of Lancashire. By the late Sir Stephen Glynne. Edited by Rev. CANON ATKINSON.

Vol. 28. Lancashire and Cheshire Wills and Inventories at Chester, 1572 to 1696; with an Appendix of Lancashire and Cheshire Wills and Inventories proved at York or Richmond, 1542 to 1649. Edited by J. P. EARWAKER.

Vols. 29, 30, 34, 35. The Poems of John Byrom. Edited by DR. A. W. WARD. 4 parts.

Vol. 32. Notes on the Churches of Cheshire. By the late Sir Stephen Glynne. Edited by REV. CANON ATKINSON.

Vol. 33. The Note Book of the Rev. Thomas Jolly, with Extracts from the Church Book of Altham and Wymondhouses. Edited by HENRY FISHWICK.

Vols. 36, 41. The Minutes of the Bury Presbyterian Classis, 1647–1657. Edited by DR. WM. A. SHAW. 2 parts.

Vol. 37. Lancashire and Cheshire Wills and Inventories. Edited by J. PAUL RYLANDS.

Vols. 38, 39, 40, 43. The Chartulary of Cockersand Abbey. Transcribed and Edited by WILLIAM FARRER. Vol. I., 2 parts. Vol. II., 2 parts.

Vols. 42, 45. A History of the Ancient Chapel of Stretford, in Manchester Parish. By H. T. CROFTON Vols. I. and II.

Vol. 44. Act Book of the Ecclesiastical Court of Whalley. Edited by MISS ALICE M. COOKE, M.A.

Vols. 46, 48. The Portmote or Court Leet Records of Salford, 1597–1669. Edited by J. G. DE T. MANDLEY. 2 vols.

Vol. 47. Chetham Miscellanies. New Series, Vol. I. Containing:

Inventories of Goods in the Churches and Chapels of Lancashire, 1552. Part III.—Amounderness and Lonsdale Hundreds. Edited by LT.-COL. FISHWICK.

An Exhortation for Contributions to Maintain Preachers in Lancashire (*Circa* 1641) by George Walker, B.D. Edited by CHARLES W. SUTTON.

The Wonderful Child. Tracts Issued in 1679 Relating to Charles Bennett, of Manchester. Edited by WILLIAM E. A. AXON.

Mosley Family. Memoranda of Oswald and Nicholas Mosley of Ancoats, with a Genealogical Introduction. Edited by ERNEST AXON.

Vols. 49, 50. The Life of Humphrey Chetham. By F. R. RAINES and CHARLES W. SUTTON. 2 vols.

REMAINS

Historical and Literary

CONNECTED WITH THE PALATINE COUNTIES OF

Lancaster and Chester.

VOLUME 50.—NEW SERIES.

MANCHESTER:

Printed for the Chetham Society.

1903.

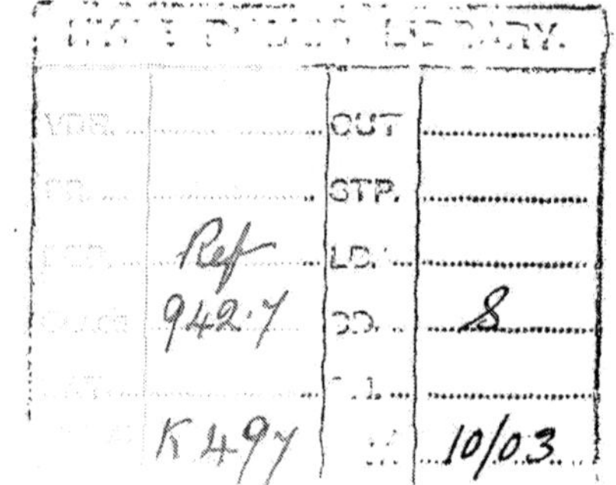

The Chetham Society.

LIFE OF

HUMPHREY CHETHAM

FOUNDER OF THE CHETHAM HOSPITAL AND LIBRARY,
MANCHESTER.

BY THE LATE

FRANCIS ROBERT RAINES, M.A., F.S.A.

VICAR OF MILNROW, AND HON. CANON OF THE MANCHESTER CATHEDRAL,

AND

CHARLES W. SUTTON, M.A.

HON. SECRETARY OF THE CHETHAM SOCIETY.

WITH A GENEALOGY OF THE CHETHAM FAMILY

BY ERNEST AXON.

VOL II.

PRINTED FOR THE CHETHAM SOCIETY.
1903.

JAMES STEWART
Printer.
36, South King St
MANCHESTER

the executors. *(b)* One hundred pounds to prepare a fit place for the library. The hospital and library were to be managed by twenty-four feoffees, who were to be incorporated. The surplus of his estate to go to the augmentation of the institution.

3.—CHURCH LIBRARIES. Two hundred pounds to be laid out in godly English books to be fixed in the parish churches of Manchester and Bolton, and the chapels of Turton, Walmsley, and Gorton. The books to be chosen by Richard Johnson, John Tilsley, and Richard Hollinworth.

One of the first cares of the executors in carrying out their trust would be to endeavour to acquire "the great house, with the buildings, out-houses, courts, yards, gardens, and appurtenances, called the College or the College House," for the purposes of the hospital and library.

On the 6th April, 1653, Major John Wigan, who before taking a commission in the Parliamentary Army had been curate of Gorton and of Birch, and Captain Jeffrey Ellatson, or Ellison, petitioned the Commissioners for compounding delinquents' estates, that they might have the farming of the College at Manchester, which formed parcel of the sequestered estate of the late Earl of Derby, and part of the jointure of the Countess Dowager. A month later a report was received from E. Aspinwall and Ro. Murray, Commissioners, embodying the following survey of the College: "One large building called the Colledge in Manchester, consisting of many rooms, with two barnes, one gatehouse very much decayed, one parcel of ground formerly an orchard, and one garden, now in the possession of Joseph Werden, gent., who pays for the same to the Commonwealth ten pounds yearly. There is likewise one other roome in the said Colledge reserved and now made use of for publique meetings of Christian conscientious people. All which wee conceive to be worth to bee lett for seaven yeares the cleare yearly rent of ten pounds."[1] The petitioners obtained the grant of a seven years' lease on 24th May, 1653.

On the 26th October, 1653, the Countess of Derby was allowed to compound for her estates, including the College at Manchester, on payment of a fine of £7,200.[2] The lease already granted to Messrs Wigan and Ellison was, however, not touched by this composition, as the executors had to come to terms with the lessees, as well as with the house of Stanley, before they could obtain possession of the College.

The feoffees at their first meeting on 6th December, 1653, agreed "that the Colledg house in Manchester should be bought, if it may be compassed uppon reasonable rate, and that a sure and fyrme estate may be made and confyrmed by the ffeoffees for the use of the hospitall and library for ever, and the executors at that tyme were desyred to endeav^r the accomplishment theroff wth all speed." At the next meeting, on the 3rd January, 1653-4, it was resolved that £350 should "be offered for the Colledg house to Mr. Wiggan and Mr. Ellison or to whom they should apoynt on their behalf."

On the 24th January the executors and feoffees offered to Mr. Holbrook and Mr. Gathorne, acting for the lessees, £400 for the College and its appurtenances, but the offer was refused. Thereupon it was determined at the "first general meeting" of the feoffees on 27th May, 1654, to seek for other property within three months. This proceeding had the effect of bringing the lessees to accept the offer of £400, and negotiations were afterwards completed for the purchase of "the great barne and Rosthorne's house, the workhouse, and the house of correction." This

[1] *Royalist Composition Papers*, vol. ii. pp. 173-4, Record Society. See also Mr. J. E. Bailey's paper in *Trans. of Library Association*, 1879, p. 114. Mr. Werden sub-let the present refectory of the College to the Presbyterians for their monthly meetings, and a large barn in the yard was used for the meetings of an Independent Church, the first of the kind in Manchester, the founder and teacher of that Church being John Wigan, the reverend major, who was a party in obtaining the above lease.

[2] *Royalist Composition Papers*, Record Society.

latter property was sold again a few months later, the purchasers being the justices, who required it for prison and other purposes.

Moneys disbursed about ye Colledge business.

June 22, 1653[-4].	Spent of Mr. Lightbowne Counsell Mr. Minshall, Anthony Cocke and myselfe in goeing to Latham to agree wt. ye Earle of Darby about ye Colledge - - - - - - -	00	15	10
June ye 4, 1654.	Spent at Mr. Halliwels at a Meeting of ye ffeoffes to veiwe ye Colledge -	00	02	11
July 17, 1654.	Pd post for Carriage of ye writings to London concerning ye Colledge -	00	05	09
July 25, 1654.	Pd Nathan Leech which hee paid post for bringing downe ye writings concerning ye Colledge - - -	00	09	03
	Spent at opening of ye writings - -	00	01	06
	Pd A messenger for to goe to Capt. Ellinson, Mr. Rigbie, 2s paid Mr. Rigbie acknowledgmt of ye ffine, Mr. Holbrooke 2s 6d, a Quart of wine 12d - - - - - -	00	05	06
August ye 8, 1654.	Spent uppon Mr. Jam. Holland, Mr. Robert Ashton and my selfe in going to Latham to take an Acknowledgmt of ye ffine from ye Earle and Countesse of Darby - - - - -	00	13	04
	Given Mr. Ashton for his paines -	00	13	04
	Given to ye Earle of Darby's Stuart for ye dispatch - - - - - -	00	05	00
	Pd my Lord of Darby for his consent	30	00	00
	Pd George Browning to goe to my Cosen Holland and another errand	00	00	06
	Pd ffranches Clayton for 13 loades of lime - - - - - - -	01	01	08
	Pd ffor A tubb to measure Lime wt -	00	01	04
	ffor a Box to putt writings in - -	00	00	02

Octob. 3, 1654.	Pd John Barne for 12 loades of Slate - - - - - - -	04	14	00
Octob. 13, 1654.	Pd Mr. Jam. Lightbowne towards ye repe of ye Colledge - - -	20	00	00
	ffor a letter by post - - - -	00	00	06
Novemb. 6, 1655.	Pd John Smith for 2 years cheese rent for ye Colledge - - - - -	00	07	06
April 19, 1656.	Pd Mr. James Lightbowne towards ye repaire of ye Colledge - - -	20	00	00
May ye 3 1656.	Pd Mr. Dutton towards ye repe - -	20	00	00
Novemb. 1653.	Spent at Mr. Greenes at ye meeting of ye ffeoffees - - - - -	01	01	06
Decemb. 1653.	More at Mr. Greenes - - -	01	12	00
	Spent at Bolton for ye Chusing of poore boyes for ye Hospital - -	00	02	06
	Pd Mr. Wiggan for ye Purchas - -	400	00	00
		590	08	02[1]

It is seen that Mr. Wigan got £400 for his bargain, and that the Earl of Derby was contented with £30 for his "consent." The amount is not stated in the Indenture between Charles, Earl of Derby, one part, and George Chetham of Clayton, and Edward Chetham of Chetham, the other, dated 2nd August, 1654, which witnessed that—

> "In consideration of a certain competent and valuable sume of good and lawfull money of England unto him by the said George Chetham and Edward Chetham already paid whereof and wherewith hee doth acknowledge himself to bee fully satisfied. And thereof and of every parte and parcell thereof doth cleerly acquitt, &c., the said George Chetham and Edward Chetham, &c., hath granted, alienated, &c., all that capitall messuage or mansion house with the appurtenances called the Colledge or the Colledge house, situate standing and being in Manchester . . . together with the scite and soyle thereof, all and singular howses, outhowses, edificies, buildings, barnes, stables, gardens, orchard, yard, backsides, courts,

[1] Allen's Papers, Chetham Library, No. 299.

court-yards, curtilages, waies, passages, lights, easements, streams, waters, water courses, woods, underwoods, tymber trees and other trees, comons, comon of pasture and turbary, liberties, priviledges, advantages and appurtencees whatsoever to the said capitall messuage belonginge, &c. . . . one buildinge standinge by itselfe and standinge towards the church yard att the upper end of one streete or place in Manchester called the Hunts Bank."

At the Restoration when the property reverted to the heirs of the Earl of Derby, it became necessary to take further steps for securing the property to the trust. A lease was obtained on 20th November, 1660, from Charlotte, Countess Dowager of Derby, the Indenture tripartite, bearing the names of Raphe Poole of Manchester, woollen draper, and John Chorlton of Manchester, apothecarie, on the second part, and of George Chetham of Turton, and Edward Chetham of Chetham on the third part, and showing that "in consideration of the sum of three score and ten pounds paid to the Countess . . . she grants a lease of the Colledge House and appurtenances . . . for and during the term and time of four-score and nineteen years from thenceforth next ensuing . . yielding and paying yearly the rent of one pepper corn."[1]

Six years later the Countess put in another claim, as appears by the following letter, which is preserved in the *Chetham MSS.*, vol. ii. p. 203.

London the 18th Sept., 1666.

Gentlemen,

I have by the laste poste receaved a letter from you occationed by some discourse which my servant Henry Ashton had with you concerning the Colledge at Manchester. I believe many of you know it to be part of my jointure, & most of you cannot be ignorant how it was taken from me without giving me the least satisfaction for the same, therefore I hope you will not take it amisse if I doe

[1] Allen's Papers, Bundle J. A part of the garden was excepted in the grant of the whole College by the Earl of Derby (Feoffees' Minutes, 27 March, 1665). A lease of this was granted and has been renewed from time to time, the rent being almost nominal.

at present desire some consideration for it; Indeed, my losses & sufferings have been such that I had neede to make what I can of that small remnant of estate which it hath pleased God to leave me, & to that purpose had given directions to Henry Ashton to looke into that businesse; but as soone as I understood you to be the feoffies in trust, I order'd him to stay all proceedings at law, because I know you to be persons of Honor & Conscience: & to the end there may be no molestation nor misunderstanding betwixt us at soe great a distance, I have desired Mr. Holt of Castleton, Mr. Richard Penington & Mr. Moseley of the Anckotes to treate with you about the businesse of the Colledge, & what they or two of them and you conclude together I shall approve of, & endeavor in what else may lye in my power to shew myself,

Gentlemen,

Your affec[te] freind to serve you,

ffor George Chetham & Ch. Derby.
Richard Holland Esq[rs] & the
ffeoffees of y[e] Colledge Howse in Manchester Theise.

Whatton states that a fresh conveyance to the feoffees was executed on 18th March, 1666[–7].[1]

The following valuation of the College buildings is unfortunately without date, but it would probably be made at the time of the purchase in 1654. The original is in the Chetham Hospital Muniments, No. 765–3.

A Survey taken by us whose names are underwritten being Masons, Carpenters and Joyners, being men that have been experienced in such work, of the Colledge house at Manchester and the outhousinge thereunto belonginge.

The outhousinge—

The Haye Barne we esteem to be worth as it nowe stands the sume of - - - -	167	00	00
The Corne Barne we value to be worth with the comon stable adioyninge - - - -	541	04	00

[1] Whatton, *History of Chetham Hosp.*, p. 178.

The Inner housinge—

The Gate house upon the East side - -	143	04	00
The buildinge being all of stone betweene the Stable and the Hall doore, eastward from ye Hall - - - - - - -	641	04	00
The outside from the Hall doore to the water being stone worke - - - - - -	1546	04	00
The roofes for these twoe buildings wth slate ffloores, p'tition walls, wainscoat and glasse	1510	00	00
The Gate house Westward - - - - -	279	12	00
The Washe house - - - - - -	118	16	00
The Garden Wall - - - - - -	220	00	00
The Slaughter house - - - - - -	013	06	08
The side Ile after the wall between the Stable and the Hall - - - - - - -	010	00	00
Three Seller ffloores - - - - - -	020	00	00
The Land whereuppon the housinge Stands with the Court and Gardens - - - -	100	00	00
Summa Totalis - -	5310	10	08
We esteem this in our Judgments to bee a true value of the house and Lands as it now stands.			
But if the housinge bee removed and pulled downe wee esteem that it will loose in the stone worke - . - . - - - -	960	00	00
Which said sum̃e subducted out of the whole there will remaine - - - - - -	4350	10	08

ffrancis F Crompton his m'ke. Richard Barlowe his N m'ke.

Arthur Crompton. John < Taylor his m'ke.

Richard Martinscrofte.

The late Mr. J. E. Bailey contributed to the *Academy*, August 14, 1886, a notice of a manuscript account in the Chetham Library, containing details of the expenses incurred in turning the College buildings into a receptacle for books and into a hospital for the education of boys. Mr. Bailey says:—

> The particulars given belong to the years 1656–8, and they exhibit in considerable detail (affording information of importance in reference to the local tradesmen and the price of materials) all the articles necessary in fitting up a library. The books in the libraries set up in the churches by the literary benefactions of Mr. Chetham were all chained, the chains being fastened to desks or fixed to the pillars or other convenient places in the buildings, charges being entered (at the rate of 8*d.* for every £1 worth of books) for the expense incurred. The Rev. Henry Newcome, minister of Manchester, says, under date of March 11, 1661–2, that he "did after dinner take order about ye chaininge of ye rest of ye bookes for ye English [*i.e.*. the Church] library, and studdyed awhile in y^e^ [great] library on 1 Cor. x. 2." It had not hitherto been known that the books in the great, or Chetham, library were likewise chained.[1] All traces of this ancient arrangement there are now lost. The expenses for fixing the chains are all recorded in the MS. under notice; and the principal person who had in hand the details of the chaining and the arrangement of the books was a clever joiner, horologist, land-surveyor, and mathematician, named Richard Martinscroft, of Manchester, who is mentioned by Newcome so late as October 30, 1661, as then working in the library; as also on December 10 following, when in the afternoon he was "with Old Martinscroft."
>
> The Rev. Adam Martindale still later, when teaching mathematics in Manchester, describes Martinscroft as being always civil and communicative, though a papist, and as having more true skill than the other teachers in the town—"old soakers with their Record's *Arithmetick*." (*Life*, page 187.)
>
> Omitting the payments, in these lengthy accounts, to the bricklayers, carpenters, joiners, labourers, and others, we may enumerate

[1] It is possible, however, that Mr. Bailey may have made a mistake in concluding that the books in the "great" library were chained. The work of preparing the "church" libraries was all done under the direction of the feoffees at the College, and Richard Martinscroft was apparently employed in his capacity as wood and metal worker on both the "great" and "church" libraries, yet did not distinguish between them in his accounts.

CHETHAM LIBRARY.

Photo by W. Ellis, 1903. GATEWAY TO CHETHAM HOSPITAL

some entries in point. The brass for clasps for books first comes into notice, 5lbs. being bought for 6*s.* 9*d.* Then follow entries for locks and keys (2*s.* 6*d.* each) and plates. Four locks for the library and a hammer for the library cost 10*s.* 10*d.* For this door no less than 17½lbs. of great nails were provided; and there is also a charge for a pair of bands for the door in the lower end of the library. Iron rods were next bought for the chaining of the books, costing 4*d.* per lb., and no less than 160 lbs. were bought. Iron pins are also mentioned, and are called *stubles* [? staples], one of which cost 8*d.* Chains are next purchased, 40 doz., costing 4*s.* per doz. Of clasps 32 doz. were bought at 2½*d.* per dozen; and 44 doz. more at the higher rate of 5½*d.* One pound and a quarter of brass at 1*s.* per lb. was provided to be made into 9 doz. clasps for the use of the library; and then are other entries for brass for the same purpose. Clasps, made in Wigan (then famous for its armorers' shops), cost 4*s.* for five dozen. Other entries are for sockets costing 4*s.* per dozen; and nails to fix the books in the library cost 3*s.* 3*d.* There is frequent mention of "Mapps" (mops) for cleaning the library floor. A kind of capp-paper for covering mats (proper) cost 4*d.*

The payments to Martinscroft apart from his other labour as a joiner, occur towards the end of the accounts, and are mostly for "cheaninge" books and for clasping them. It is noticeable that only one of the Manchester booksellers is mentioned in the accounts, viz., Raphe Shelmerdyne, who is paid 2*s.* 6*d.* on April 8, 1658, "for covering ye Great Byble in ye Hall." Martinscroft also set up in the college yard the great dial, an indication that the trees in the college garden and in the churchyard obstructed the view of the old church clock.

Robert Browne, the son of old Robert Browne of the Ancoats, was about this time one of the Fellows of Manchester College, and he became first deputy-librarian of the library. A chamber was provided for him in the college; and there are numerous payments in the accounts for making the room as comfortable as possible for a bookish man. Entries occur for "trimming" the chamber and for the "painting-stuff" in it. A fire-iron weighing 21lbs. was placed therein, and a charge made for a lock and key for his chamber door. "A pair of bands to be used for Mr. Browne's chamber" cost 4*d.*; and "an hobb" was set in the same place. "Four hooks and stubles for the book-frame in Mr. Browne's chamber" cost 4*d.* After all this trouble Mr. Browne, who had no love for his position there, was discharged in 1658. He got an underhand presentation to Salford Chapel, under a promise to resign when asked; but he would not resign. He ultimately settled as minister of Hoole, near Preston, and "carried vainly and poorly." In 1662 he became chaplain of Manchester, and afterwards curate of Salford. Newcome was confident that a sermon which he heard him preach at the old church, October 5, 1662, was stolen. (*Diary*, page 129.)

On the 5th August, 1656, the conversion of the College to its new uses having been completed, "the Hospitall boyes were removed from theire severall private quarters where they had been tabled, into the hospital and lodged there."[1] On the same day a dedication meeting was held, when Richard Hollinworth delivered a speech, the following outline of which has been preserved in the Feoffees' Minute Book.

Thursday the 5th day of Augt. 1656.

A meeting for the dedication of the hospitall, where many of the ffœffees and other p'sons were assembled in the hall of the said hospitall, Mr. Richard Hollinworth, one of the ffœffees (and two other ministers assisting in prayer and praising of God), did first breifely shew the lawfulnes and fittnesse of dedication of houses, especially of publicke houses, from the 20th of Deuteronomie, and 5th verse ["and the officers shall speak unto the people, saying What man is there that hath built a new house, and hath not dedicated it?"], and the 30th Psalm, and 1st verse [the Psalm *Exaltabo te*, sung at the dedication of the house of David], and the manner of such dedication. And afterwards in a large speech shewed that the house had formerly bin the Haule or Manor house of the Grelles or Gredleyes, Lords of Manchester, and was then called Barons Court or Barons Yerde. And afterward it was built colledg-

[1] Feoffees' Minute Book.

wise for the cohabitation of the warden and ffellows of the Collegiate Church of Manchester, and called the College, and about one hundred years agoe was alienated to the Earle of Derbie, and was accounted the Earle of Derbies house in Manchester, whence hee tooke occasion to complain of the late sale of the Lands of the appropriated Rectory in Manchester, wch hee affirmed was most vnjust and Illegall. Hee shewed alsoe that from hence forth the saide house could fytly and justly be named by noe other name than by the name of Mr. Cheethams Hospitall. Hee shewed further that God had not onely a general title and interest in the house as hee hath in all other houses, but that hee hath alsoe a speciall and peculiar title to it above other houses, by virtue of former grants, of Mr. Cheethams late donation, and [of] this present dedication; and hee shewed alsoe what an abhominable and accursed thing it would bee for any one to alienate or injure it. Hee gave several directions and Exhortations to the ffœffees, to the governour, to the hospitall boyes, and to the people present. And then haveing severall tymes sang certaine verses selected out of Davids Psalmes suitable to the occasion, hee (as the other ministers alsoe did) praysed God that gave vnto Mr. Cheetham both mind and meanes to doe this great good worke, prayed to God for his blessing on the Hospitall, the ffœffees, the Governour, and hospital Boyes, and soe dismissed the Assembly.[1]

The choice of the books for the public library, as for the Church libraries, was left to Richard Johnson, John Tilsley, and Richard Hollinworth, but the actual purchasing seems to have been deputed to Johnson, the first librarian of the Chetham Library, who was at this time Master of the Temple and lived in London. The early records of the library contains the titles and prices of many of the books. Some of them are noticed by Canon Raines in his life of Johnson in the *Fellows of the Collegiate Church of Manchester*, vol. i. page 125, and by Mr. Edward Edwards in his

[1] Quoted in an interesting article by Mr. J. E. Bailey in *Local Gleanings*, No. 754, July 5, 1878; also by Mr. J. E. Gregan in a paper on "Humfrey Chetham and his Foundations" in the *Journal of the British Archæological Association*, 1850, vol. vi. pp. 294–302.

Manchester Worthies, 1855, page 29. The following statement shows that it took about three years to spend the £1000 set aside for books :—

A particular Account of what Moneys is Lay^{d} out in Books for Manchester Library, together with ye Charges for Carriage, Globes, Mappes, etc.

Date	Item	£	s.	d.
1655, August 2.	The first Parcell sent - -	238	2	0
Septemb^{r} 20.	The Second parcell - - -	51	18	6
1656, May 21.	The third Parcell - - -	200	15	0
Oct. 18.	Fourth Parcell and Carriage payd in London - - - -	70	13	0
1657, May 7.	The fift Parcell - - - -	78	9	0
July 28.	The Sixt Parcell - - -	66	2	6
	For the Orientall Bible (not yet sent) - - - - - -	12	0	0
1658, Aprill 29.	The Seaventh Parcell sent - -	121	19	0
	English Bookes Bought of Mr. Playford - - - - -	15	10	0
	More English Bookes bought of Mr. Rothwell - - -	14	17	0
	Bought of R. L. in English Books - - - - - -	77	9	6
	More bought of Mr. Rothwell and sent wth ye 5th parcell -	13	4	0
	More in English Books and sent with the sixt Parcell - -	8	9	6
	A paire of Large Globes - -	16	0	0
	To Rich. Ell., Locksmith - -	1	12	6
	Chaines, and for sending to Bromingham - - - -	0	4	3
	Carriage of the first parcell to Manchester - - - -	9	9	0
	Carriage of the second parcell -	5	0	0
	Carriage of the third parcell -	8	13	10
	Two Large Mappes - - -	2	3	6
	Carriage of the fift Parcell - -	2	5	6

Carriage of the Sixt Parcell -	1	12	6
Carriage of the Seaventh Parcell	2	19	6
	1019	9	7[1]

In 1661 the feoffees began to think about obtaining the charter of incorporation, according to the will of the founder, and on 27th May in the following year they made the following note in their minutes, "Mr. Johnson and Mr. Edward Chetham at the desyre of the other ffeoffees doe intend to meet at London about this day six weeks to endeavour the incorporating of the Hospital and Librarie from his Majestie." The following instructions in the matter were drawn up about this time, but it was not until the 10th November, 1665, that the Charter of King Charles II. was granted.[2]

A Copy of ye Instructions for London about the Hospitall and Library.

1.—The Hospitall and Library to be Incorporated and called (if it may be obtained) The Hospitall of Humphrey Chetham Esqr deceased, in Manchester in ye Countie Pallatine of Lanc^r. Together wth the Library there Incorporated and founded by his Gracious Matie King Charles ye Second uppon the humble petition of his heir and surviving Executor and Trustee appointed by his wil. (Sutton Hospitall was thus The Hospitall of King James founded in &c. at the Humble petition and onely costs and Charges of Tho. Sutton Esqr.)

2.—And y^t ye ffeoffees or Trustees shall be called Masters or Governours thereof.

3.—That the Corporation may beare the Coat-Armour of the ffounder wth this motto subscribed Quod tuum tene. And wth this circumscription about the Scale

[1] Allen's Papers, N. 301, endorsed "An accompt of what is laid out by Mr. Johnson for books in ye Library at Manchester." The original invoices of the books are still in existence, in the custody of the Solicitors to the Hospital (Messrs. Taylor, Kirkman and Colley).

[2] Allen's Papers, N. 300. For the Charter see Appendix IV.

Sigillum Humfred Chetham Arm
(and if there be roome) in Manchester.

This may be graven at home.

4.—That after the Incorporation the present p'sons incorporated or the greater number of them Present (upon a months notice to such as live in England) may fill up the number of the foure and twenty according to the will and afterwards as any one or more dies then to chuse another in his or their roomes at a publique meeting upon an Easter Monday.

To have power to choose Governours Library-Keep[r] and other officers and servants and to give them an Oath for the due execution of their offices places and trusts whilst they continue therein.

5.—The Hospitall House to be called as in the deed of Purchase (w[ch] see) . . . The Capitall mesuage in Manchest[r] called the Colledge or Colledge house &c.

6.—The Heire of the founder w[ch] is James Chetham the sonne of George, and Edward the surviveing Executor of Humphrey and his nephew, and the heire males of the Body of the same George and Edward for ever to be visitours and to visit them every Easter Monday or every other Easter Monday or 3[d] or 4th as they please not exceeding once a yeare and also they to have votes wth the rest in the election of ffeoffees officers and poore boyes and buying of bookes and all other things concerning the premises. But not to be interested in the Estate because the estate comes from them til after they have purchased Lands and settled the same according to the wil and then they to be ffeoffees wth the rest to all intents and purposes if it may be or visitours at their owne Election.

It is feared they cannot be ffeoffees in regard the rents issue out of their Lands and it might extinguish the same.

And there to be noe other visitors for if nothing be said y[e] Governours shall themselves visit.

7.—To get the originall will out of the Prerougative Court of Canterbury (if you can) and leave a copy or else to inroll it in

Chancery or exemplifie it under the great seale and your Counsel shall advise for it is the life of our Interest.

8.—To have power to make orders and constitutions as is praied in the petition.

9.—To take up a copy of the will and such deedes as shall be requisite above.

10.—And to send up what monies may be thought fit.

11.—Mr. Johnson to be named the present Library Keeper in the foundation for his life (if heele accept of it) wth such yearely stipend and salarie as shall be thought fit by the ffeoffees.

James Chetham.

Edmund Hopwood.	Rich. Howorth.
Robert Hyde.	Jo. Lightbowne.
Nicholas Mosley.	Richard Johnson.
Will. Radley.	Ralph Worsley.
	Tho. Mynshull.
	Ralph Brooke.

To buy all the Statutes at Large old and new wel bound wth the Preambles thereof and an Index or table thereunto very usefull for a publick Library and in a few hands . . . in three or 4 volt.

The subsequent history of Humphrey Chetham's foundations having been treated at length by several writers it is not proposed to recount it here. It will suffice to refer to William Robert Whatton's *History of Chetham Hospital and Library,* 1833; Edward Edwards' *Manchester Worthies and their Foundations,* 1855; Richard Copley Christie's *Old Church and School Libraries of Lancashire,* 1885 (with regard to the Church Libraries); and Gilbert J. French's *Bibliograpical Notices of the Church Libraries at Turton and Gorton, bequeathed by Humphrey Chetham,* 1855. Reference should also be made to a paper on Chetham's Library, by John Eglington Bailey, in the *Transactions of the Library Association* for 1879 (London, 1880), and to a pamphlet by Albert Nicholson on *The Chetham Hospital and Library*, 1899. The architectural history of the Chetham Hospital is admirably given in Henry Taylor's *Old Halls in Lancashire and Cheshire*, 1884, pp. 31 *et seq.*

About twenty years after Humphrey Chetham's death the feoffees of the Hospital had it in their minds to mark his resting place by a suitable tomb, and to adorn the Hospital hall with his statue. In the minutes of their meeting of the 4th October, 1675, the following resolution is found :—

> "That there bee soe soone as conveniently it can be done a Tomb erected over and uppon the place where now Humfrey Chetham Esqr lyeth interred in his Chappell in Manchester Church coverred wth a marble stone wth an Inscription thereuppon of his pious guift And also a statue of his body carved as neare as may bee to his lykenes And the same to be fixed within the Hospitall Hall in Manchester in the most convenient place therein as shall by the said Governors be appointed, And that Mr. Henry Dickenson and Mr. John Sandiforth see to the effecting hereoff."

This was followed on the 27th March, 1676, by the additional minute :—

> "That whereas a statue was formerly agreed to be erected in the Hospitall for Humfrey Chetham Esqre deceased, it was agreed that the said statue should be cut in white marble of six foot in height with a pedestall and suiteable appurtenances wch is refferd to the care of the twoe form^r gentlemen, and that Mr. Richard Fox and Mr. Samuell Harmer be joined to them to assist and promote the same with all convenient speed."

For some reason with which we are unacquainted these resolutions were not carried into effect, and nearly two centuries were allowed to pass before any monument to the founder was erected. No tomb has even yet been placed over his mortal remains.

In the year 1853, exactly two hundred years after Chetham's death, Mr. George Pilkington, formerly an inmate of Chetham's Hospital, was moved by his gratitude to the founder to erect a

MEMORIAL TO HUMPHREY CHETHAM IN THE MANCHESTER CATHEDRAL.

beautiful marble monument in Manchester Cathedral. The sculptor of the statue was Mr. William Theed. Chetham is seen seated and in a contemplative posture, and at his feet, resting on the pedestal, is a College boy with open book. The inscription on the monument is as follows:—

> Humfredo Chetham, Hospitii et Bibliothecæ Fundatori D.D. Gratus Alumnus MDCCCLIII. "He that followeth after Righteousness and Mercy findeth Life, Righteousness and Honour."
>
> Prov. xxi. 21.

Upon the book held open by the College boy is the following:

Psalm cxii. verse 9.

He hath dispersed abroad, and given to the poor	and his righteousness remaineth for ever.

The cost of this monument was about £1000.[1] Mr. Pilkington also placed in the Cathedral a stained glass window dedicated to the memory of Humphrey Chetham.

Humphrey Chetham naturally finds his place among the Manchester Worthies whose statues are fixed on the Albert Square front of the Manchester Town Hall, which was opened in 1877. These admirable figures were executed under the direction of the architect, Mr. Alfred Waterhouse, by Messrs. Farmer and Brindley, 43, Westminster Bridge Road, London, the sculptor being Monsieur Guilleman.

In February, 1886, a pictorial memorial of Chetham was placed in the large room of the Manchester Town Hall. This is

[1] A photograph of the statue is given in R. W. Procter's *Memorials of Manchester Streets*, 1880, and a wood engraving appeared in the *Illustrated London News*, November 26, 1853. A miniature model is kept in the Reading Room of Chetham's Library. A portrait and brief memoir of George Pilkington will be found in John Evans's edition of Parkinson's *Old Church Clock*. Pilkington died on 24 February, 1864, aged 64. He was buried in All Saints' Churchyard, Oxford Road. His tomb having fallen into decay it was restored in 1900 by public subscription.

Mr. Ford Madox Brown's fresco (panel No. 8), entitled "Chetham's Life Dream," where the founder is represented as studying his will in the garden of the college, which in imagination he has peopled with his "forty healthy boys" and their pedagogue.

Of literary memorials the first of any importance after Fuller's notice of him in the *Worthies of England*, was W. R. Whatton's valuable *History of Chetham's Hospital and Library* published in 1833, on which all subsequent memoirs, including that most readable one by Mr. F. Espinassé in his *Lancashire Worthies*, have been based.

Lastly, the Chetham Society, under whose auspices the present volume is published, must be mentioned, as by its means the founder's name has been carried far beyond the town of his birth and life's work. The Society was established in 1843 at a memorable dinner held at the house of Mr. James Crossley. An organisation was then determined upon with the object of printing "Remains Historical and Literary connected with the Palatine Counties of Lancaster and Chester"; and the happy thought of appropriating the name of Chetham was doubtless due to the sentiments of gratitude entertained by the founders of the Society to their eponymous hero for the great library that had so long been a place of resort of local scholars.

The only portrait of Humphrey Chetham extant is the painting that hangs over the fireplace of the reading room in the Chetham Library. The artist's name is not known, nor is there any record in the Feoffee's minute-books as to the date when it was received by its present custodians. It was exhibited in the first Exhibition of National Portraits, in 1866, and is thus described in the catalogue: "No. 769. To waist; yellow embroidered cap, falling wide collar, dark dress; glove in right hand. Canvas, 32 x 25 inches." The photographs of it, taken by the Arundel Society during the Exhibition, are already fading. A miniature copy of the portrait was made by Patrick McMorland about 1790, and is now in the house-governor's room. An engraving from this miniature forms the frontispiece to Radcliffe's *Catalogue* of 1791.

It is a beautiful specimen of James Heath's art, but the engraver, following the miniaturist, has made Chetham a much older man than in the original. It was re-engraved in 1831 for Baines's *History of Lancashire* by W. Holl, who followed McMorland's miniature or Heath's engraving. A third engraving is that by Charles Pye, from a drawing by Henry Wyatt, published in the *History of the Foundations in Manchester* (1828–33). This, while more closely following the painting, is still unsatisfactory, since it makes the Founder's face too broad, and the features too hard. Many engravings have since been published, but as they are merely copies of one or other of those mentioned above it is unnecessary to specify them.

APPENDIX I.

THE WILL OF HUMPHREY CHETHAM.

THE will of the Founder was proved on the 21st March, 1653–4, in the Prerogative Court of Canterbury in London. The Feoffees, when they were applying for their Charter, desired to obtain possession of the original will from that Court, "or else to enrol it in Chancery or exemplify it under the Great Seal," but no evidence has been found that either wish was accomplished. The will is now at Somerset House, fol. 303 Alchin. The following copy is taken from that printed by order of the Feoffees in 1761, and has been compared and corrected with the probate copy in the possession of the solicitors to the trust. The version given in Whatton's *History* is evidently from the 1761 edition, but is incorrect in several particulars.

In the Name of GOD Amen The sixteenth day of December in the yeare of our Lord God one thousand six hundred fifty and one, I Humfrey Chetham of Cleyton, in the county of Lancaster, Esq^{e}, being mindfull to dispose and settle my estate and being of sound and perfect memory (praised be God for the same) doe make this my last Will and Testament in manner and forme following (that is to say) first of all I bequeath my soule to Almighty God hopinge to bee saved by his mercy through the merritte and mediac̄on of Jesus Christ my blessed Saviour and Redeemer and my body to be buried in the Parrish Church of Manchester within the county of Lancaster within my Chappell there in such decent manner as my executors hereafter herein named shall thinke fitt. And I do constitute ordaine and make my two kinsmen George Chetham and Edward Chetham sonnes of my brother James Chetham gentleman executors of this my last Will and Testament. And itt is

George Chetham and Edward Chetham appointed executors.

my mind and will that all such debts as I shall owe unto any person or persons uppon the day of my decease (if any such be) shalbee discharged by my said executors within three months afterwards. And I doe give and bequeath unto the said George Chetham sonn of James Chetham my said brother (whome I have nominated one of my executors) the sume of five thousand and three hundred pounds of good and lawfull money of England, to the intent and purpose that hee shall therewith, soe soone after my decease as conveniently may be purchase and buy lands, tenements, rents, or other hereditaments, of and for a good and firme estate in fee simple, in the name of and to the said executors or the survivor of them, and their or his heires forever, of the cleere yearely value of three hundred and eighteene pounds of good and lawful money of England. And in case the said sume of five thousand and three hundred pounds will not bee sufficient to purchase lands, tenements, rents, or hereditaments, of the cleere yearely value of three hundred and eighteene pounds as aforesaid, then I doe charge and require the said George Chetham, to make up the said sume of five thousand and three hundred pounds soe much out of his owne estate as may be sufficient to purchase lands, tenements, rents, or hereditaments, of the cleere yearely value of three hundred and eighteene pounds, in regard of the greate estate I have given him, or settled uppon him as hereafter is herein expressed. Alsoe I doe give and bequeath unto the said Edward Chetham (whom I have nominated the other of my executors) the sume of one thousand and seaven hundred pounds of good and lawful money of England, to the intent and purpose, that he shall therewith, soe soone after my decease as conveyniently may be, purchase and buy lands, tenements, rents, or other hereditaments, of and for a good and firme estate, in fee simple, in the name of, and to the said executors, or the survivor of them, and their or his heires for ever, of the cleere yearely value of one hundred and two pounds of lawful money of England. And in case the said sume of one thousand and seaven hundred pounds will not be sufficient to purchase lands, tenements, rents, or hereditaments, of the cleere yearely value of one hundred and two pounds as aforesaid, then I doe charge and require the said Edward Chetham to make up the said sume of

£5,300 given to George Chetham to purchase lands &c., of the clear yearly value of £318.

£1,700 given to Edward Chetham to purchase lands &c., of the clear yearly value of £102.

one thousand and seaven hundred pounds so much with or out of his owne estate as may be sufficient to purchase lands, tenements, rents, or hereditaments, of the full cleere yearely value of one hundred and two pounds, in regard of the great estate I have given him or settled uppon him as hereafter is herein expressed. And I desire if they soe please that my said executors shall and will joine in the purchase of the said lands and hereditaments by them to be bought and purchased as aforesaid and in the settlement and assurance thereof for the uses and purposes herein mencõned att and by the oversight and advice of my overseers hereafter herein named. The which said lands, tenements, and hereditaments, and every of them to bee so by my said executors or either of them purchased and bought as aforesaid, my will and mind is further, that the same shall within as short a time as may bee after the purchase or respective purchases thereof bee conveyed, granted, and assured by my said executors or the survivor of them, or by such of them as shall purchase the same or by his heires unto Richard Holland of Denton in the county of Lancaster Esq. Alexander Barlowe of Barlowe in the said county of Lancaster Esq. Edmund Hopwood of Hopwood in the same county Esq. Robert Hyde of Denton in the same county Esq. Richard Howorth of Manchester in the same county Esq. Richard Radcliffe of the same Esq. Henry Wrigley of Chamber within Ouldham in the said county of Lancaster Esq. Nicholas Mosley of Ancoates in the said county of Lancaster Esq. John Lightbowne of Salford in the same county Esq. Robert Booth of Salford aforesaid Esq. Francis Mosley of Collihurst in the same county Gentleman William Radley of Ouldfeild within Salford in the same county Gentleman Richard Johnson Clerke late one of the Fellows of the Colledge in Manchester aforesaid Richard Hollinworth of Manchester aforesaid Clerke John Tildesley of Rumworth in the same county of Lancaster Clerke Edward Johnson of Manchester aforesaid Gentleman James Marler Thomas Mynshull and James Lightbowne of the same Gentlemen John Cunliffe of Hollins in the same county Gentleman Raphe Worsley of Platt in the same county Gentleman Alexander Norres and John Okey of Boulton in the Moores in the same county of Lancaster Gentlemen and Raphe Brooke of the same Yeoman, theire heires and assignes

Executors directed to join in the purchase of the said lands, &c.

Executors to convey the said lands, &c., to the first Feoffees.

for ever, or to the survivors and survivor of them, and the heires and assignes of such survivor and survivors for ever, to the use of my said executors and of the survivor of them, and of the said Richard Holland, &c. &c. [names as before] and the survivors and survivor of them, and of the heires and assignes of my said executors and of the survivor of them, and of the heires and assignes of the said Richard Holland &c. &c. and of the survivors and survivors of them for ever, under and uppon this trust and confidence nevertheles and to the onely use, intent, and purpose, that the whole cleere profitts, issues, benefitts, and revenues thereof and thereby to bee raised and received shall and may to the pleasure of Almighty God bee ordered, disposed of, employed, and converted from time to time for ever, in for and about the releife, maintenance, educacon, bringing up, and binding apprentice, or other preferment of soe many and such poore boyes or male children, and in such sorte, manner, and forme as in and by this my last Will and Testament is and are or shalbee in such behalfe sett downe and expressed, appointed or declared. And it is my further will and mind, that when there are, or shalbee onely twelve of them, the said Richard Holland &c. &c. [names as before, with the addition of George and Edward Chetham] remaininge in full life, then my will and mind is, that the same twelve surviveinge shall enfeoffe other twelve honest, able, and sufficient persons, inhabitinge within twelve miles of the said towne of Manchester at the time of such enfeoffeinge, and to be nominated and elected by such twelve surviving persons as aforesaid (respect being had to such townes and places respectively, in which such feoffees and persons intrusted as aforesaid as shalbee then deceased did inhabite and dwell in theire life-time, that others may be chosen out of the same townes and places, or as neere thereunto as conveniently may bee) and the heires and assignes of the said other twelve persons to bee soe newly elected, nominated and enfeoffed as aforesaid of the said lands, tenements, rents, and hereditaments, soe to be purchased and bought as aforesaid, to the use of the same survivors feoffors, and of the said other twelve persons to bee soe newly ellected, nominated, and enfeoffed as aforesaid, and of the heires and assignes of the said survivors feoffors, and of the said other twelve

The profits of these lands to be laid out in the mainten-ance and education of poor boys.

Feoffees when reduced to twelve, shall elect and en-feoff other twelve.

Persons elected to dwell within twelve miles of Manchester.

Respect to be had to the towns and places of abode of the deceased feoffees.

persons to be so ellected, nominated, and enfeoffed as aforesaid, for ever, under, and uppon the like trust and confidence, and to the use, intent, and purpose aforesaid, for the performance of this my last Will and Testament, for and concerning the releife, maintenance, educac̃on, bringing upp, and binding apprentice, or otherwise preferringe or providinge for such said poore boyes, in manner and forme as aforesaid forever as by Counsell learned in the lawes shall bee advised, or devised, and that the like course bee kept forever, when and as often as there shall bee onely twelve feoffees or persons alive to whose use the said lands, tenements, and hereditaments, shalbee soe or in like manner conveyed, and assured as aforesaid, according to the true meaneing of this my last Will and Testament: and that itt bee soe expressed in the feoffments and assurances thereof hereafter to be made as aforesaid. And itt is my will and minde, that soe longe as any of my name, blood, or kindred, shall dwell att Turton, Cleyton, or Chetham aforesaid, and in Ordsall and Crumsall, in the county of Lancaster aforesaid, or elswhere neere unto the same places, and shall bee fitt to bee made feoffees, that they be used for the same purpose, and nominated feoffees with and as the rest. Alsoe it is my will and minde and I doe desire that whereas I have in my lifetime taken upp and maintained fourteene poore boyes of the towne of Manchester aforesaid, and six of the town of Salford aforesaid, and two of the town of Droylsden in the aforesaid county of Lancaster, being two and twenty in all, that the same may, and shalbee made upp the number of forty, by the addition of eighteene more poore boyes, every of them to be above the age of sixe and under the age of tenn yeares, at the time of theire severall ellections, and the same eighteene poore boyes to bee ellected and taken upp within three moneths after my decease, out of such townes or towneshipps onely and by such numbers or proportions as are herein hereafter menc̃oned (that is to say) in or out of the said towne or towneshipp of Droylsden one, in or out of the towne or towneshipp of Crumsall aforesaid two, in or out of the towne or towneshipp of Boulton in the Moores aforesaid tenne, and in or out of the towne or towneshipp of Turton in the aforesaid county of Lancaster ffive, and not elswhere or otherwise. And my mynd and will is, that after the

The like course to be kept for ever, as often as there shall be only twelve feoffees alive.

The founder's kinsmen to be feoffees if fit.

Twenty-two poor boys maintained in his life time, to be increased to forty.

Age of the boys to be added.

Out of what townships, and in what proportion the additional boys are to be elected.

number of fforty is compleated by such numbers and proporc̃ons as aforesaid, that then and in case of any vacancie of the said poore boyes by death, or beinge above such age as hereafter is herein expressed or by misorder, or misgovernment, or inffecc̃ous or incurable sickness or disease of any of the said poore boyes, or otherwise att the discretion of the feoffees and persons intrusted or authorized, or hereafter to bee intrusted or authorized, as is hereafter herein mentioned in that behalfe, the same shalbee supplyed by new ellections successively forever out of the respective townes and places out of which such boyes whose places shalbee come vacant by any the meanes aforesaid were taken upp and chosen and not otherwise; nor out of any other place if there bee poore boyes enough within the same place to bee chosen, soe as there may be from time to time successively forever fourteene out of Manchester, sixe out of Salford, three out of Droylsden, two out of Crumsall, tenn out of Boulton in the Moores, and five out of Turton as aforesaid. And furthermore my will and minde is, that the same poore boyes from time to time, and att all times after my decease to bee ellected and taken upp as aforesaid, shalbee children of honest, industrious, and painfull parents, and not of wandering or idle beggars or roages, nor that any of the said boyes shalbee basterds nor such as are lame, infirme, or diseased att the time of theire ellection. And my will and minde is, that the same poore boyes shall have a Treasurer or Receiver and a Governor, with Officers and Servants fitt and requisitte for the orderinge and manageinge of the same children and of the affaires of the hospitall hereafter herein mentioned; and that the same Treasurer or Receiver, Governor, Officers and Servants, shall have some competent allowance, stipends, or sallaries, answerable to theire paines in and touching the premises. Alsoe my will and mynd further is, that the said Richard Holland, &c. &c. and all and every such other person and persons for the time beinge, to whome or to whose use the said lands and premises, or in default thereof, the annual rents or yearely sumes of money hereafter named by this my last Will bequeathed, are or shall be or are hereby mentioned, or intended to bee willed, devised, bequeathed, limitted, appointed, granted, assigned, conveyed, or assured, according to the true

Vacancies of poor boys to be supplied out of the same townships, from which the boys whose places are vacant, had been elected.

Boys elected to be children of honest, industrious parents, and not bastards, or diseased.

A treasurer, governor, and other officers to be appointed

The majority of the feoffees that meet, to have power to elect, or displace the boys.

meaneinge of this my last Will, or the greater number of soe many of them as shall yearely meete for or about the performance of this my last Will, according to the true meaneinge thereof shall for the time being respectively from time to time for ever, have full, onely, and absolute libertie, power, priviledge, and authoritie, for and concerning the ellecting, appointinge, placeinge, displaceing, orderinge, governinge, mainteyninge, bringinge upp, and bindinge apprentice, or otherwise preferringe, or provideinge of and for the said fortie poore boyes to be elected and taken up as aforesaid for ever. And alsoe for and concerninge the ellectinge, nomminateinge, appointinge, placeinge, and displaceinge of such Treasurer or Receivour, Governor, Officers and Servants, as shalbee thought fitt to be imployed about the premises, and for the limittinge, appointinge, and alloweinge of the stipends, or sallaries of the said Treasurer or Receivour, Governour, Officers, and Servants respectively and other charges whatsoever in anie wise concerninge the said poore boyes or the Hospitall hereafter herein named, and for and concerninge the issueinge, orderinge, payeinge, employeinge, and bestoweinge of the benefitts, issues, and profitts of the said lands, tenements, rents and hereditaments for the uses and purposes aforesaid, accordinge to the rules, direccons, and true meaneinge of this my last Will and Testament and the trust therein declared. And for the better accomplishment of the ellections of the said poore boyes, my will is and I doe desire that the Churchwardens and Overseers for the poore for the time beinge of the said respective townes or towneshipps or the greater number of them shall and will within six weeks after my decease for the said eighteene to be first ellected and afterwards when as often as there shall be cause, prepare severall and respective bills of the names of double the number of such said poore boyes to be taken up in and out of theire respective townes or towneshipps, according to the true meaninge of this my last Will, uppon request thereof to them to be first made by anie the persons before herein mencconed, authorized or appointed for the makeinge of the same ellections, which said bills respectively shall togeather with the names of such said children expresse theire said severall ages, and theire fathers names, and the name of the towne or towneshipp whereof they are, and

And to elect, and displace officers, and employ the revenues, according to the directions of the will.

Church wardens and overseers of the respective towns, to prepare lists of double the number of boys to be elected, with their ages, &c.

the day and yeare when the same bills were made and subscribed with the hands of the said Churchwardens and Overseers of the poore of the said townes and towneshipps respectively, or the greater number of them, and shall bee delivered to some of the persons before menconed, authorized or appointed for makeinge of the said ellections that the same may bee communicated to the rest, to the end such ellections as aforesaid may bee made of the said poore children in the said bills to be named, or some of them, or of anie others of the same townes respectively, according to the good discrecons of the said persons before menconed, authorized or appointed for the making of the said ellections, whome I desire to take the advice or assistance of the said Churchwardens and Overseers, but my mind is not that they shalbee bound to followe the advice or directions of such said Churchwardens and Overseers nor concluded thereby. Alsoe it is my will and minde and I do hereby devise and appointe that the said two and twenty poore male children by mee taken upp and mainteyned in my lifetime, and such eighteene others as shalbee added unto them to make upp and compleate the said number of forty by such new ellections as aforesaid, and all other such poore male children as shall at any time or times forever happen to bee ellected and appointed to succeed or come in or to anie the roomes, steeds, or places of anie of the said fortie poore children, according to the true meaneinge of this my last Will and Testament, shall bee respectively well and sufficiently mainteyned and kept with meate, drinke, lodgeinge, and apparrell, and alsoe educated and brought upp to learninge or labour in the townes of Manchester and Salford aforesaid or one of them by and with the profitts, issues, benefitts, and revenewes of the said lands, tenements, rents, and hereditaments soe by my said executors or either of them to bee purchased as aforesaid, the said children and every of them to be soe mainteyned, kept, educated, and brought upp as aforesaid respectively for soe longe time, and untill they and every of them shall accomplish his and their respective age of fourteene yeares, and for such time afterwards as untill they may bee conveniently bound apprentice or otherwise preferred or provided for, according to the true meaneinge of this my last Will and noe longer. Nevertheles my will and minde is that

The lists to be subscribed by the churchwardens and overseers.

Feoffees not to be concluded or restricted by the bills of the churchwardens and overseers.

The poor boys to be well and sufficiently maintained, and to be brought up to learning, or labour, in Manchester or Salford.

The boys to be kept and educated till they arrive at the age of fourteen.

the said Feoffees or Trustees or the greater number of them that shall bee present att any meetinge of the said Feoffees or Trustees concerninge the performance of this my last Will, upon cause of misorder or misgovernment, refractorines, infectious or incurable sicknesses or diseases of any of the said poore boyes or other just cause conceived by the said Feoffees or Trustees or such greater number of them as aforesaid shall and may remove and displace anie of the said poore boyes, att any time or tymes before they come to their said age of fourteene yeares, and shall and may alsoe withould from and denie or refuse to pay or allowe unto or for all and every or any such said boyes as shalbee soe displaced, all or anie parte of the benefitt, meanes or maintenance which otherwise to him or them should have belonged by virtue of this my last Will, accordinge to the discrecons of the said Feoffees or Trustees or such greater number of them as aforesaid. Alsoe it is my will and minde and I doe hereby devise, order, and appoint, that when and after the said children come to fourteene yeares of age respectively from time to time for ever, that then or after as aforesaid, they bee placed and putt forth apprentice to some honest masters, or otherwise preferred or provided for with some parte of the issues and profitts before menconed, or with the profitts of such easie labour as they shall be set unto to keep them from idlenese dureinge such time as they shall bee betwixt tenne and fourteene yeares of age or more, or by both the meanes aforesaid or otherwise as the greater number or soe manie of the feoffees or trustees aforesaid as shall yearely meete for that and other purposes concerneinge the performance of this my last Will, shall thinke fitt and convenient. And nevertheles my last will and minde is that such poore boyes as are or heareafter shall bee ellected and chosen within the parrish of Boulton aforesaid, shall after they attaine to their severall ages of fourteene yeares or more as aforesaid bee bound apprentice or otherwise preferred and provided for within the said towne or parrish of Boulton or elswhere, except in the parrish of Manchester aforesaid, and that for that purpose at the time of theire beinge ellected and chosen as aforesaid, it be assented unto by the churchwardens and overseers for the poore of and for the said parish of Boulton, and such of the inhabitants of

Feoffees to to have power to displace boys for misbehaviour, incurable sickness, or any other just cause.

The boys, when of the age of fourteen, to be bound apprentice, or otherwise provided for, as the Feoffees shall think fit.

Boys elected within the parish of Bolton, not to be bound apprentice in the parish of Manchester, and this to be assented to by the Overseers of Bolton, at their election.

the same parrish, as shalbee thought fit by the said feoffees or trustees for the time beinge, that they may returne to bee bound apprentices or inhabitt within the towne or parrish of Boulton aforesaid, after their severall ages of fourteene yeares or more, or after such removall or displacing as aforesaid before their said ages of fourteene yeares. And furthermore, my will, desire, and minde is, that there bee in the Parrish Church of Manchester aforesaid, upon every Mundy in Easter weeke yearely for ever, and oftner there or elsewhere if neede shall bee, and as often as the said Feoffees or Persons intrusted or to be intrusted as aforesaid, or the greater number of them shall for the time then beinge thinke fitt, yearely meetings of the said Feoffees or Trustees and Persons aforesaid, or of soe manie of them as cann be present to make such ellections as aforesaid, to place or displace the said children, as there shalbee cause, and to give directions for theire maintenance, educacon, bringing up, and binding apprentice, or other preferments as aforesaid, to make leases of the lands, and hereditaments to be purchased by my executors or either of them as aforesaid, to audit accompts and to order all other the affaires and busineses touchinge the premises accordinge to such orders, instructions, and directions, and in such sorte, manner, and forme as is or are in this my last will conteyned and expressed, which said meetinge to be yearely kept upon every Easter Munday, my will is that the same shall beginn about one of the clocke in the afternoon of the said Mundyes yearley for ever. And my minde is that notice be given unto or left att the house of every of the said Feoffees or Trustees for the time beinge of the time and place of every meetinge touchinge the premises (except the said constant yearely meetinge upon Easter Munday as aforesaid.) And my will and minde further is, that wherein the same orders, instructions or directions are or heareafter by experience or alteration of times or affaires or otherwise, shalbe found defective, short, or insufficient for the well orderinge, governinge, or manageinge of the said poore boyes and the affairs of the said Hospitall, that the same shall bee from time to time for ever suplied, altered, or amended by the wisdomes, and good discreations of the said Feoffees or persons intrusted or to be intrusted, to whom or whose use or uses the said lands and premises or in default

The Feoffees to meet yearly, every Monday in Easter week in the parish church of Manchester, or elsewhere, to elect boys, and do all other business.

The aforesaid meeting to begin about one o'clock in the afternoon, and notice to be given to the feoffees of all other meetings except this.

The Feoffees empowered from time to

time, as they see fit, to supply, alter, or amend any rules or directions laid down.

thereof the annuall rent or yearely sumes of money aforesaid are or shalbe or are hereby meant or intended to bee willed, devised, bequeathed, limitted, or appointed, graunted, assigned, conveyed, or assured for or in behalfe of the said poore boyes, or by the wisdoms and discrec̃ons of the greater number of them for the time beinge. And whereas I have heretofore in or by my indenture or deed beareinge date the ninth day of August which was in the yeare of our Lord God one thousand six hundred and fiftie, and made betweene mee the said Humfry Chetham upon thone parte and William Langton of Broughton in the said county of Lancaster Esquire, Robert Mawdesley of Mawdesley in the said county of Lancaster Esq., Oswald Mosley of Manchester aforesaid Gentleman, and John Lomax of Chetham aforesaid Gentleman, uppon thother parte, given, granted, enfeoffed, and confirmed, or otherwise conveyed and assured unto the said William Langton, Robert Mawdesley, Oswald Mosley, and John Lomax and their heires, all that and those the mannor or Lordshipp of Turton, with the rights, members, and appurtenances thereof in the aforesaid countie of Lancaster, and all that the capital messuage or mansion house of or in Turton aforesaid, then or theretofore called or known by the names of Turton Tower, and all and every the demesnes and demesne lands and other hereditaments thereunto belonginge; and alsoe all and singular other the messuages, cottages, houses, millnes, lands, tenements, demesnes, and demesne lands, and other lands, and grounds, meadows, pastures, fields, closes, feedings, moores, commons, wastes, mynes, tythes, and other hereditaments whatsoever, with theire and every of theire appurtenances, scituate, lyeing and beinge in Turton aforesaid, and in Harwood in the parrish of Boulton in the Moores aforesaid, and in Westleigh and Horwich in the said county of Lancaster, and in Bolton nigh Bolland in the county of Yorke, and in every or any of the parrishes, townes, towneshipps, villages, hamletts, feilds, precincts, or territories of Turton, Harwood, Westleigh, Horwich, and Bolton nigh Bolland aforesaid, in whose tenures, possessions, or occupac̃ons soever, the aforesaid mannor, messuages, lands, tenements, and hereditaments last before herein mentioned, or anie of them, then were or had beene, whereof or wherein I the said Humfrey Chetham

Recital of the settlement of his lands in Turton, with power to charge the same.

then had anie estate of inheritance in possession, reverc̃on, remainder, or otherwise, to have and to hold the said mannor, messuages, lands, tenements, and hereditaments, last mentioned, with their and every of theire appurtenances, unto the said William Langton, Robert Mawdesley, Oswald Mosley, and John Lomax, and their heires for ever, to the use and behoofe of mee the said Humfrey Chetham, and the heires of my body lawfully to be begotten, and for default of such issue then to the use and behoofe of the said George Chetham (sonne of my said brother James Chetham) and the heires males of the body of the same George Chetham lawfully begotten and to bee begotten, and for default of such issue, then to the use and behoofe of the aforenamed Edward Chetham and the heires males of his body lawfully begotten and to bee begotten, and for default of such issue then to the use and behoofe of George Chetham then of Cleyton aforesaid in the same county of Lancaster Gent. (sonne of Raphe Chetham Gent. deceased) late brother of mee the said Humfrey Chetham and to the heires males of the body of the said George Chetham, sonne of the said Raphe Chetham, thereafter lawfully to bee begotten, and for default of such issue, then to the use and behoofe of the right heires of mee the said Humfrey Chetham for ever. And to the further use and intent, and itt was in and by the said indenture or deed amongst other things expressed or provided, that itt should and might be lawfull to and for mee the said Humfrey Chetham att all times thereafter duringe my naturall life, by any my deed or deeds in writing to bee sealed and delivered in the presence of twoe or more sufficient witnesses, or by my last Will and Testament in writeing, to be published in the presence of twoe or more witnesses, to graunte, limitt, bequeath, devise, will, appointe, or assure unto any person or persons, and for any estate or estates whatsoever, one or more annuall or other rent or rents, sume or sumes of money, to bee yearely issueinge, payable, perceived, goeinge or taken out of, and in all and every or any of the said mannor, messuages, lands, tenements, hereditaments, and premises last before menc̃oned, or out of or in any parte or parcel thereof, and the same to have such continuance, and to bee soe yearely, or otherwise payable, and to and for such uses, behoofes, intents, and purposes, and under and uppon such sume and sumes of money, in name of penalty or other forfeiture for non-payment thereof, or of any parte thereof, and att such feast daies and times, and in such sorte, manner, and forme absolutely, limitably, or condic̃onally as to mee the said Humfrey Chetham should seeme meete and expedient: and further, as in and by the said indenture or deed (relation thereunto being had more fully and att large) it doth and may appeare, now my full will and minde is, for and towards the better performance and accomplishment of this my last Will and Testament, toucheing the releife, maintenance, educac̃on, bringeing upp and binding apprentice the said poore boyes as aforesaid, and the purchase and settlement of lands for that purpose; and least the said George Chetham (sonne of my said brother James Chetham) should not for his parte perform this my last Will and Testament, and accomplish the Trust by mee in him reposed, for and concerninge the purchase of lands, tenements, rents, or hereditaments, and the settleinge and assuringe thereof for the releife, maintenance, educac̃on, and bringing up, and binding apprentice of the said poore boyes as aforesaid, within convenient time after my decease, I doe therefore hereby will, devise, and bequeath, limitt, and appointe, accordinge to my said power, libertie, or authority unto the aforesaid Richard Holland, Alexander Barlow, &c. &c. and their heires and assignes forever, one annuall rent or yearely sume of nine score pounds, of good and lawful money of England, to be yearely issueinge, payable, perceived, received, had and taken out of, and in all and singular the said mannor, messuages, lands, tenements, and hereditaments, in or by the said last-menc̃oned deed, or indenture graunted, conveyed, or assured, as aforesaid, and out of and in everie parte and parcell thereof, to have and to hould and yearely to perceive, receive, and enjoye, and take the said annuall rent, or yearely sume of ninescore pounds, and every parte and parcel thereof, unto the said Richard Holland, Alexander Barlow, &c. &c. and their heires and assignes forever, imediately from and after the decease of me the said Humfrey Chetham, under and uppon the provisoe or condic̃on heareafter herein nextly menc̃oned, the same annuall or yearely rent or sume of nine score pounds, to bee payable, and payd yearely unto the

He devises the yearly rent charge of £180 to the Feoffees, out of his lands in Turton, towards the pious uses aforementioned.

said Richard Holland, Alexander Barlow, &c. &c. and their heires and assignes in or uppon the feast dayes of the birth of our Lord God, and the Nativitie of St. John Baptist, by even and equall portions, at or in the south porch of the parrish church of Manchester aforesaid; and the first payment thereof to commence and begin in or upon such of the same feast daies, which shall next happen after the decease of mee the said Humfrey Chetham. Provided alwaies, and upon condiĉon and nevertheles my will and minde is, that in case the said George Chetham, (sonne of my said brother James Chetham), and the heires males of the body of the same George Chetham, shall and doe att any time after my decease purchase or buy some lands, tenements, rents, or hereditaments, of the cleare yearely value of nine score pounds as aforesaid of and for a good estate in fee simple and shall sufficiently and effectually convey, settle, and assure, or cause the same to bee sufficiently and effectually conveyed and assured as aforesaid unto the said Richard Holland, Alexander Barlow, &c. &c. and their heires and assignes or the survivors or survivor of them their and his heires and assignes as aforesaid, to and for the uses, behoofes, intents, and purposes before mentioned and in manner and forme as aforesaid, that then and from thenceforth, that is to saie, from and after such purchase, settlement, and assurance as aforesaid, the said yearely rent charge or yearely sume of nine score pounds charged or chargable upon the said mannor, messuages, lands, tenements, hereditaments, and premises in the said deed mentioned, shall cease and be noe longer paid or payable in any wise; but that the said mannor, messuages, tenements, lands, and hereditaments last mentioned, shall bee for ever thereafter discharged, freed, and acquitted, of and from the payment thereof, and of every parte and parcel thereof. And my will and minde is that the same annuitie, annuall and yearely rent or sume of nine score pounds, shall and may be used, imployed, and disposed of, for and dureing the continuance thereof as aforesaid, to and for the releife, maintenance, educaĉon, bringeing upp, and binding apprentices, or other preferment of the said poore boyes, in such manner and sorte as the profitts, issues, rents, and revenues of the aforesaid lands, tenements, and hereditaments, to bee purchased and bought by the

The above rent charge payable at Midsummer & Christmas, in the south porch of Manchester church

This rent to cease upon the settlement of other lands of the same yearly value, by George Chetham.

This rent charge to be employed for the pious uses aforesaid.

said George Chetham (sonne of my said brother James Chetham) by and with the sume of three thousand pounds, parcell of the aforesaid sume of five thousand three hundred pounds to him by mee formerly herein bequeathed in that behalfe, in case the same were purchased, should bee and are herein and hereby limitted and appointed. And I do hereby further limitt, devise, bequeath, and appointe, that they the said Richard Holland, Alexander Barlow, &c. &c. and their heirs and assigns, and the survivors and survivor of them, their and his heires and assignes, and every of them, shall, and may distraine for the said annuall or yearely rent, or sume of nine score pounds, in or uppon the aforesaid mannor, messuages, lands, tenements, hereditaments, and premises, in, or by the said last mencōned deed or indenture granted, conveyed, or assured as aforesaid, or anie parte or parcell thereof, in case the same be in arreare, at any the daies and times before mencōned as in a case of a rent charge. And whereas alsoe I the said Humfrey Chetham have in or by my deed or indenture, beareinge date the eight day of this instant December, and made betweene mee the said Humfrey Chetham upon thone parte, and the before named William Langton, Robert Mawdesley, Oswald Mosley, and John Lomax, upon thother parte, given, graunted, enfeoffed, and confirmed, or otherwise conveyed and assured unto the said William Langton, Robert Mawdesley, Oswald Mosley, and John Lomax, and their heires and assignes for ever, all that capital messuage, or mannor house, scituate and being in Cleyton in the said county of Lancaster, commonly called or known by the name of Cleyton Hall, with the rights, members, and appurtenances thereof in the aforesaid county of Lancaster, and all and singuler the messuages, howses, edifices, buildings, dove howses, barnes, stables, cowhowses, oxe-howses, millnes, killnes, orchards, gardens, curtilages, parks, lands, tenements, demesnes and demesne lands, and other lands and grounds, meadows, pastures, fields, closes, feedings, rents, reversions, services, courts leete, view of franck pledge, courts baron, perquisites, and profits of courts and leetes, franchizes, jurisdictions, priviledges, preheminences, wastes, commons, mynes, profitts and hereditaments whatsoever, with their and every of their appurtenances, scituate, lyeinge and beinge in Cley-

The Feoffees to distrain for the said annual rent, if not paid.

Recital of his settlement of Clayton, with power to charge the same.

ton aforesaid, or elsewhere in the said county of Lancaster, to the said copihold messuage or mannor-house lyeing, belongeinge, or in anie wise apperteyninge, and alsoe all and singuler other the messuages, cotages, howses, edifices, buildings, dove howses, barnes, stables, millnes, dammes, millnepooles, streams, currents of water and waters, water courses, soken suite, multure and grist, killnes, curtilages, orchards, gardens, parkes and impalled or inclosed grounds or lands, lodges, tenements, demesnes and demesne lands, and other lands and grounds, meadowes, pastures, feildes, closes, feedinges, woods, wast grounds, underwoods, highwaies and other waies and passages, and the soyle and ground of the same, rents, reversions, services, courts leete, view of franck pledge, courts baron, perquisites and profitts of courts and leetes, franchizes, jurisdictions, priviledges, preheminences, commons, common of pasture, moss and turbary, and the ground and soyle of the same mosse and turbary, fishinges, free warren, mynes, profitts and hereditaments, whatsoever, with theire and every of theire appurtenances, scituate, lyinge, and being within the townes, towneshipps, villages, hamletts, fields, precintes, and territories of Cleyton and Manchester aforesaid, and Faylesworth, Droylsden, Gorton, and Newton, within the parrish of Manchester aforesaid, and in Woodhayes within the parrish of Asheton under Lyne, and in every or any of them in the said county of Lancaster, or elsewhere in the parrish of Asheton under Lyne aforesaid, in whose tennures, possessions, or occupacons soever the aforesaid hereditaments and premises or any of them then were or had beene whereof or wherein I the said Humfrey Chetham then had anie estate of inheritance in possession, revercon, remainder or otherwise, and the revercon and revercons, remainder and remainders, of all and singuler the same premises, and of every parte and parcell thereof, to have and to hold the said capitall messuage or mannor howse, and all and singuler other the messuages, lands, tenements, hereditaments, and all and every other the premises, with theire and every of theire appurtenances, in or by the said last mentioned deed or indenture graunted, or ment, or mentioned to bee therein or thereby graunted, conveyed, or assured as aforesaid, unto the said William Langton, Robert Mawdesley, Oswald

Mosley, and John Lomax, and their heires for ever, to the use and behoofe of mee the said Humfrey Chetham, and the heires of my body lawfully to be begotten and for default of such issue, then to the use and behoofe of the aforenamed George Chetham, (sonne of my said brother James Chetham) and of the heires males of the body of the said George Chetham, (sonne of my said brother James Chetham) lawfully begotten or to bee begotten, and for default of such issue, then to the use and behoofe of the afore named Edward Chetham, and the heires males of his body lawfully begotten and to bee begotten and for default of such issue then to the use and behoofe of the said George Chetham, (sonne of my said brother Raphe Chetham) and of the heires males of the body of the same George Chetham, thereafter lawfully to bee begotten; and for default of such issue, then to the use and behoofe of the right heires of mee the said Humfrey Chetham for ever. And to the further use and intent, and itt was in and by the same indenture or deed amongst other things expressed or provided that it should, and might bee lawfull to and for mee the said Humfrey Chetham, att anie time or tymes thereafter dureing my naturall life, by any my deed or deeds in writeing, to bee sealed and delivered in the presence of two or more sufficient witnesses, or by my last Will and Testament in writeing, to be published in the presence of two or more witnesses, to grante, limitt, bequeath, devise, will, appointe, or assure unto any person or persons, and for any estate or estates whatsoever, one or more annuall rent or rents, sume or sumes of money to be yearely issueing, payable, perceived, goinge or taken out of, and in all, and every, or any the said capitall messuage, and other the messuages, millnes, lands, tenements, hereditaments, and premises last before herein mentioned, or out of, and in any parte or parcell thereof, and the same to have such continuance, and to be soe yearely, or otherwise, payable, and to, and for such uses, behoofes, intents, and purposes, and under, and uppon such sume and sumes of money, in name of penalty or other forfeiture for nonpayment thereof, or any parte thereof, and att such feast daies and times, and in such sort, manner, and forme absolutely, limittably, or condic̃onally, as to mee the said Humfrey Chetham should seeme meete and expedient;

and further as in and by the same indenture or deed (relation thereunto being had), may more fully and att large appeare. Now my will and minde is and for and towards the better performance and accomplishment of this my last Will and Testament, touchinge the releife, maintenance, educacon, bringeing up, and binding apprentice of the said poore boyes as aforesaid, and the purchase and settlement of lands for that purpose. And least the said George Chetham (sonne of my said brother James Chetham) should not for his parte performe this my last Will and Testament and accomplish the trust by mee in him reposed, for and concerneinge the purchase of lands, tenements, rents, and hereditaments, and the settlinge and assuringe thereof for the releife, maintenance, educacon, bringinge up, and bynding apprentice of the said poore boyes as aforesaid, within convenient time after my decease, I doe therefore hereby will, devise, bequeath, limitt, and appoint accordinge to my said power, libertie, and authoritie, unto the aforesaid Richard Holland, Alexander Barlow, &c. &c. and their heires and assignes for ever, one annuall rent, or yearely sume of one hundred thirty and eight pounds more of like lawful money of England to bee yearely issuing, payable, perceived, received, had, and taken out of, and in all and singular the said capitall messuage, and other the messuages, millnes, lands, tenements, hereditaments, and premises, in or by the said last menconed deed or indenture granted, conveyed, or assured as aforesaid, or out of or in any parte or parcell thereof, to have, hould, and yearely to receive, perceive, enjoye, and take the said annuall rent, or yearely sume of one hundred thirty and eight pounds, and every parte and parcell thereof, unto the said Richard Holland, Alexander Barlow, &c. &c. and their heires and assignes forever, under or upon the provisoe or condition hereafter herein nextly menconed, the same annuall or yearely rent or sume of one hundred thirtie and eight pounds to bee payable and paid yearely unto the said Richard Holland, Alexander Barlow, &c. &c. their heires and assignes, in or uppon the feast daies of the birth of our Lord God, and the Nativitie of St. John Baptist, by even and equall porcons, att or in the south porch of the parrish church of Manchester aforesaid and the first pay-

He devises to the Feoffees the clear yearly rent charge of £138, out of his lands in Clayton, &c.

This rent charge to be paid at Christmas and Midsummer in Manchester church porch.

ment thereof to commence and begin in or uppon such of the same feast daies which shall first happen next after the decease of mee the said Humfrey Chetham. Provided alwaies and uppon condition, and nevertheles my will and minde is, that in case the same George Chetham, or the heires males of his body, shall and doe at any time after my decease, purchase and buy some lands, tenements, or hereditaments of the cleare yearely value of one hundred thirty and eight pounds as aforesaid, of and for a good and firme estate in fee simple, and shall sufficiently and effectually convey, settle, and assure, or cause the same to bee sufficiently and effectually conveyed and assured unto the said Richard Holland, Alexander Barlow, &c. &c. and their heires and assignes, or the survivors and survivor of them, theire and his heires and assignes as aforesaid, to and for the uses, behoofes, intents, and purposes before mencōned, and in manner and forme as aforesaid, that then and from thenceforth, that is to say, from and after such purchase, settlement, and assurance as aforesaid, the said yearely rent charge or yearely sume of one hundred thirty and eight pounds, so charged, or chargeable upon the said capitall messuage, and other the messuages, millnes, lands, tenements, hereditaments, and premises, in, or by the said last mentioned deed granted or conveyed as aforesaid, shall cease and bee no longer paid, or payable in any wise; but that the said capitall messuage, and other the messuages, milnes lands, tenements, hereditaments, and premises last mentioned, shalbe forever thereafter discharged, freed, and acquitted of and from the payment thereof, and of every parte and parcell thereof. And my will and minde is that the same annuity, yearely rent, or sume of one hundred thirty and eight pounds, shall and may bee used, imployed, and disposed of for and duringe the continuance thereof as aforesaid, to and for the releife, maintenance, educacōn, and bringing upp, and bindinge apprentice, or other preferment of the said poore boyes, in such manner and sorte as the profitts, issues, rents, and revenues of the aforesaid lands, tenements, and hereditaments, to bee purchased and bought by the said George Chetham (sonne of the aforesaid James Chetham), by, and with the sume of two thousand and three hundred pounds, residue of the aforesaid sume of five thousand and three hundred pounds, to him by me

This rent to cease upon the settlement of lands of the same clear yearly value upon the feoffees by George Chetham or his issue male.

This yearly rent of £138 to be employed for the pious uses aforesaid.

formerly herein bequeathed, in case the same were purchased, should bee and are herein and hereby, limitted and appointed. And I doe hereby further limitt, devise, bequeath, and appointe that they the said Richard Holland, Alexander Barlowe, &c. &c. and theire heires and assignes and the survivors and survivor of them their and his heires and assignes and every of them shall and may distraine for the said annuall or yearely rent, or sume of one hundred thirty and eight pounds in, or upon the aforesaid capitall messuage and other the messuages, millnes, lands, tenements, hereditaments, and premises, in or by the said last menc̃oned deed or indenture granted, conveyed, or assured as aforesaid, or any parte or parcell thereof, in case the same be arreare, att any the daies or times before menc̃oned, as in case of a rent charge. And whereas I have likewise in or by one other indenture or deed, beareing date the aforesaid ninth day of August, which was in the said yeare of our Lord God one thousand six hundred and fifty, and made between mee the said Humfrey Chetham upon thone parte, and the said William Langton, Robert Mawdesley, Oswald Mosley, and John Lomax, upon the other parte, given, granted, enfeoffed, and confirmed, or otherwise conveyed, or assured unto the said William Langton, Robert Mawdesley, Oswald Mosley, and John Lomax, and their heires, all those the messuages, barnes, and other buildings, with thappurtenances, lately erected by mee the said Humfrey Chetham, scituate and beinge in Ordsall and Pendleton or either of them, in the county of Lancaster, then or late in the tenure or occupation of mee the said Humfrey Chetham or of my assignes; and all those lands, tenements, closes, clausures, parcells of land, and hereditaments of mee the said Humfrey Chetham, with their appurtenances, scituate, standing, and beinge in Ordsall and Pendleton aforesaid or in either of them, or elsewhere within the parrish of Eccles, in the said county of Lancaster, or within Salford aforesaid, in the said county of Lancaster, or in any of them, commonly called or known by the several or other name or names of the Massie Bottoms, the Thorny Sholsworth otherwise Suzeworth, the Barne Stidds, the Little Showlsworth otherwise Suzeworth, the Hall Stidds, the Lady Meadowe, the two Pin gatts, the Dobb feild, the Broad hey, the Great Sawfeild, the Flatt Shouls-

The feoffees to distrain for this rent, in case it be in arrear.

Recital of the settlement of lands in Ordsall and Pendleton, with power to charge the same.

worth or otherwise Suzeworth, the Warth, the Withens, the Brookes, the Hyde Acre, the Roadley otherwise Rodley, the Gatley Bankes, the Little Sawfield, the Milnefield, and the Tunstall otherwise Gunstall, or by what other name, or names soever, the same closes, clausures, and parcells of land, and every or any of them theretofore had beene, then were, or might be called or knowne late or theretofore, in the severall or other tenures or occupations of Sir Alexander Radcliffe Knight of the Bath, Humphrey Booth Gentleman, then deceased, and Lawrence Bradshaw Gentleman, or their assignes, and then in the tenure of mee the said Humfrey Chetham, or of my assignee or assignes, and all and singuler other the messuages, houses, edifices, buildings, barnes, stables, lands, tenements, and hereditaments whatsoever, of mee the said Humfrey Chetham, scituate and beinge in Salford, Ordsall, and Pendleton, aforesaid, or in anie of them, or elswhere within the said parrish of Eccles to have and to hold the said messuages, barnes, buildings, lands, tenements, closes, and parcells of lands, hereditaments, and premises last before mentioned, with their and every of their appurtenances unto the said William Langton, Robert Mawdesley, Oswald Mosley, and John Lomax, and their heires forever, to the use and behoofe of mee the said Humfrey Chetham, and the heires of my body lawfully to bee begotten, and for default of such issue then to the use and behoofe of the aforenamed Edward Chetham, and the heires males of his body lawfully begotten, and to bee begotten, and for default of such issue then to the use and behoofe of the said George Chetham (sonne of my said brother James Chetham) and of the heires males of his body lawfully begotten, and to be begotten, and for default of such issue, then to the use and behoofe of the said George Chetham (sonne and heire of my said brother Raphe Chetham), and to the heires males of his body lawfully to bee begotten, and for default of such issue, then to the use and behoofe of the right heires of mee the said Humfrey Chetham, forever. And to the further use and intent, and itt was in and by the same indenture or deed, amongst other things expressed or provided, that itt should or might be lawful to and for me the said Humfrey Chetham, att all times thereafter dureing my naturall life, by any my deed or deeds in writeinge, to bee sealed and delivered in the presence of two or more sufficient witnesses, or by my last Will and Testament in writeinge, to be published in the presence of two or more witnesses, to grante, limitt, bequeath, devise, will, appointe, or assure unto any person or persons, and for anie estate or estates, whatsoever, one or more annuall or other rent or rents, sume or sumes of money, to bee yearely issuing, payaple, perceived, goeing or taken out of, and in all and every or any the said messuages, barnes, lands, tenements, closes, and parcells of land, hereditaments, and premises last before menc̃oned, or out of and in anie parte or parcell thereof, And the same to have such continuance, and to bee soe yearely or otherwise payable, and to and for such uses, behoofes, intents, and purposes, and under and upon such sume and sumes of money, in name of penalty or other forfeiture for non-payment thereof or any part thereof, and at such feast daies or times, and in such sorte, manner, and forme, absolutely, limittably or condic̃onally, as unto me the said Humfrey Chetham should seeme meete and expedient, and further as in and by the same indenture or deed (relation thereunto being had) may more fully and att large appeare. Now my full will and minde is and for, and towards the better performance and accomplishment of this my last Will and Testament, touchinge the releife, maintenance, educac̃on, bringing up, and binding apprentice of the said poore boyes as aforesaid, and the purchase and settlement of lands for that purpose; and least the said Edward Chetham should not for his parte performe this my last Will and Testament and accomplish the trust by mee in him reposed for and concerneinge the purchase of lands, tenements, rents, hereditaments, and the settling and assureing thereof for the releife, maintenance, educac̃on, bringing up, and binding apprentice of the said poore boyes as aforesaid within convenient time after my decease, I doe therefore hereby will, devise, bequeath, limitt, and appointe according to my said power, libertie, or authority, unto the aforesaid Richard Holland, Alexander Barlow, &c. &c. and theire heires and assignes forever, one annuall rent, or yearely sume of one hundred and two pounds of good and lawfull money of England, and to bee yearely issuinge, perceived, received, had, and taken out of and in all and singuler the messuages, barnes,

He devises to the feoffees the clear yearly rent of £102 out of his lands in Ordsall, &c.

lands, tenements, closes, and parcells of land, hereditaments, and premises in or by the said last mencõned deed or indenture granted, conveyed, or assured as aforesaid, or out of or in any parte or parcell thereof, to have, hould, and yearely to receive, perceive, and take the said annuall rent, or yearely sume of one hundred and twoe pounds, and every parte and parcell thereof, unto the said Richard Holland, Alexander Barlow, &c. &c. and theire heires and assignes forever, imediately from and after the decease of mee the said Humfrey Chetham, under and uppon the provisoe or condicõn hereafter herein nextly mencõned, the same annuall rent or yearely sume of one hundred and two pounds, to be payable and paid yearely, unto the said Richard Holland, Alexander Barlow, &c. &c. theire heires and assignes, in or uppon the feast daies of the birth of our Lord God, and the Nativity of St. John Baptist, by even and equall portions at or in the south porch of the parrish church of Manchester, and the first payment thereof to commence and begin in or uppon such of the said feast daies which shall first happen next after the decease of mee the said Humfrey Chetham. Provided alwaies, and uppon condicõn, and nevertheles my will and minde is, that in case the said Edward Chetham or the heires males of his body shall and doe att any time after my decease purchase and buy some lands, tenements, rents, or hereditaments of the cleere yearely value of one hundred and two pounds as aforesaid, of and for a good and firme estate in fee simple, and shall sufficiently and effectually convey, settle, and assure, or cause the same to bee sufficiently and effectually conveyed, and assured unto the said Richard Holland, Alexander Barlow, &c. &c. and their heires and assignes, or the survivors or survivor of them, theire and his heires and assignes as aforesaid, to, and for the uses, behoofes, intents, and purposes before mencõned, and in manner and forme as aforesaid that then and from thenceforth, to wit, from and after such purchase, settlement, and assurance as aforesaid, the said yearely rent charge, or yearely sume of one hundred and twoe pounds so charged or chargeable upon the said messuages, barnes, lands, tenements, closes, and parcells of land, hereditaments, and premises in or by the last mencõned deed granted or conveyed as aforesaid, shall cease and bee no

This rent of £102 to be paid at Christmas and Midsummer, in the south porch of Manchester church.

This rent-charge to cease upon the settlements of

longer paid or payable in any wise, but that the said messuages, barnes, lands, tenements, closes, and parcells of land, hereditaments, and premises last before mencõned, shalbee forever thereafter discharged, freed, and acquitted of and and from the payment thereof, and of every parte and parcell thereof. And my will and minde is that the same annuitie, yearely rent, or sume of one hundred and two pounds shall and may bee used, or ordered, imployed, and disposed of, for and dureing the continuance thereof as aforesaid, to and for the releife, maintenance, educacõn, bringinge upp, and binding apprentice, or other preferment of the said poore boyes, in such manner and sorte as the profitts, issues, rents, and revenewes of the aforesaid lands, tenements, and hereditaments, to bee purchased and bought by the said Edward Chetham, by and with the said sume of one thousand and seaven hundred pounds, to him by me formerly herein bequeathed (in case the same were purchased) should bee and are herein and hereby limitted and appointed. And I doe further hereby limitt, devise, bequeath, and appointe, that they the said Richard Holland, Alexander Barlow, &c., &c., and their heires and assignes and the survivors and survivor of them, theire and his heires and assignes, and every of them shall and may distraine for the said annuall or yearely rent, or sume of one hundred and two pounds, in or uppon the aforesaid messuages, barnes, lands, tenements, closes, and parcells of land, hereditaments, and premises in or by the last mencõned deed or indenture granted, conveyed, or assured as aforesaid, or any parte or parcell thereof in case the same bee arreare at any the daies or times before mencõned, as in case of a rent charge. And furthermore my will and minde is, that the said severall yearely rents, charges, or sumes of money shall, and may be granted, conveyed, and assigned by the survivors of the said Richard Holland, Alexander Barlow, &c., &c., when there are onely twelve of them in full life, or sooner, if the survivors of them shall thinke fitt, for the time beinge, in like manner and forme as the aforesaid lands and hereditaments, in case the same were purchased, are by the true intent and meaneinge of these presents to be conveyed and assured under and uppon the trust and confidence, and to and for the uses, purposes, and intents before mencõned; nevertheless under and uppon

other lands, of the same clear yearly value, to the same use by Edward Chetham.

This rent of £102 to be employed for the pious uses aforesaid.

The feoffees may distrain for the said rent, if in arrear.

The feoffees, when there are only twelve of them in full life, or sooner, to grant over to others the same rents, to the same uses.

the severall provisoes and condicons respectively before herein menconed, and accordinge to the tenor or purporte, true intent, and meaninge hereof, savinge that the said George Chetham (sonne of my said brother James Chetham) or Edward Chetham, nor the heires males of their bodies, are to bee grantees or feoffees thereof or therein, in regard they may have estates in the said lands and premises soe to be charged and chargeable with the said rents and sumes of money as aforesaid. And because my will and minde is, that the same poore boyes may cohabite, and live together in one house, or two, as may bee thought convenient, and under good gouernment; I doe give, devise, and bequeath unto my executors the sume of five hundred pounds of good and lawful money of England, to the intent and purpose that they shall buy and purchase therewith, some fittinge and convenient house or houses, in Manchester or Salford aforesaid, or some convenient parcell of land in or near Manchester or Salford aforesaid, and thereuppon to erectt an house or houses, which said house or houses soe to be bought or built shalbe an hospitall for the habitacon of the said forty poore boyes, theire governor, officers, and servants (other then theire treasurer or receiver), successively forever, to the pleasure of Almighty God. And my desire is that the great howse, with the buildings, outhouses, courts, yards, gardens and appurtenances, in Manchester aforesaid, called the colledge or the colledge house, may bee purchased and bought for the same purpose (if it may bee had, and obteyned uppon good termes and for a good estate), and I doe devise and desire, the same course may be taken for the setleinge, estatinge, conveyinge, and assureinge of the said house or houses and premises soe to bee bought or built for an hospitall or habitacon of fortie poore boyes and theire officers as aforesaid, unto and uppon the said Richard Holland, Alexander Barlow, &c., and theire heires and assignes forever, for the use, and behoofe of them the said Richard Holland, Alexander Barlow, &c., &c., and of my said executors and the survivors and survivor of them, and the heires and assignes of the said Richard Holland, Alexander Barlow, &c., &c., and of my said executors and of the survivors and survivor of them forever; nevertheles to and for the habitacon of the same governour, poore boyes, officers, and servants

George and Edward Chetham and their heirs male not to be grantees.

The poor boys to live together.

He devises £500 to his executors, to buy or build a house for that use in Manchester or Salford.

He desires that the College may be purchased, if it may be had, and conveyed to the feoffees, as the other lands.

(other than the said treasurer or receivour), and under and uppon such condicõn of infeoffinge over, as the said other lands and hereditaments to bee purchased are to bee, and if it may conveniently bee, the same to bee conveyed and assured to the said feoffees in and by the same deed or assurance, as the said other lands, rents, or hereditaments are to bee conveyed and assured. And my will and minde is, that if hereafter itt may bee obteyned, that the said hospitall may bee incorporated and made a body pollitick for the better orderinge, governinge, and manageinge thereof, and of the estate and meanes by mee to the same left or given that the same bee done in as good forme, way, and manner as cann or may bee contrived, procured, or obteyned. And my will and minde is, that there bee at all times hereafter fortie pounds in the treasurer or receivours hands, for the necessarie suply of necessarie occasions touching the premises, as defence or maintenance of the right and title belonginge to the said feoffees and hospitall. And if any overplus or surplusage bee of the said issues and profitts, rents and revenewes before mentioned, or of the said seaven thousand pounds given unto my cozens George and Edward as aforesaid, over and beside the discharge of the premises, then my will and minde is, that the same overplus bee ordered and imployed and disposed of to and for the augmentacõn of the number of poore boyes, or for the better maintenance and binding apprentice of the said forty poore boyes, in such manner as to the said feoffees for the time beinge, and persons intrusted and to be intrusted as aforesaid, or the greater number of soe manny of them as shall yearely meete as aforesaid shalbee thought fitt; and that my executors or the said feoffees or other persons trustees last before mentioned, shall have noe private benefitt by such overplus; and in case there bee not enough to binde any of them apprentice, then that which should have mainteyned him in the hospitall shalbee imployed for that purpose; and until that bee done no other is to succeed him in his place. And my will and minde is, that the said feoffees, or trustees for the time being, or the greater number of them, shall and may from time to time sett or lease any parts, or parcells of the said lands and hereditaments, to bee purchased as aforesaid (excepting the Hospitall Howse), with th'appurtenances, for anie

And in the same deed, if it conveniently may be.

He desires that the Hospital may be incorporated.

£40 to be always in the treasurer's hands, for necessary occasions.

The overplus of the revenue, if their be any, to augment the number of poor boys.

If there be not enough to bind any of them apprentice, his place not to be filled up till that money is saved

The feoffees to have power to set or lease the lands for eleven years, reserving the full rent.

number of yeares not exceeding eleaven years in possession, att any one time; and so as uppon the same therebee reserved the full rent or value, that cann be obteyned for the same, and with such covenants and conditions for repaire and payment of the rent or otherwise as shalbee thought fitt by the said lessors. Alsoe I give and bequeath unto my said executors and to the survivor of them to be sould for and towards the performance and accomplishment of this my last Will and Testament, all and every mannors, or reputed mannors, messuages, lands, tenements, rents, reverc̃ons, services, and hereditaments, with theire and every of their appurtenances, which are or were conveyed, sold or mortgaged unto mee or to and for my use, by Robert Tatton of Withenshawe in the county of Chester Esq., and Anne his wife, Richard Bannester of Brightmett in the said county of Lancaster, Gentleman, Catherine his wife, Alexander Bannester Gentleman, now deceased, late sonne of the said Richard, and by every or any of them, together with all other mannors, messuages, lands, tenements, rents, reverc̃ons, services, and hereditaments, with theire and every of theire appurtenances, in the said county of Chester, or in Aynsworth, Tonge, or Brightmett in the said county of Lancaster, whereof or wherein I the said Humfrey Chetham, or any other person or persons intrusted for me or to my use, have any estate, terme, or interest whatsoever, in possession, reverc̃on, remainder, use or otherwise.

He gives all lands mortgaged to him, to be part of his personal estate, and towards the performance of his will.

A lease granted by Isabel Chetham, in trust for the testator, to be part of his personal estate.

Alsoe whereas Isabel Chetham widdowe, lately deceased, by indenture dated the second day of August, which was in the yeare of our Lord God one thousand six hundred fortie and one, did demise, bargaine, and sell unto the said George Chetham (sonne of my said brother James Chetham), and to my nephew George Traves, their executors, administrators and assignes, certain messuages, lands, tenements, rents, reverc̃ons, services, and hereditaments, in the same indenture mentioned, for the terme of nine hundred yeares, which was nevertheles in trust for mee and to and for such uses as I by my last Will and Testament or otherwise, should direct, limitt, and appointe, albeit itt was not soe expressed in the said indenture, I doe hereby declare my mind and will to bee that the said lease, bargain, and sale, and all the benefitt and profitt, by vertue thereof, to bee reised and made out of or by the said messuages, lands, tenements, rents, reversions, services and hereditaments, in the same indenture expressed, or any of them, shalbee as parte of my personall estate, and shall goe and bee as assetts in the hands of my executors, for and towards the performance of this my last Will and Testament. Provided alwaies and my will and minde further is, that in case anie of the lands or hereditaments aforesaid which have been sould, conveyed, or mortgaged unto mee or to my use by the said Robert Tatton and Anne his wife, and Richard Bannester and Katherine his wife, and Alexander Bannester, and by every or any of them as aforesaid, as in the said last mentioned indenture expressed, may or ought to bee redeemed, either in lawe or equitie, by vertue of any condicõn annexed to the estate thereof or otherwise, and that the same bee hereafter redeemed accordinglie: That then my executors shall have all the moneys due and to be received for all such redemptions, in leiw of the said lands and hereditaments formerly herein bequeathed or intended, and soe to bee redeemed as aforesaid, for and towards the performance of this my last Will; and the said redemption money, my will is, shalbee imployed accordingely as the moneys which otherwise might be reised by the sale of the said lands and hereditaments should have done. And my will and mind is, that the interest of the moneys, and profitts of the said lands which shall bee reised or received out of all and every of the said lands, tenements and hereditaments, before sale or redemption thereof shalbee assetts in my executors hands, and goe towards the performance of this my last Will and Testament as parte of my personall estate. And I give and bequeath unto the said George Chetham (sonne of my brother James Chetham), all the estate, right, title, inheritance, terme, interest, and demands, which I have of in out of or unto anie messuages, lands, tenements, rents, revercõns, service, or hereditaments, in the parish of Boulton nigh Bolland, in the county of Yorke, or in the forest of Gisburne in the said county of Yorke, to have and to hold the same unto the same George Chetham (sonne of my said brother James Chetham), and to his heires, executors, administrators, and assignes, to and for his and their owne onely uses, benefitts and behoofes, for and dureinge and accordinge to my severall estates, termes, and interests thereof

The money arising from the redemption of the aforesaid mortgaged lands to be part of his personal estate

The interest of the profits of the said lands, before redemption, to be part of his personal estate

He gives his lands in Bolton near Bolland to George Chetham.

Particular legacies to his relations, friends, and servants, to be paid within six months after his decease.

or therein, respectively. Alsoe I doe give and bequeath unto my said brother James Chetham the sume of one hundred pounds, and unto my sister Alice Chetham one hundred pounds, and I give unto my cozen Jane Key widdow (one of the daughters of my said brother James Chetham), one hundred pounds, and to my cozen Isabel (one other of the daughters of the said James Chetham and now wife of one Richard Lomax) one hundred pounds. Alsoe I do give unto the said George Chetham (sonne of my said brother Raphe Chetham) two hundred pounds, and unto my cozen Mary, one of the daughters of the said Raphe and now wife of the said John Cunliffe two hundred pounds, and unto my cozen Margarett now wife of the said John Tildsley and one other of the daughters of the said Raphe Chetham two hundred pounds, and unto my cozen Eilzabeth, one other of the daughters of my said brother Raphe and now wife of Edward Croston two hundred pounds, and I do give unto the said Edward Croston fiftie pounds more. Alsoe I doe give and bequeath unto my nephew George Traves fifty pounds (the which said George doth now live with mee att Cleyton), and unto my cozen Richard Traves fifty pounds, and unto my cozen Raphe Traves fifty pounds, and unto my cozen James Traves fifty pounds. Alsoe I give unto Roger Walkden of Sharples in the county of Lancaster yeoman fortie ponnds, and unto my cozen Alice, wife of Richard Cowper fortie pounds. Alsoe I give unto my loveinge freind Mr. Richard Johnson aforesaid, preacher att the Temple London three score pounds. Alsoe I doe give and bequeath unto my loveinge freind before-named John Lightbowne fifty pounds. And I doe give and bequeath unto every of my servants which shall dwell or live with mee or in my service, att the day of my decease twentie shillings apeece, all and every which said legacies my will is shalbee paid to the several legatees aforesaid, their executors or administrators, within six moneths after my decease. And furthermore my will and minde is, and nevertheles the aforesaid guifts, legacies, bequests, and sumes of money soe by mee before herein given or bequeathed unto the said George Chetham, sonne of my said brother Raphe Chetham, Marie now wife of John Cunliffe, Margarett now wife of the said John Tildsley, Edward Croston, Elizabeth his now wife,

The legacies to his brother Ralph's children, his bro-

George Traves, Richard Traves, Raphe Traves, James Traves, Roger Walkden, Alice now wife of the said Richard Cowper, Jane Key, and Isabell wife of the said Richard Lomax, shalbe, and are by mee ment and intended to bee given and bequeathed upon this condic̃on followeinge, That is to witt, that in case the said George Chetham, sonne of the said Raphe Chetham, John Cunliffe, John Tildsley, Edward Croston, George Traves, Richard Traves, Raphe Traves, James Traves, Roger Walkden, Richard Cowper, Jane Key, and Richard Lomax, or anie of them, shall refuse, deny, or neglect to give, seale and deliver generall releases and acquittances to my said executors for and from all claimes, matters, and demands whatsoever, att such time or times as my executors shall make payment of the said severall legacies to them or any of them or anie of theire wives respectively given or bequeathed as aforesaid; and soe as upon the sealeinge and delivery of the said releases and acquittances respectively, they shall and may receive theire said legacies, gifts, and bequests before menc̃oned, to them or theire wives given as aforesaid, that then the said gifts, legacies, and bequests before menc̃oned, of and belonginge to such of them or theire wives, as shall soe refuse, denie, or neglect to give, seale and deliver generall releases and acquittances as aforesaid, shall respectively cease and bee voyd and determine and not bee paid to such of the same person or persons soe denieinge, refuseinge or neglectinge to give, seale and deliver generall releases and acquittances as aforesaid; for my will and minde is, that the said persons last mentioned and theire wives shall give such generall releases and acquittances in the law for and from all claimes, matters and demands whatsoever as aforesaid, as they shalbee respectively required by my executors as aforesaid at the time of theire respective receipts of the gifts or legacies before menc̃oned. Saveinge that my will and minde is, that the releases, which the said John Cunliffe, John Tildsley, Edward Croston, and George Traves, are hereby required to give, shall noe waies prejudice nor bee construed to prejudice the trust in them before herein or hereafter herein by mee reposed with the other persons before menc̃oned nor the settlement of lands to bee purchased, or devises or grantes of annuities or rente charges to them with others, by or accordinge to this my last Will, nor any-

ther James's daughters, and his sister Travis's children, are given upon condition that they seal general releases to his executors.

These releases not to prejudice the trust reposed in John Cunliff, John Tildsley, Edward Croston, & George Traves; nor to prejudice George Traves in the lands given him by the testator.

thinge touchinge the same nor anie guift of lands, tenements, or hereditaments, settled uppon the said George Traves by mee; but the same shall and may bee excepted in their severall releases or acquittances, if need bee, and that itt be soe thought fitt by my overseers. And I doe hereby ratifie, approve, and confirme the aforesaid three deeds or indentures before herein mencõned, to bee by mee made unto the said William Langton, Robert Mawdesley, Oswald Mosley, and John Lomax, and theire heires, and the estates, and uses thereby by mee graunted or mencõned to bee by mee graunted, accordinge to the severall tenors and purports thereof, and under and uppon the powers, provisoes, liberties, and limittations therein respectively conteyned and expressed. And whereas I have in and by the aforesaid deed or indenture, beareinge date the eight day of this instant December, charged the capitall messuage, lands, hereditaments, and premises (therein mentioned and comprized), with the payment of the sume of two thousand pounds to the said Edward Chetham for his owne use, accordingly as is therein expressed, my will and desire is, that the same sume of two thousand pounds be accordingly paid as is therein mentioned, and that the same Edward doe therewith soe soone as hee can conveniently after he hath received the said sume of two thousand pounds lay the same out upon the purchase of some lands, tenements, or hereditaments, and settle the same upon himselfe and his children in such manner as hee shall thinke fitt. And touching the number of mourneinge garments or blackes to be worn for mee, and all the charges of my funerall, I doe wholly leave and referr the same to my two executors, to bee by them considered of and ordered accordinge to theire discreations. Alsoe I doe hereby give and bequeath the sume of two hundred pounds to be bestowed by my executors in godly English Bookes, such as Calvins, Prestons, and Perkins workes, comments of annotacõns uppon the bible or some parts thereof, or such other bookes as the said Richard Johnson, John Tildsley, and Maister Hollinworth or anie of them shall thinke most proper for the edificacõn of the common people, to be by the discrecõn of my said executors chained uppon deskes, or to bee fixed to the pillars or in other convenient places, in the parrish churches of Manchester and Boulton in the Moores aforesaid,

He ratifies and confirms the three deeds before mentioned, made to William Langton, Robert Mawdsley and others.

Edward Chetham to lay out £2,000 given to him, upon lands, &c., and to settle the same upon himself and his children.

Mourning and funeral expenses to be at the discretion of his executors.

He gives £200 to be laid out in godly books, to be fixed in Manchester and Bolton.

and in the chappels of Turton, Walmisley, and Gorton, in the said county of Lancaster, within one yeare next after my decease. Alsoe I give unto my said executors one thousand pounds to be by them bestowed in such bookes as the said Richard Johnson, John Tildsley, and Richard Hollinworth or any two of them shall thinke fitt for or towards a librarie within the towne of Manchester, for the use of schollars and others well affected to resort unto; and if the said colledge or colledge house in Manchester may be obteyned and purchased as aforesaid, then I would have some convenient parte or place thereof or therein, such as my executors and the said three persons last menc̃oned, together with my overseers hereafter herein menc̃oned, shall think fitt to be the place for the same library, and where the same bookes may be laid and disposed of for the use of schollars and others well affected as aforesaid; and if the same cannot be obteyned, then I leave the ellection of the same place for the said librarie to the discrec̃ons of my said executors and overseers, and of the said Richard Johnson, John Tildsley, and Richard Hollinworth, or of the greater number of them, soe as the same bee in some of the chappells of the said church of Manchester, if the same cann bee obteyned, or elsewhere in the said towne of Manchester; the same bookes there to remaine as a publick librarie forever; and my minde and will is, that care be taken that none of the said bookes be taken out of the said librarie att anie time. And my will, minde, and desire is, that the ordereinge and disposing of the said bookes and library may bee by such persons from time to time forever, as I have herein formerly appointed to bee Feoffees and persons intrusted for the orderinge of the said poore children. And my will and minde is, that the same bookes bee fixed or chained as well as may bee within the said librarie for the better preservac̃on thereof. And I doe hereby give and bequeath unto my said executors one hundred pounds, to bee by them bestowed in purchaseinge, providinge, prepareinge, and repaireing of some fitt place for the said librarie and necessaries and conveniences for the same purpose, the same to bee settled and assured, as the same hospitall house as aforesaid. Alsoe I will that my said executors shall be allowed all the charges, expenses, costs, and damadges to the full, which they shall make appeare to my

Also others for the chapels of Turton, Walmsley and Gorton.

About £1000, to be bestowed in books for a public library in Manchester, to be in the College if it may be obtained, or elsewhere at the discretion of his executors, &c.

The ordering of the books to be by the feoffees for the ordering the poor boys.

The books to be fixed or chained within the said Library.

He gives £100 to purchase or prepare a place for a library.

The executors to be allowed all the expenses they shall

be put to in the execution of the will.

overseers hereafter named, that they or anie of them shall have expended, disbursed or susteyned, or shall bee putt unto by reason of the proveinge, executeinge of this last will, or otherwise concerninge the same, or in anie wise touchinge my funerall charges before menconed. And as touchinge and concerneinge all the rest, residue, and remainder of all my goods, chattles, plate, leases for yeares, household stuffe, and personal estate whatsoever, after all the guifts, legacies, and bequests before menconed, debts, funerall expenses, and other charges whatsoever, concerning this my last will or the execucon thereof, being paid and performed, and my said executors satisfied and saved harmelesse and indemnified of and for the same, out of my estate as aforesaid, I doe will and devise that all the said rest, residue, and remainder of my said personall estate shalbee bestowed by my executors in bookes, by the discrecon of the said Richard Johnson, John Tildsley, and Richard Hollinworth, or anie of them, to be bought, and disposed of, ordered, and kept in such place, and in such sorte as the said other bookes are to bee, which are to bee bought with the said sume of one thousand pounds, formerly herein by mee for that purpose bequeathed; and the same shall bee for the further augmentacon of the said librarie.

The residue of his personal estate to be employed for the augmentation of the library.

And I doe desire and appoint my said very loveinge friends, John Lightbowne and Raphe Worsley, and my said cozens Edward Croston and George Traves, to bee overseers of this my last Will and Testament, and to see the same performed by the executors, accordinge to the great trust by mee in them reposed. And if after my decease there shall happen any controversie, doubt or difficultie to arrise concerneinge this my last Will and Testamentarie disposicon, or any parte thereof, or of any ambiguitie or doubt to growe by reason of the imperfection or defect of or in any the words, sentences, or clauses herein conteyned, itt is my will and minde that the whole decideinge, determinacon, and exposicon thereof shalbee by the wisedomes and good discretions of my said overseers.

He appoints overseers to see that his will be performed by his executors.

All doubts that may arise concerning the will, or any part thereof, to be determined by the said overseers.

And furthermore I doe hereby revoke all and every former and other wllls, legacies, bequests, executors, and overseers by mee in any wise before the day of the date of theis presents made, willed, bequeathed, or named.

He revokes all former wills

And lastly I doe approve, publish, and declare this writeinge, conteyned in fower skins of

Declares this writing, contained in the

parchment, uppon every of which I have written my name, to conteine my true, whole, and onely last Will and Testament; and for further confirmac̃on thereof I have sett my seale, the day and yeare first above written, to witt the before herein mentioned sixteenth day of December in the abovesaid yeare of our Lord God one thousand six hundred fiftie and one.

four skins of parchment, to be his true, whole, and only last will.

HUMFREY CHETHAM.

Sealed, signed, published, and declared, by the within named Humfrey Chetham, Esq., to be his last Will and Testament—theis words (or of the said seaven thousand pounds given to my said cozein George and Edward as aforesaid)—and theis words (And in case there bee not enough to bind any one of them apprentice then that which should have mainteyned him in the hospitall shalbee imployed for that purpose and untill that bee done noe other is to succeed him in his place)—and theis words (nor any guift of lands tenements or hereditaments setled uppon the said George Traves) by mee being first interlyned in the last skin of parchment. And the said Humfrey Chetham to every of the foure skins did write his name with his owne hand, in the presence and witnesse of (being after the sealeinge and delivery of the within mentioned deed or indenture beareing date the eight day of this instant moneth of December) and after the same deed or indenture was executed by attornment.

Theophilus Howorth — Robert Haulgh
John Lomax — John Chorlton
Thomas Baron — Richard Hartley
Peter Assheton

The following certificate is attached to the "probate" copy of the will:—

Oliver Lord Protector of the Com̃onwealth of England Scotland and Ireland and the Dominions thereunto belonging To all persons to whome theis p'sents shall come Greeting Know yu that uppon the one and twentieth daie of March one thousand sixe hundred fiftie three before the Judges for probate of wills and grauntinge Adc̃ons lawfullie authorized the last will and testament of Humfrey

Chetham late whilst hee lived of Cleyton in the Countie of Lancaster deceased was in due forme of Lawe prooved which will is to theis presents annexed Adcon of all and singuler ye goods chells and debts of the said deced which may any manner of way concerne hym or hys—said will was graunted and comitted to George Chetham and Edward Chetham ye extors named in the said will, they having first taken theire oaths well and trulie to administer ye said goods chells and debts of the deced according to ye tenor and effect of the same will and to make or cause to bee made a true and perfect Inventorie of all and singuler the goods chells and debts of ye said deced wch have shall or may come to their hands possion or knowledge and alsoe a iust Accompt in and concerning their said Administracon when yey [they] shalbee assigned or lawfullie called soe to doe which touching an Inventorie they were presentlie assigned to performe at or before last daie of this instant moneth of March, ye aforesaid will beeinge pronounced for by a diffinitive sentence formerlie read. Given att Westm under the Seale of ye Court for pbate of wills and grauntinge adons the said one and twentieth of March 1653.

THO. SERLE Deputy Regr. MARK COTTLE Regr.

R. SANKEY.

APPENDIX II.

INVENTORY OF HUMPHREY CHETHAM'S GOODS.

THE following inventory is entered on a parchment scroll, ten feet long, among the documents belonging to the Feoffees of the Hospital, and is copied by permission of Henry Taylor, Esq., Solicitor to the Feoffees.

A TRUE AND PERFECT INVENTORIE of all the goods and chattells of Humphrey Chetham late of Clayton in the County of Lancaster Esquire deceased apprised by us Thomas Strangways of Gorton Esquire Raphe Worsley of Platte Gentleman John Lomax of Chetham gentleman and Henry Dickonson of Manchester gentleman : At Clayton the ffive and Twentyeth day of October in the yeare of our Lord God one Thousand sixe hundred ffifty and three.

	li	s	d
Imprimis in Apparell with some small Remlants of cloth and one ould Watche at - - - - -	20	00	00
Item in plate in - - - - - - - -	75	00	00
Item in Gold Rings and litle Cupp at - - -	07	00	00
Item three paire of ffine sheet at - - - -	01	10	00
Item two paire Round sheets at - - - -	00	08	00
Item fourteene Table Napkins Three Table Cloaths two Towells and Two Pillow beeres at - -	01	00	00
In the Hall.			
Item one longe Table on the Northside and three long fformes at - - - - - - - -	01	06	08
Item three cheares one Livery Table and one quishion at - - - - - - - -	00	06	08

*In the Great Parlo^r^*

Item one long Table with a greene Carpet at - -	02	00	00
Item two square Tables at - - - - - -	00	10	00
Item one Cubboard Table wth an ould Greene Carpet at - - - - - - - - -	00	10	00
Item one litle Livery Table at - - - - -	00	04	00
Item sixe Stooles covered with sett worke at - -	00	15	00
Item foure Stooles covered with Blewe at - -	00	08	00
Item two covered Cheeres at - - - - - -	00	08	00
Item one Back Stoole and plaine stoole covered with greene at - - - - - - - -	00	02	00
Item sixe Quishions at - - - - - - -	00	10	00
Item one paire of ould Tonges at - - - - -	00	00	06

In the Parlour Closet.

Item one Table and one quishion at - - -	00	10	00
Item in the Wall Twenty Boxes at - - -	00	06	08
Item one Portmantle with twoe Cloath bags at -	00	10	00
Item two paire of Gold weights with some other small things at - - - - - - - -	00	04	00

In the Closet in the end of the Gallery.

Item in Bookes at - - - - - - - - -	20	00	00
Item one Table one stoole and a Quishion at - -	00	05	00

In the Greene Chamber.

Item one square Table at - - - - -	00	01	00
Item one Cubboard Table at - - - - - -	00	10	00
Item two covered Cheares and two covered stooles at	00	18	00
Item three soiled formes at - - - - - -	00	06	08
Item five soiled stooles at - - - - - -	00	10	00

In his lodginge Chamber.

Item one standinge Bed at - - - - - -	02	00	00
Item four paire of newe sheetes at - - - - -	01	04	00
Item two feather beds two bolsters and one pillowe at - - - - - - - - - - -	03	15	00
Item one Caddowe and three Blankets at - -	01	02	00
Item in Curtaines and Rods at - - - - -	00	13	04
Item one litle Round Table at - - - - -	00	03	00

Item one soiled Cheare at - - - - -	00	03	04
Item one faire Presse at - - - - -	01	06	08
Item one covered Stoole and three quishions at -	00	05	00

In the Corner Chamber.

Item one Bedstead at - - - - - - - -	01	04	00
Item one Truckle Bed at - - - - -	00	04	00
Item one Chest at - - - - - - -	00	06	00
Item two Back Stooles at - - - - - -	00	04	00
Item four soiled Stooles at - - - - - -	00	08	00
Item one Table at - - - - - - -	00	06	00
Item one feather bed one Bolster and two Pillowes at	02	08	06
Item two white Caddowes three blankets and a paire of Sheetes at - - - - - - -	01	04	00
Item one paire of Tongs and ffire shoole at - -	00	02	00

In the Closet next to the Corner Chamber.

Item one Presse at - - - - - -	00	13	04
Item one litle Table at - - - - - - -	00	04	00
Item sixe litle Boxes at - - - - - -	00	03	00

In another Closet adioyneinge to the Corn^r Chamber.

Item in Gunpowder at - - - - - - -	03	00	00
Item in armour three ould Bills two swords and three paire of Bandalears at - - - - - -	00	13	04

In the Maids Chamber.

Item one standinge bed and one Truckle bed at -	00	14	00
Item one feather bed three bolsters and two Pillowes at - - - - - - - - - - -	02	07	00
Item one Chaf bed at - - - - - - -	00	03	00
Item sixe Blankets two coverlets and two paire of sheetes at - - - - - - - - -	01	08	00
Item one Truncke at - - - -	00	04	00
Item one Box at - - - - - - - -	00	02	06
Item one Chest at - - - - - - - -	00	05	00
Item in Remlants of Lynnen Cloath at - - -	00	09	04
Item ffive Sheets at - - - - - - -	01	04	00
Item two Pillow beeres at - - - - -	00	03	04
Item two Towells at - - - - -	00	02	00

In the Closet next to the Maids Chamber.

Item one Presse at - - - - - - - -	00	05	00

In the White Chamber.

Item two standing Beds at - - - - - -	02	00	00
Item one Canopy Bed and one Truckle bed at -	00	13	04
Item three ffeather beds ffive fether bolsters a chaffe bolster and one Pillowe at - - - - - -	07	10	00
Item sixe Blankets a coverlet and a Cadowe at -	01	04	00
Item two paire of sheets at - - - - - -	00	12	00
Item two Chests at - - - - - - - -	00	16	08
Item one Covered Cheare and foure covered Stooles with two plaine soiled Stooles at - - -	00	14	00
Item one fire Iron at - - - - - - - -	00	04	00

In the Gatehouse Chamber.

Item one bedstead curtaines and valens at - -	02	00	00
Item one Truckle bed at - - - - - - -	00	04	00
Item two feather beds two bolsters and two Pillowes at - - - - - - - - - - -	04	04	00
Item one Caddow one coverlet and Sixe blanckets at	02	04	00
Item one Chaffe bed at - - - - - - - -	00	03	00
Item in window Curtaines at - - - - -	00	02	00
Item in Square Table at - - - - - - -	00	04	00
Item one Livery Cubboard at - - - - -	00	10	00
Item one Chest at - - - - - - - - -	00	06	00
Item two Desks at - - - - - - - -	00	06	08
Item one Covered Cheare one covered stoole one covered back stoole and two joyned stooles at -	00	14	00
Item one litle Carpet and two quishions at - -	00	04	00

In the litle Parlour.

Item one Bedstead at - - - - - - - -	00	06	08
Item one ffeather bed two Pillowes and one flock bolster at - - - - - - - - - -	01	16	00
Item three blanckets one Cadow and one paire of sheetes at - - - - - - - - - -	01	02	00
Item one Table and one cheare with three joyned stooles at - - - - - - - - - -	00	10	00

In the Ward Roabe Parlour.

Item one Bedstead at - - - - - - -	00	10	00
Item one Chest at - - - - - - - -	00	05	00

In the Nursery.

Item one ould bed and one ould forme at - -	00	04	06

In the Fellowes Parlour.

Item one standinge Bed and two ould low bedsteads at - - - - - - - - - - -	00	12	00
Item foure Coverings two blanckets and a Caddowe at	01	00	00
Item one feather Bolster at - - - - -	00	06	00
Item two paire of Sheetes at - - - - -	00	08	00
Item two flock bolsters three chaffe bolsters and three chaffe beds at - - - - - - -	00	14	00
Item a hammer and a paire of pincers - - -	00	00	06
Item two formes and one Lanterne at - - -	00	02	00

In the Buttery.

Item one Round Table at - - - - - -	00	06	08
Item one Tennell five painted dishes and some other small things at - - - - - - - -	06	06	08

In the Closet by the Buttery.

Item fifteene glasse Bottles at - - - -	00	02	06
Item in shelve boards at - - - - - -	00	02	06
Item in the Entry one great Chest at - - -	00	10	00

In the ould Buttery.

Item fouer Throwes to sett Barrells upon at - -	00	05	00
Item three juggs at - - - - - - - -	00	00	09

In the Sellor.

Item ffoure Throwes to sett Barrells upon at - -	00	06	08
Item three hogsheads at - - - - - - -	00	07	00
Item five Barrells at - - - - - - - -	00	13	04
Item one Tundish at - - - - - - -	00	01	00
Item eight glasse Bottles and foure stone bottles at -	00	03	00

In the Roome over the Sellor.

Item three ould Tubbs a broken throwe one Eashen and two Rodds of Iyon with some other small thinges at - - - - - - - - -	00	04	00

In the Deyry howse.

Item one long Table with three Tresses whereon it stands at	00	05	00
Item one ould Cubboard Table at	00	05	00
Item one square Table at	00	03	04
Item on[e] Safe at	00	13	04
Item one Lead Tub at	00	16	00
Item one great Turnnell at	00	05	00
Item one great salting Tub and one litle one at	00	13	04
Item one long forme two long boards and one ould bast at	00	04	00
Item sixe milke Runges at	00	04	00
Item six butter potts at	00	03	00
Item in Butter at	01	00	00
Item two little Stands one great Canne and a little Bason at	00	04	00

In the Cheese Chamber.

Item in Cheese at	01	10	00
Item in Lead Weights at	01	03	04
Item in Cheese boards and trests at	00	04	00
Item one beame and scales at	00	05	00
Item one ould presse one ould Arke Lid and a cheese grate at	00	03	00

In the Kitchine.

Item one Plancke at	00	05	00
Item one Chest at	00	08	00
Item one litle Cubbard at	00	02	06
Item one ould forme at	00	00	06
Item two Easehens at	00	02	06
Item three cheares one back stoole and five quishions at	00	08	04
Item three Racks one crosse barr of Iron two paire of Tongs three chafing dishes one fire shoole one tosting Iron two little Brundaithes with a broad peace of Iron at	00	10	00
Item three hatchinge knives two pesteles and one fleshhooke at	00	04	06

Item three drippinge Pannes wth other small things of tinne at - - - - - . - - -	00	03	00
Item one smoothinge iron at - - - - - -	00	02	00
Item one batrell and Rouling Pin at - - -	00	00	02
Item twelve muskets and one dragoone at - -	02	00	00
In the Pastery next to the Kitchen.			
Item two stooles at - - - - - - -	00	04	00
Item one frying Panne one hand peele and one grater and one handbasket at - - - -	00	03	00
In the other Pastery.			
Item one Cubbard at - - - - - - -	00	13	04
Item one Chest at - - - - - - - -	00	06	08
Item in Pitchers Pots and glasse bottles two litle Cans and one wisket at - - - - -	00	02	06
Item in Pewter at - - - - - - - -	11	00	00
Item in Brasse pot mettle at - - - - -	02	15	10
Item in Panne mettle at - - - - - -	01	06	8
Item one warmeinge Pann at - - - - -	00	04	00
Item three Skellets and a Ladle at - - - -	00	04	06
In the Roome next to the Kitchine.			
Item one Table and forme at - - - - - -	00	06	8
Item one thick Trest at - - - - - -	00	02	6
Item two Lanterns at - - - - - - -	00	01	4
Item two costrels one Eashen foure Chessuds and one great Bason at - - - - - - -	00	06	00
Item foure litle Cans and a boule at - - -	00	00	10
In the Back house.			
Item three Cheese presses at - - - - -	00	10	00
Item six Spitts with other small things of Iron at -	00	12	00
Item one eashen one ould chest one Throwe & one trest wth other smal things at - - - - -	00	05	00
In the darke howse at the end of the Hall entry.			
Item one paire of Racks at - - - - - -	00	06	8
Item one Tubb and one Asboard at - - -	00	01	00
In the Brewhowse.			
Item two great Keares and two Brewing Keares at -	01	10	00

Item one Ironing Tub and two great Runges at -	00	07	06
Item three Milke Runges at - - - - -	00	02	00
Item foure Eashens at - - - - - - -	00	05	00
Item four Piggins at - - - - - - -	00	02	00
Item one Churne and Curdle at - - - -	00	05	00
Item in Basons throwes chessuds cans two trests and other small things at - - - - - - -	00	06	08
Item one Keare to steepe Mault in at the Brewhouse doore at - - - - - - - - -	00	06	8

At Clayton the 26th day of October, 1653.

Item in the Large Entry one frame for Boxes at -	00	02	06

In the Chamber over the Kitchine.

Item one great Maulte Arke at - - - - -	01	10	00
Item another lower Maulte Arke at - - -	01	06	8
Item the Highest Meale Arke at - - - - -	01	04	00
Item the Meale Arke with two locks upon it - -	01	04	00
Item one ould bolting Arke at - - - -	00	05	00
Item two litle Chests at - - - - - - -	00	06	00
Item two lead weights at - - - - - -	00	05	00
Item in Mault ffive Loads at - - - - -	03	06	8
Item in Meale three Loads at - - - - -	02	00	00
Item in wheat flower at - - - - - - -	00	05	00
Item in groats at - - - - - - - -	00	05	00
Item fouer sacks at - - - - - - -	00	08	00
Item in Tallowe at - - - - - - -	00	02	00
Item in the Onyon Chamber in Onyons at - -	00	06	8
Item one ould bedstead one ffeath^r Tub and a window Lid at - - - - - - - - -	00	02	00
Item in the Chamber over the Henhouse one ould bedstead at - - - - - - - -	00	02	00

In the Chamber over the Backhouse.

Item in Spoakes at - - - - - - -	02	10	00
Item in Axle trees at - - - - - - -	00	12	00
Item in Netherheads at - - - - - - -	00	03	4
Item in Plowe sheathes at - - - - - -	00	03	4
Item in spade shafts and shooe shafts at - - -	01	00	00
Item in cloven wood and cart staves at - - -	00	02	00

In the Chamber over the Brewhouse.

Item in ffelies for wheeles at - - - - - -	01	12	00
Item in Harrowes and Chaines to them at - -	02	13	4
Item in Oxe Yoakes with bowes and chaines belonginge to them at - - - - - - - -	01	05	00
Item one Gill Roape with an Iron hooke at - -	00	09	00
Item in Cart Roapes at - - - - - - -	00	11	00
Item one ffanne at - - - - - - -	00	06	8
Item in Rakes and Soales at - - - -	00	10	00
Item in Iron Chaines and Clevisses at - - -	01	00	00
Item on Hopper and other small things at - -	00	02	00

In the Porters Ward.

Item in spades and shooles at - - - - -	00	10	00
Item in fforcks and mattocks at - - - -	00	10	00
Item two Iron Crowes at - - - - - -	00	08	00
Item two Pickforcks at - - - - - -	00	03	4
Item in shares and colters at - - - - -	00	10	00
Item in Sythes at - - - - - - - -	00	06	8
Item in Bills and axes with a hamer at - - -	00	13	4
Item in Iron wedges at - - - - - -	00	04	00
Item in Sawes Nogres Chisels Wimbles Goarges one Trowel one Spoakeshave and a hamer at - -	00	09	00
Item in Water piles and mawes wth other odde things in that place at - - - - - -	00	05	00

In the Lyme howse with those in the Gallery adioyneinge.

Item in Inch boards and halfe inch boards at - -	35	00	00
Item one ould Truckle bed with other small things at	00	03	04

In the Coale house.

Item in Coales one wisket and a shovell at - -	04	00	00
Item in Turves in all at - - - - - - -	02	10	00

In the Corne Chamber.

Item in Windowed Oates at - - - - - -	30	00	00
Item in Sacks at - - - - - - - -	01	00	00
Item in measures, sives and scuttles wth two shovels and two planks at - - - - - - -	00	12	00
Item one ould cubboard at - - - - - -	00	05	00

In one of the Chambers over the Gatehowse.

Item in Wheat threshed and windowed at - -	05	10	00
Item in Barley windowed in the same Roome wth some odd timb^r^ at - - - - - - -	06	00	00
Item in the other Gatehowse Chamber in windowed Beanes at - - - - - - - - - -	05	10	00
Item in the Chappell in Latts and ould Sparthes at -	00	05	00

In the ould Barne.

Item two muck Carts with one Harvest Cart and the Wheeles at - - - - - - - -	09	00	00
Item another Cart with wheeles in the new Barne at	01	00	00
Item three Coale Carts and two harvest Carts at -	03	10	00
Item one pair of Bolster Bowes and some other odde Timber at - - - - - - - - - -	00	03	00

In the Stable.

Item in seaventeene Barks and fouer Cart Saddles at	00	11	00
Item nyne Halters at - - - - - - - -	00	10	00
Item ffower Redgwiths and fouer Belly bands at -	00	10	00
Item two swingletrees and thaives at - - - -	00	04	00
Item in Iron Trease at - - - - - - - -	01	00	00
Item in Hempen Trease at - - - - - - -	00	16	00
Item in three paire of Thilhames and harrowinge Teights and hempen halters at - - - - -	00	04	00
Item one paire of hindmost Gheeres at - - -	00	01	00
Item two Sleads at - - - - - - - -	00	06	8

In the Oxe house.

Item three Turfe carts and two cart chests at - -	01	15	00
Item in ould shod wheeles with axletrees at - -	01	16	00
Item two ould coale baskets at - - - - -	00	01	00

In the New Stable.

Item one Chest at - - - - - - - - -	00	05	00
Item five hackney saddles and foure bridles with furniture at - - - - - - - - -	02	00	00
Item one shovel and a halter wth other small things in the same place at - - - - - - -	00	03	4
Item in Slate at - - - - - - - -	03	10	00

Item in Bricke at - - - - - - - - -	00	15	00
Item the Boate with fouer plowes and some other small timber in it at - - - - - - -	01	00	00
Item ffive Ladders at - - - - - - - -	00	15	00
Item in Oats in both Barnes unthreshed at - -	80.	00	00
Item in wheate unthreshed at - - - - - -	35	00	00
Item in Beanes unthreshed at - - - - -	27	00	00
Item in Haye at - - - - - - - - -	55	00	00
Item nyne worke horses at - - - - - -	36	00	00
Item one white Mare at - - - - - -	06	00	00
Item three Coltes all three yeares ould past at -	17	00	00
Item foure ffilly Coults at one yeare ould at - -	10	00	00
Item two wained Colts at - - - - - -	03	10	00
Item five Oxe stirkes at - - - - - - -	10	00	00
Item eight Cowe stirks at - - - - - -	15	00	00
Item seaven twinter stewers at - - - - -	20	00	00
Item eight Twinter heifers at - - - - - -	25	00	00
Item three fatt Oxen at - - - - - - -	16	00	00
Item one Bull at - - - - - - - - -	03	13	4
Item sixteene Melch kine at - - - - - -	44	13	4
Item nyne Calves at - - - - - - - -	10	10	00
Item sixe shoates at - - - - - - - -	04	00	00
Item two swine at - - - - - - - - -	02	05	00
Item two fatt swine at - - - - - - - -	04	00	00
Item one Chest at Thomas Minshalles in Manchester at - - - - - - - - - - - -	00	05	00

At the New Barne in Ordsall the 27th of October, 1653.

Imprimis in the Chamber one ould Bedstead one Chaffebed one Chaffe bolster one fether Bolster one Coverlet two blancketts and one paire of Sheets at - - - - - - - - - -	01	00	00
Item in Oxe Teames and foure Oxe yoaks at - -	01	00	00
Item one fire Iron and a Lanterne at - - - -	00	10	9
Item one great Roape at - - - - - -	00	16	00
Item in Plowe Sheaths and other odde Timber at -	00	01	06

Item one frameinge Sawe two ould shovels two nogres two Chisels one paire of Plow Irons three

mucke scratches one hopper and one ould axe at	00	10	00
Item fouer Pickforks one ould Bill foure ould Riddles two ould scutles two short Chaines and three Iron forks at - - - - - - - - -	00	10	00
Item one ould window sheete with some litle timbr at	00	03	00
Item windowed Oats at - - - - - - -	00	16	00

In the Great Stable.

Item fouer plowes one swingletree one Chaine and two paire of plowe Irons - - - - - -	00	16	00
Item fouer harrowes with Chaines and swingletrees at - - - - - - - - - - -	01	04	00
Item one Iron crowe at - - - - - - -	00	05	00
Item one Cart Saddle two paire of Trease and a paire of hindmost gheeres at - - - - - -	00	10	00
Item one Carte Roape at - - - - - -	00	03	04
Item in ffelies at - - - - - - - - -	00	08	00
Item one ould paire of shodd Wheeles at - -	00	10	00
Item one Dearne powle with its furniture at - -	01	00	00
Item twenty soales at - - - - - - -	00	03	04
Item three Ladders at - - - - - - -	00	12	00
Item two fleakes at - - - - - - -	00	01	00
Item one Cart Chest - - - - - - -	00	04	00
Item one ould harvest Cart at - - - - -	00	10	00
Item in Timber about the Barne at - - - -	01	10	00
Item in Bricke at - - - - - - - -	00	16	00
Item in the Barne in Oats unthreshed at 60li - -	60	00	00
Item in Haye at - - - - - - - -	20	00	00
Item in Dunge at - - - - - - - -	03	00	00
Item seaventeene fatt Oxen one Bull and three heifers at - - - - - - - - - -	105	00	00
Item two Colts at - - - - - - - -	10	00	00

At Turton the Last day of October, 1653.

Imprimis in the Hall one Longe Table at - -	01	00	00
Item one soiled forme at - - - - - -	00	03	4
Item one Court Cubboard at - - - - - -	00	06	8

In the Buttery.

Item one ffaire Cubboard - - - - - - -	01	06	8

Item one Throw to lay Hogsheads upon & one thick Board at - - - - - - - - -	00	05	00
In the Dineinge Chamber.			
Item one longe Table at - - - - - -	01	06	8
Item one short Table at - - - - - -	00	10	00
In the Greene Chamber.			
Item one standing bed with mat and coards at -	01	06	08
Item one Chest bound with Iron at - -	01	06	08
In the Chamber over the Porch.			
Item one standing bed with mat and coards at -	00	18	00
In the Closett over the Porch.			
Item one Presse and one Table at - - - -	01	03	4
In the Parlour.			
Item one Table at - - - - - - -	01	00	00
In the lower Kitchine.			
Item two presses at - - - - - - -	00	04	00
Item in the Pastry one ould presse at - - -	00	06	8
In the Brewhowse.			
Item one Stone Throughe and one Cheese presse at	00	12	00
In the Brewhowse Chamber.			
Item two Meale Arks at - - - - - -	03	00	00
Item one Chest at - - - - - - - -	00	10	00
In the Kitchine.			
Item one Beame and Scales a barre of Iron and a Racke which hangs at it at - - - - -	00	04	00
In the Chamber over the Deyryhouse.			
Item three ffformes one dripper and one ould cheare at	00	05	00
In the Servants Chamber over the Kitchine.			
Item ffive bedstocks at - - - - - - -	00	10	00
In the Deyry howse.			
Item one Lead Saltinge Tub and four fflags at -	02	10	00
Item in the back Kitchinge one ould Table at -	00	05	00
Item one Litle Table in the Porche at - - -	00	03	4
Item in the Killne three great Garners and two great Keares at - - - -	05	10	00

In the Millne.

Item one great Arke and a Chest at - - -	00	16	00
Item one Crowe Two ham̄ers and twelve Picks at -	00	08	00
Item one Millne Roape at - - - - - -	00	04	00
Item twoe Millne stones at - - - - - -	00	13	4
At Okenbothome the first day of November, 1653.			
Imprimis in Oates unthreshed at - - - - -	02	10	00
Item in Haye at - - - - - - - - -	05	10	00
Item the Okenbothome howse the Millnes Kilne and the Appurtenances together with the Land within the Towneshippe of Breightmet at 400li - -	400	00	00
Item in all Huslements at - - - - - -	00	10	00
The Totall of the goods and Chattells -	1459	18	10
In ready moneyes - - - - - - - -	6748	03	05
In debts whereof some are doubtfull and some desperate and in Mortgages - - - - -	5688	18	11
	13897	01	02

This Iñry was Ex̃ted the 29th day of Decembr in the year 1655 by Mr. John Allen Procter for the Executors for a true and perfect Inventory yett under Protestac̄on to add if need, &c., require, &c.

Jo. Ham̄ond.

A true Copie of the Copie granted out of the Prorogative Court Examind by us

Nathan Leech.
Jeremy Hargreaves.

NOTE to page 264, line 21. This item of twenty pounds' worth of books in the "closet at the end of the gallery" proves that Chetham possessed a not inconsiderable number of volumes. Compare the reference on page 125 to the 225 books in James Jollie's possession at Clayton, which Canon Raines thought it was "tolerably clear" had been secured by Chetham. Mr. Edward Edwards (*Manchester Worthies*, p. 29) has remarked that the Chetham Library "does not possess a single book that was the founders's."

In the Manchester Free Library there is a copy of Heylyn's *History of the Sabbath*, 1636 (bound up with Francis White's *Treatise of the Sabbath Day*, 1635), with the inscription of "Humphrey Chetham his Book, 1644." This volume came from the library of Mr. James Crossley, who in a *MS.* note declares his conviction that the autograph is genuine. Another book with an autograph inscription by Humphrey Chetham is mentioned in the *Palatine Note Book*, vol. iv. p. 118: *Considerations of Present Use concerning the Danger resulting from the Change of our Church-Government*, London, 1644. It was then (1884) in the possession of the late Mr. R. H. Sutton, having been purchased by him at the sale of Mr. Richard Wood's library. A third volume is noticed as follows in the catalogue of a sale of books at Sotheby's, London, on December 7, 1900: "No. 1304. Richard Rolle of Hampole, The Prick of Conscience. *MS.* xiv. cent." To this description the following note is appended: "This important old English manuscript was formerly the property of the famous Manchester philanthropist Humphrey Chetham, and was found in a loft at Pennington Hall near Haigh in Lancashire, the seat of the Hiltons, intimate friends of Chetham." The *MS.* was purchased by Mr. Toplis for £8 15*s.*

It is of great interest to find that a member of the Chetham family of Nuthurst was the possessor of manuscripts of early English poems. Mr. G. C. Macaulay in his edition of Gower's *English Works*, published by the Clarendon Press (vol. ii. p. cxli.), has a valuable note on a *MS.* of Gower's *Confessio Amantis*, in the Chetham Library (No. 6696), and a *MS.* of the *Destruction of Troy*, now in the Hunterian Museum, Glasgow University, both of them bearing evidences of former ownership by the Nuthurst Chethams. May not the above-mentioned copy of *The Prick of Conscience* have come from the same source before passing into the hands of Humphrey Chetham?

APPENDIX III.

Bills of Expenses at Humphrey Chetham's Funeral, extracted from the Originals in the Clowes Family Papers.

October 13th 1653.

Rec^d^ from Mr. Edward Chetham the sume of thirteene pounds and ten shillings in satisfaction for my paines and all other demands concerneing the funerall of Humfrey Chetham esq^r^ - - - - 13^li^ 10^s^

By mee Randle Holme [1]
deputy to the Office of Armes.

given to his servant - - - - - - - - 4^s^

An Accompt of the materialls and Charges for the Hearsse of Humphrey Chetham Armiger.

ffor materialls and working them upp for the Hearsse	06	13	04
ffor siz Eschocheons over and besyds those of the hearsse - - - - - - - - - -	02	00	00
ffor 100 Pennons for the poore and the Blewecoates	10	00	00
ffor 7 dozen and a halffe of ffringe - - - - -	00	15	00
	19	08	04

[Receipt Signed] Tho. Wroe
17 Oct.

A note of some worke done unto ye Chappell windowes at Manchester Church belonging to Humphry Chetham at Clayton esq.

348 quarrells 1^d^ per quarell - - - - - -	01	08	04
for leading and sodering 14 panes - - - -	00	07	00

[1] This bill is omitted from the summary on page .

for banding—88 foote at 1ᵈ per foote - - -	00	07	04
for 2 foote and a quarter new glasse - - -	00	01	00
	02	03	08

William Sorocould
17 Oct.

A note of Church dues for Humphrey Chetham of Clayton Esqr.

Imp^is for 6 houres passing peale - - - -	00	06	00
for ye grave and mason - - - - - - -	00	02	00
for 7 houres Ringing all ye Bells overnight - -	00	14	00
ffor Ringing all ye Bells from 8 aclocke in ye morneinge untill 9 a clocke at night ye Sermon while excepted - - - - - - - - -	01	04	00
for bringeing ye Beere to Clayton - - - -	00	02	00
for ye Bellmans paines and for Raphe Baguley -	00	08	00
for Reg. Stronge - - - - - - - -	00	00	04
	02	16	04
Paid Edmund Williamson for pointing ye Leades and ye Chappell Windowes and for morter - -	00	05	06
Paid Wm Hilton for 53 pound of Iron Barrs for ye Chappell Windowes at 4ᵈ per pound - - -	00	19	00
For a new Kaye mending ye locke - - - -	00	00	08
For an Iron to fasten ye great steeleing - - -	00	00	08
	01	01	02

[Recᵈ 17 Oct.]

Evan Clarke
Samuel Holinworth
Edmund Williamson
Wm. Hilton marke W H
Henry Walker

A note of Cleton.

It. a Cossen - - - - - - - - - -	1	0	0
the Hearse - - - - - - - - - -	1	0	0
for Caringe the Cossen - - - - - - -	0	3	0

for Caringe the hearse - - - - - - - -	0	4	0
for takinge downe the wenscot - - - - - -	0	2	0
for setinge the wenscot up - - - - - - -	0	3	0
for a pice of timber for the Crest - - - - -	0	1	0
	2	12	0

[Rec^{d} 13 Oct.]

Peter Lingard.

From Tho. Mynshull, Oct. 11° 1653.

ffor the funerall of the Worp^{ll} Humfrey Cheetham of Clayton Esq.

Three Boxes conteineing as follows

No. 1.	Allmond Comfetts	16^{li} - - - - -	01	12	0
	Cinamon Comfetts	15^{li} - - - - -	01	10	0
	Ginger Comfetts	11^{li} - - - - -	01	2	0
	Clove Comfetts	9^{li} - - - - -	00	18	0
	Coriand^{r} Comfetts	8^{li} - - - - -	00	16	0
	Orring Comfetts	6^{li} - - - - -	00	12	0
	Rose Comfetts	7^{li} - - - - -	00	14	0
	Violett Comfetts	9^{li} - - - - -	00	18	0
	Anniseed Comfetts	4^{li} - - - - -	00	08	0
	Muske Comfetts	2^{li} - - - - -	00	04	0
	Mixt Comfetts	2^{li} - - - - -	00	04	0
92^{li}	Smooth Allmon	3^{li} - - - - -	00	07	6
No. 2.	Allmon Comfetts	10^{li} - - - - -	01	00	0
	Ciñamon Comf.	6^{li} - - - - -	00	12	0
	Coriand^{r} Comfetts	6^{li} - - - - -	00	12	0
	Violett Comfetts	7^{li} - - - - -	00	14	0
	Orring Comfetts	4^{li} - - - - -	00	08	0
	Ginger Comfetts	4^{li} - - - - -	00	08	0
	Clove Comfetts	6^{li} - - - - -	00	12	0
45^{li}	Rose Comfetts	2^{li} - - - - -	00	04	0
No. 3.	Allmon Comfetts	8^{li} - - - - -	00	16	0
	Ciñamon Comfetts	6^{li} - - - - -	00	12	0
	Coriand^{r} Comfetts	6^{li} - - - - -	00	12	0
	Violett Comfetts	6^{li} - - - - -	00	12	0
	Rose Comfetts	2^{li} - - - - -	00	04	0
	Clove Comfetts	4^{li} - - - - -	00	08	0

No.	Item	£	s	d
	Ginger Comfetts 4^{li}	00	08	0
40^{li}.	Orring Comfetts 4^{li}	00	08	0
	Seaven Boxes of Naples Bread.			
4.	58^{li} 12^{oz} t^{r} 12^{li} 4^{oz} net 46^{li}	06	02	8
5.	42^{li} 8^{oz} t^{r} 10^{li} net 32^{li} 8^{oz}	04	06	8
6.	40^{li} 8^{oz} t^{r} 8^{li} 8^{oz} nett 32^{li}	04	05	4
7.	32^{li} 8^{oz} t^{r} 7^{li} 8^{oz} net 25^{li}	03	06	8
8.	38^{li} 6^{oz} t^{r} 8^{li} 6^{oz} net 30^{li}	04	00	0
9.	62^{li} t^{r} 11^{li} 8^{oz} net 50^{li} 8^{oz}	06	14	8
10.	in the Box w^{th} $leath^{r}$ dishes and Mack roones 11^{li} 8^{oz}	01	10	8
	Towe great boxes of Bisketts conteineing			
11.	120^{li} t^{r} 35. 8^{oz} nett 85^{li} 8^{oz}	06	8	3
12.	189^{li} 14^{oz} t^{r} 53. 6^{oz} nett 136^{li} 8^{oz}	10	4	9
13.	1 box of Candyed Orring and Lymon cont. 26^{li}	04	6	8
	and 2^{li} Cand. Greene Cytrã	00	9	0
	and 1^{li} 12^{oz} of Quince	00	7	0
14.	1 box of fyne paisl. of fruites conteineing 25^{li}	05	00	0
15.	1 box conteineing 3^{li} 11^{oz} of Rocke Candy	01	09	6
	and 3^{li} 6^{oz} $Ering^{g}$ Cand.	01	07	0
16.	1 Box Mackroones net 27^{li}	03	13	4
	more Mackroonẽs in the box w^{th} $leath^{r}$ dishes and Nap. bred 7^{li} 8^{oz}	01	00	0
17.	1 Box conteineing of Lump Sug^{r} 35^{li}	02	12	6
	1^{li} dry Cloves	00	09	8
	1^{li} Larg Cinamõ	00	06	8
	ij^{li} best $Ging^{r}$	00	02	8
	v^{li} best Nutt megs	00	03	6
18.	1 box more of Candyed Orring and lymon conteineing 8^{li} 11^{oz}	01	9	0
	Some is	87	11	8

Alsoe delivered to Geo. Travis the 24th of $Sept^{r}$ 1653.

Item	£	s	d
3^{li} best Corrans	0	3	0
3^{li} raisons son	0	2	0

2^{oz} large mace - - - - - - -	0	2	8
2^{oz} dry Cloves - - - - - - -	0	1	6
1^{oz} Cinamō - - - - - - -	0	0	6
1^{li} Browne Sug^r - - - - - - -	0	0	11
1^{li} Lump Sug^r - - - - - - -	0	1	6
1^{li} Bisketts - - - - - - -	0	1	6
xijth of Octob^r 1653.			
franke nuttmegs ? ^{li} - - - - -	0	1	10
best Corrans 2^{li} Raisons 2^{li} - - - - -	0	3	4
Alsoe x^{li} Lump Sug^r more the same day, wch was rec^d backe the day aft^r - - -	0	0	0
Some is - -	0	18	9
The Some &c. - -	88	10	5
The Spices and odo^{rs} for the Embalmeing of Mr. Cheetham - - - - - - -	23	00	00
	111	10	5

Rec^t 19 Oct. 1653

(Signed) Tho. Mynshull.

October 12, 1653. A noate of the Charges laid out at the funerall of Humfrey Chetham Esquire by me John Bordeman.

13 yards of silke fringe at 13^d - - - - - -	00	14	1
for Coveringe the Hearse (an nayles) - - -	00	10	0
for my dewes for the hanginge of blacke cloth at Hall and Church - - - - - - - -	00	10	0
(Rec^d 18 Oct.) John Bordeman.	1	14	1

Imp. for making ye pillian cloth - - - - -	00	06	00
for lethēr buckels and making the bridle and bresplat - - - - - - - -	00	10	00
for a black bit - - - - - - -	00	02	06
for a pear of black crul^e raines - - -	00	02	06
for a pear of black spurs - - - -	00	02	08
for a black sterup - - - - -	00	02	06

for a bridle and black bit - - - - -	00	04	06
for making 3 covers and 3 clothes - - -	00	03	06
for a bridle and blacke bit - - - - -	00	04	06
(Rec[d]) Thomas Barker.	01	18	08

Imp. for y[e] Sadle sterupes lethers and gerthes -	00	12	06
for making y[e] Cloth - - - - - -	00	06	00
for mending y[e] pillian - - - - - -	00	00	08
for making 2 Covers and a cloth - - -	00	01	08
for bridle and bit - - - - - -	00	04	06
for a pear of spurs - - - - - -	00	02	04
for a footstoole - - - - - - -	00	00	06
(Rec[d] 22 Oct. 1653) Thomas Barker.[1]	01	07	02

For the Fun[r]all of the Wott Humphrey Cheatom Esq[r]

For Mrs. Tilsley
Mrs. Croston
Mrs. Cundife.

17 yrds. q[r]ter rich Ducape at 12[s] 4[d] - -	10	12	09
30 yrd. Naples silke penella 7[s] 4[d] - -	11	00	00
11 yrd. quarter flor[d] sersnett at 10[s] 4 - -	05	16	03
for trimge these 3 gownes - - - -	03	07	05
3 Ducape hoods - - - - - - -	00	19	06

For Mr. Edward Cheethom } wifes
Mr. Richard Lomax }
Mrs. Jane Key.

43 yrd. 3 staled fine heire Callymanco 5[s] 9[d] -	12	18	09
22 yrd. $\frac{5}{8}$ heire prunella at 5[s] 10[d] - -	06	11	11
22 yrd. $\frac{1}{4}$ florr. sersenett at 10[s] 4 - - -	06	06	07
3 yrds. $\frac{5}{8}$ ducape for quoyfes and scar. 12. 4 -	02	04	08½
for trimge of these three gownes - - -	02	01	06

For yo[r] Maid Alce Hilton.

11 yrds. fine heire prunella 5[s] 10[d] - -	03	04	02
06 yrds. fine Italliano at 3[s] 8[d] - - -	01	02	00

[1] Thomas Barker's bills do not appear in the summary, pp. 206-207.

	£	s	d
for trim̃ge her gowne and petticoats	00	10	02
1 yrd. blã florrance sersnett 10s 4d	00	10	04
For Ann Baylif yor maide.			
6 yds. ha. Paddua seardge at 10s	01	06	00
for trim̃ge her gowne	00	09	06
1 yrd. florrance sersnett 10s 4d	00	10	4
For Raph Trevis, James Trevis, Rich. Coopr } wifes			
26 yrds. fine blã Italliano at 3s 4d	04	05	04
14 yrd. bla. flanders serdge 4s 8d	03	05	04
2 yrd. florrance sersnett 10s 4d	01	00	08
For Ann Trevis.			
6 yrd. ha. flanders serdge at 4s 8d p yrd.	01	10	10
For my brothers Maide.			
6 yrds. ½ Paddua seardge at 3s 8d	01	03	10
For Ann Ravald.			
12 yrd. blã flanders Cheney at 2s 10 p yrd.	01	14	00
4 yrd. ha. bla. Paddua serdge 3s 8d	00	16	06
For Mrs. Cheathom of Nuthurst.			
5 yrd. 3 quarters rich duc̃pe 12s 4d	03	10	11
11 yrds. ha. Naples Silke Prunella 7s 4d	04	04	04
for trim̃ge	00	15	08
For Mrs. Leightbowne of Salford.			
5 yrd. 3 quarters rich Ducape 12s 4d	03	10	11
8 yrds. fine Silke prunella broad 8s 2d	03	05	04
For Mrs. Mynshull.			
5 yrd. 3 qrters rich Ducape at 12s 4d	03	11	11
8 yrd. ⅞ broad silke prunella at 8s 2d	03	12	06
For my Mother Johnson.			
5 yrds. 3 quarters Ducape at 12s 4d	03	10	11
8 yrds. ⅞ Silke prunella 8s 2d	03	12	06
	113	02	4½
For John Trevis wife of Milhouses.			
7 yrd Paddua seardge 3s 4d	01	03	04
For ould Mrs. Alce Cheathom.			
10 yrd. ha. broad Silke prunella 8s 2d	04	05	09

3 yrd. ha. florrance sersnett 10^s 4^d - -	01	16	02
1 yrd. broad blã ribon at 2^s 6 - - -	00	02	06
1 Taffita hood at 6^s 6^d - - - -	00	06	06
1 broad lone [? lawn] hood at 6^s 6^d - -	00	06	06
for trim̃ge her gowne - - - - - -	00	13	00
For yor 3 doughters Gownes and petticoates.			
59 yrd. fine silke Morrella at 5^s 9^d - -	16	19	03
9 yrd. florrance sersnett at 10^s 4^d - -	4	13	00
2 yrd. ducape for neckcloths - - -	01	04	08
a hood 6^s 9^d - - - - - - -	00	06	09
for trim̃ge theire 3 gowne and peticõts - -	03	06	03
For yor father James Cheathom.			
Coate and trim̃ge his sute - - - - -	02	11	01
For Mr. Tilsley.			
trim̃ge sute and Cloake - - - - -	02	18	00
for Mr. Cundlife, Trim̃ge - - - - - -	02	09	00
for Mr. Croston, Trim̃ge - - - - - -	01	13	01
for Mr. Lomax, Trimm̃ge - - - - - -	01	00	00
for Mr. Livsey, Trim̃ge - - - - - - -	01	02	08
for Mr. Holmes - - - - - - - -	00	02	08
for ye Bew Coates Thred and buck[ram] - -	00	13	00
for ye Trumpeter 1 dz. ha. ribon and silk - -	00	10	07
	48	04	07
For my Brother George Cheathom Esqre his owne use.			
36 yrds. best broad 12^d Taffita ribon 10^s -	01	10	00
33 yrd. 10^d Taffita ribon at 9^d - - -	01	04	09
18 yrds. 6^d Taffita ribon - - - -	00	09	00
12 yrds. halfe dimidy - - - - -	00	15	04
3 yrd. ha. fine Normandy Camus - -	00	07	09
6 yrds. wide Linnen 14^d - - - -	00	07	00
3 yrds. 6^d firritt ribon 4^d - - - -	00	01	00
2 ounce ha. quarter Silke - - - -	00	05	00
4 dozen Gimpe butts at 6^d - - -	00	02	00
8 doz^n flagon butts at 3^d - - - -	00	02	00
3 doz. Cass. Gimp butts at 10^d - - -	00	02	06
5 yrd. ha. Cotton Tape - - - -	00	00	11

2 doz. 8 pr ho. and eys [hooks and eyes] thrid 12d - - - - - - -	00	01	09
3 Coll. 3 pr Bellipec ½ yrd. Callico - -	00	02	08
3 inches [?] Ducape - - - - -	00	02	03
3 yrds. ⅜ boulton fustian - - - -	00	03	04
1 yrd. ha. bobbin, bone 3d - - -	00	00	06
Pd for double Taggings poynts 3s 1d - -	00	03	01
Pd for tagging James poynts 9d - - -	00	00	09
10 yards gallowne 4 Cloake butts - -	00	05	06

For my sister Cheathom Gowne

14 yrd. halfe of 3 staled rich Naples Silke Callimando 13s 4d - - - - -	09	13	04
7 yrd. ha. broad rich Silke prunella at 8s 2d	03	01	03
1 yrd. 3 quarters dimidy - - - -	00	02	04
3 quarters Sympiterium - - - -	00	02	00
1 yrd. ha. blã Callico, 1 yrd. white - -	00	03	04
4 yrds. broad ribõ at 18d - - - -	00	06	00
3 yrds. 6d Taffita ribon - - - -	00	01	00
3 yrds. gallowne lace - - - - -	00	00	09
3 quarters Silke - - - - -	00	01	09
A Rowle and a buske - - - -	00	02	08
2 laces - - - - - - - -	00	00	08
5 yrd. 6d ribon 1 yrd. 4d - - - -	00	02	10

For Sister her Sadle Cloath.

2 yrd. ha. buckerum, thrid 3 - - -	00	03	04
29 yrd. blã Silke gallowne - - - -	00	08	03
10 ounce quarter-Silke - - - -	00	02	11
1 dozen blã 4d ribon - - - - -	00	04	00

For yor sonn Henry sute and cloake.

5 yrd. ha. fine blã flanders seardge at 5s 4d -	01	09	08
6 yrds. bd Taffita ribon - - - -	00	03	00
3 yrds. fustian 15d - - - - -	00	03	09
halfe yrd. boulton fustian - - - -	00	00	08
2 yrd. ha. Tape Coll. Bell. Clas. thrid and bobin lace - - - - - - -	00	01	06
3 doz. Butts 3d ⅜ Silke - - - -	00	01	02

halfe ellne Camus. 1 y. litle butts - -	00	01	07
For Tho. Orrall.			
¼ Camuis Silke 3ᵈ 1 long button - -	00	01	04
	23	06	02
For Cosin Mr. Edwurd Cheathom.			
5 yrd. ha. flanders serdge at 5ˢ 4ᵈ - -	01	09	04
6 yrd. paddua seardge at 3ˢ 6ᵈ - - -	01	01	00
3 quarters Camuis 1 yrd. buckerm - -	00	03	00
quarter and ha. Silk bone and thrid 18ᵈ -	00	02	04
quarter and halfe Sympiteruum - - -	00	01	00
1 yrd. ha. dimidy 3 quarters Callico - -	00	02	02
2 yrd. 6ᵈ firritt ribon ⅝ gall. - - -	00	00	10
2 yrd. la. blã taffita ribon at 8ᵈ - - -	00	01	08
4 Cloake buttons 10 yrds. gallowne - -	00	05	06
12 dosin flaggon butts at 3ᵈ - - -	00	03	00
28 yrds. broad 12ᵈ ribon at 10ᵈ (3ˢ 4ᵈ to much)	01	06	08
24 yrds. bᵈ Taffita ribon - - - -	00	12	00
Pd for tagginge yoʳ poynts - - - -	00	01	02
2 yrd. halfe buckerm at 16ᵈ for sadle cloth -	00	03	04
12 yrd. 4ᵈ Taffita ribon - - - -	00	04	00
2 dosin best blã gallowne - - - -	00	06	00
ha. quarter ounce Silke - - - -	00	00	03
Coll and bell Clas. Bobin lace - - -	00	01	04
3 quarters yrd. blã Ducape - - -	00	09	03
12 yrd. dimidy at 15ᵈ - - - - -	00	15	00
3 yrd. 3 quarters fine Camuis - - -	00	05	08
2 Coll 3 pr. Bell. 2 doz. hoo. and eyˢ pastbord and bobin lace - - - -	00	02	06
7 yrd. ha. Cotton tapes ⅝ Callico - -	00	01	09
thrid 4ᵈ 1 ounce ½ and dram Silke - -	00	04	00
bone 2ᵈ quarter Ducape - - - -	00	03	03
2 doz. 6ᵈ Taffita ribon - - - -	00	12	00
6 doz. buttons at - - - - -	00	03	00
2 yrds. 3 quarters fustian - - - -	00	04	00
For wifes ridinge coate.			
7 yrds. ⅝ fine mild [? milled] seardge at 4ˢ 4ᵈ	01	14	02

2 dozin blã 6d ribon - - - - -	00	12	00
quarter and halfe Silke - - - -	00	00	09
ha. yrd. ducape 3 yrd. 6d firritt ribō 4d -	00	07	00
quarter and ha. Sympiteruũ Clas. 2d - -	00	01	02
3 yrds. 2d ribon 2 yrd. ha. 4d ribon - -	00	01	04
For your Man Charles Nuttall.			
3 doz. butts 3d thrid Silke 9d 1 yd. ½ ribō -	00	02	03
5 yrd. 6d ribon 1 yrd. 4d ribon - - -	00	02	10
2 yrds. Gallowne lace - - - -	00	00	06
1 yrd. Cotten tape 6 yrds. 6d ferritts - -	00	02	02
for a childs coate.			
2 yrd. blã serdge at 5s 2d - - - -	00	10	04
quarter Camuis, quarter buckeram - -	00	00	10
bone and thrd ⅝ fustian ⅝ Callico - -	00	01	10
	13	02	02
Ribons for the funrall.			
144 yrd. broad 12d ribon at 10½d - - -	06	06	00
288 yrd. 12d ribon at 8½d - - - -	10	04	00
324 yrds. 10d ribon at 7½d - - - -	10	02	06
144 yrd. of fourtene peney broad at 12½d -	07	10	00
208 yrd. broad double 10d at 17½d p yrd. -	07	17	06
208 yrds. broad ribon at 20½d - - -	09	04	06
072 yrd. broad scarfe ribon at 2s 5½d - -	08	17	00
36 yrds. broad ribon at 15½d - - -	02	06	06
128 yrds. broad ribon at 20½d - - -	09	04	c6
18 yrd. halfe scarfe ribon at 2s 5½d - -	02	05	06
33 yrds. broad ribon at 19½d - - -	02	13	07
135 yrd. broad ribon at 17½d - - -	09	17	07
216 yrd. broad 12d ribon at 10½d - - -	09	09	00
36 yrd. broad ribon at 18d p yrd. - -	02	14	00
40 yrd. 12d ribon at 10½d - - - -	01	15	00
05 yrd. broad ribon at 14d - - - -	00	05	10
36 yrd. broad ribon at 18d - - - -	02	14	00
13 yrd. halfe 12d at 9d - - - -	00	09	09
10 yrd. ha. 12d at 10½d - - - -	00	09	02
09 yrd. ribon at 9d - - - - -	00	06	09

22 yrd. 12^d^ at 10½^d^ - - - - -	00	19	03
17 yrds. More 12^d^ ribon at 10½^d^ - - -	00	10	06
07 yrds. broad ribon at 20½^d^ - - -	00	12	00
18 yrd. broad ribon at 15^d^ - - - -	01	02	06
20 yrd. broad lone 5^s^ 8^d^ - - - -	05	13	04
25 yrd. ½ narrow lone 4^s^ 8^d^ - - - -	05	19	00
	120	03	00
Rec. back the 20 yrd. broad lon. 5^s^ 8^d^ - -	05	13	04
Rec. back 4 yrd. ¼ lone 4^s^ 8^d^ - - -	00	19	10
	06	03	02

[Summary]

	048	04	09
	113	02	04
ye ribons - -	120	03	00
y^r^ note for selfe -	023	06	02
ye other nte. - -	013	06	02
Totall of All - -	317	18	05
Rec^d^ in lone - -	06	03	00
rest - -	311	15	05

Rec^d^ the 19th of October 1653 of Mr. George Chetham and Edward Chetham Execut^rs^ (&c.) £311 15 0

John Johnson.

Rec'd the 19th of Octob^r^ 1653 of Mr. George Chetham and Edward Chetham Executo^rs^ of the last will and testament of Humfrey Chetham Esqre deceased the sume of seaven pounds which moneys I payd at London unto Mr. Richard Johnson Clarke for a mourneinge suite by the appointment of the said Executors beeinge p^r^te of the funerall charges of the said Humfrey Chetham I say Recd. the some of 07 00 0.

ꝑ mee John Chorlton.[1]

Moneys layd out as followeth.

For triminge for Raphe Travis morneing sutte -	00	11	00

[1] This is not in the summary.

for a morneinge hatte and band - - - -	00	08	00
for triminge of Raphe Travis wiffe morneinge sute -	00	15	00
for a morneinge hatt and band for her - - -	00	11	00
	02	05	00
for triminge for Richard Coup morneinge sute -	00	08	00
for a morneinge hatt and band for him - - -	00	06	00
for triminge of Richard Coup wiffe morneinge sutte	00	07	08
for a morneinge hatte and band for her - - -	00	06	00
	01	07	08
for triminge for James Travis morneinge sutte and his wives morneinge sutte - - - - - -	00	18	11
for two morneinge hatts for them and bands - -	00	14	03
(Recd. 6. 4. 2. Raphe Travis 24 Oct. 1653)	01	13	02
for triminge for my morneinge sute - - - -		11	0

George Travis 24 Oct. 1653.

A not for the funerall of Mr. Chetam.

to Mr. Tilslei delivered 5 bands cost 2^{s} 4 - - -	0	11	8
to Mr. Tilslee 3 fine Castores cost 1^{li} 18^{d} - -	3	4	6
one Castor more for Mr. Cunlef cost 1^{li} 18^{d} - - -	1	1	6
to Mr. Richard Lomas 3 fine Castors - - - -	3	4	6
for Mr. Edard Chetam one fine Castor - - -	1	1	6
Mr. Tilslei and his wife 2 fine Castors - - - -	2	3	0
for Mr. Edard Chetam 2 black felts - - - -	0	8	2
2 mornin bands - - - - - - - - - -	0	3	0
2 Lings [? linings] - - - - - - - -	0	1	4
one felt more Line for your son - - - - - -	0	4	0
one hatt cas [case] for your self - - - - -	0	01	0
one band for your yong son - - - - - -	0	1	2
for Mrs. Ales Chetam one fine Caster band and Ling -	1	3	10
for Mr. Croston wifes one fine Castor band and Ling -	1	3	10
Mr. George Chetam 2 Castores - - - - - -	1	4	0
One Castor - - - - - - - - - -	0	5	6
One Castor - - - - - - - - - -	0	16	0

2 Morning band	0	03	8
3 Morning bands	0	04	6
One hat case	0	01	0
Mr. Tilslei 2 best bands	0	4	8
To Mr. George Traves 2 London felts	1	1	4
2 Lings and Caridg	0	3	0
2 bands	0	3	8
Mr. Edward Chetam 4 bands	0	7	4
Mr. Richard Lomas one London felt	0	10	8
One Ling Caridg and band	0	3	0
Mr. James Chetam one Caster	0	14	0
One band cost 22[d] Ling and Caridg	0	3	4
One London felt Mr. Croston	0	10	8
One best band and lings	0	3	10
One felt Line with Calico		3	00
3 Lings and Caridg for Mr. Geordg Chetam		3	0
best Lining		1	6
	22	00	8
Profet	01	16	4
In all	23	17	0
Deduct for 2 hat cases which are to be paid for by the p[r]ticular persons	00	02	4
	23	14	8

Rec[d] 17 Oct. 1653 Edward Bowker.

Bought of Edward Johnson.

7 yards fine blacke serge att 7*s.* ℘ yard	02	09	00
¾ yard black Dewcape 9*s.* 6*d.* 18 yards 6*d.* Ribbin 9*s.* 6 yarns 4*d.* Ribbin 2*s* Cannie 18*d.*	01	02	00
1 yard buckram 16*d.* ¼ stiffening 4*d.*	00	01	08
4 (?) oz. threede 8*d.* ½ ℔ bone 8*d.* ½ oz. ⅛ silke 17*d.*	00	02	09
first Octob[r] 1653 Hugh Hobson 2 yards blacke buckram 22*d.*	00	03	08

2 dozen 11 yard ½ b^d Ribbin att 6*s.* 8*d.* - -	00	17	09
6 yards 4*d.* ferrett att 3*d.* p yard - - -	00	01	06
	04	18	04

Recd. 19 Oct. 1653 George Travis.[1]

Bought of Arth^r Bulkeley Sept. ye 23rd 1653.

Imp^rs 16 yards super fine Black Clo. at 23*s.* yd. - -	18	08	00
19 yards fine Black Cloth at 18*s.* 6*d.* yd. -	17	02	06
3 yds. ½ Black bais at 22*d.* p yd. - -	00	06	05
	35	16	05
			(*sic*)

Recd. 17 Oct. 1653 Samuel Walker
for the use of my Mast^r Arth^r Bulkeley.

Bought of Katherin Done the 9th of October 1653.

6 paire of the best Treblepointed Drawne for gentlemen 2*s.* 6*d.* a paire - - - - -	00	15	0
one dozen of the Best Treblepointed Mens at 20*d.* a paire - - - - - - - -	01	00	00
one dozen of the Best Treblepointed Mens at 20*d.* a paire - - - - - - - -	01	00	00
one dozen [as before] - - - - -	01	00	00
one dozen [&c.] for gentlewomen - - -	01	00	00
18 paire [&c.] - - - - - -	01	10	00
14 paire of Treblepointed for women at 18*d.* a paire	01	01	00
one dozen [&c.] for men - - - -	00	18	00
one dozen [&c.] 16*d.* a paire - - -	00	16	00
one dozen of pricksheame Girles Gloves 16*d.* a paire	00	16	00
one dozen of Treblepointed Mens large Gloves 18*d.*	00	18	00
one dozen [&c. the same] - - - -	00	18	00
18 paire of Treblepointed for Women 18*d.* a paire	01	07	00
16 paire of Womens prickesheame Gloves at 16*d.* a paire - - - - - - -	01	01	04
2 doz. of Mens Gloves 12*d.* a paire - -	01	04	00
one dozen of Womens at 10*d.* a paire - - -	00	10	00
4 paire of Youths of the best at 16*d.* a paire -	00	05	04
6 paire of the Best Childrens at 8*d.* a paire -	00	04	00

[1] Not in summary.

8 paire of Childrens 6*d.* a paire - - -	00	04	00
6 paire of the Best Childrens 6*d.* a paire - -	00	03	00
one paire of Mens Gloves - - -	00	01	08
one paire of Manacles - - - -	00	00	02
2 paire of Treblepointed Womens - -	00	03	04
	16	15	06
Receyved backe 7 paire of Womens Gloves at 10*d.* a paire - - - - - -	00	05	10
Rests in all - -	16	10	00

[Recd. 18 Oct. 1653] Katheren Done.

Bought of James Lightbowne 3° Oct. 1653.

598 yeards of black minikin at 22*d.* yerd is - -	54	16	4
4 yerds of blacke bays at 14*d.* a yerd - -	00	03	6
a yerd 3 q^rs^ of blacke brod cloth at 7*s.* yerd is -	00	12	3
	55	12	1

[Recd. 18 Oct.] James Lightbowne.

Bought of Arthur Scolfeild 22 Septr 1653.

For Mr. Geo. Cheetam 7 yards of fine black cloth 28*s.* yard - - -	009	16	00
For Mr. Cunliffe 5 yards of the same black -	007	00	00
„ Mr. Edw. Cheetam 7 yards of fine black att 19*s* - - - - -	006	13	00
„ Mr. Humphrey and Geo. Travis 11 yards of same black att 19*s.* - -	010	18	06
„ Mr. Rich. Lomax 7 yards of same black att 19*s.* - - - -	006	13	00
„ Mr. Hollinworth 7 yards of same black at 19*s.* - - - -	006	13	00
„ Mr. Lightboune 7 yards of same black att 19*s.* - - - -	6	13	0
„ Mr. Tho. Cheetham 7 yards q^r^ black cloth 17*s.* - - - -	006	03	03
„ Mr. Rich. Cropper 6 yards 3 q^rs^ of same black - - - -	005	4	09

	£	s.	d.
For Mr. Croston 7 yards of black cloth 19*s.* -	006	13	00
„ Mr. Herick „ „ „ -	006	13	00
„ Mr. James Cheetham 8 yards of fine black 25*s.* yard - - - -	010	00	00
„ Mr. Geo. Ch. a Jumpe 2 yards halfe q^r^ same black - - -	002	13	01½
„ his yong^r^ sone 4 yards q^r^ and halfe of blacke 17*s.* - - - -	003	14	04½
„ Mr. Humphrey a yard ½ and naile fine black 21*s.* 6*d.* - - -	001	13	07½
„ Mr. Ed. Cheetams Children 9 yards ½ of black cloth att 15*s.* - -	007	02	06
„ Mr. Livesley 7 yards of that black cloth 17*s.*	005	19	00
„ Mr. Geo. Cheetam yong^r^ 7 yards q^r^ of black cloth 19 - - -	006	17	09
„ Mr. Roger Walkden 7 yards of black cloth 15*s.* 4*d.* - - - -	005	07	04
„ Richard Travis 7 yards ¼ of same &c. -	005	11	02
„ Raphe Travis 7 yards of same - -	5	7	4
„ James Travis 7 yards 17*s.* - -	5	19	0
„ Fra. Prockter 6 yards ½ of black 13*s.* 4*d.*	004	06	08
„ Jo. Welsh 7 yards of the same - -	4	13	4
„ Mr. Wiggon schoolm^r^ 5 yards q^r^ of black 19*s.* yard - - - -	4	19	9
„ Mr. Birch Schoolm^r^ 4 yards 3 q^rs^ of that black 15*s.* 4*d.* - - -	3	13	1
„ Mr. Dutton Schoolem^r^ 4 yards 3 q^rs^ of black 13*s.* 4*d.* - - -	3	3	4
„ the Bellman 4 yards of black cloth 12*s.* 6*d.*	2	10	0
„ Evan Clarke 4 yards of same - -	2	10	0
„ Sam̃ Hollinworth 4 yards of same -	2	10	0
„ Mr. Isack Ashton 6 yards of black at 19*s.*	5	14	0
„ Dr. Howorth sute 2 yards of the same &c. - - - - -	1	18	0
„ Mr. Cunliffe 2 yards halfe q^r^ of same -	2	0	4½
„ Mr. James Chetam a q^r^ of black clo. to lyne skirts 18*s.* - - -	0	4	6

	£	s.	d.
For Schoolm^r at Bolton 5 yards of that black do. 15*s.* 4*d.* - - - -	3	16	8
" Mr. Smith att Turton 5 yards of the same &c. - - - -	3	16	8
" the Trumpitter 2 yards 3 q^rs black cost me 15*s.* 6*d.* - - -	2	2	7½
" ye Herrald 5 yards of same 15*s.* 4*d.* -	3	16	8
" Mrs. Allis Cheetam 4 yards halfe q^r of blacke att 19*s.* - - -	3	18	4½
" Jonathan Edge 4 yards ½ of black do. 8*s.*	1	16	0
" Saxton at Church a yard 3 q^rs of same black 8*d.* - - - -	0	14	0
" 7 Coates 13 yards of same cloth 8*d.* -	5	4	00
" Jo. Travis 5 yards of black cloth 10*s.* 6*d.*	2	12	6
" Mr. Ed. Cheetam and Child^n 4 yards ½ of black bays for Lyneinge 20*d.* -	0	7	9
" 6 Mens Breeches 5 yards 3 q^rs of black clo. 6*s.* 8*d.* - - - -	1	18	4
" Hen. Travis 2 yards and half q^r att 6*s.* 8*d.*	0	17	6
" Jo. Wroe 3 yards of black cloth att 6*s.* 8*d.*	1	0	0
" Charles Nuttall 2 yards 3 q^rs of black cloth att 6*s.* 8*d.* - - - -	0	18	4
" pillion do. and cov^r 3 yards att 6*s.* 8*d.* -	1	0	0
" a Sadle cloth a yard of black ker^s att 4*s.* -	0	4	0
" noyntler 3 q^rs and di. of black 8*s.* yrd. -	0	7	0
" Mr. Ed. Ch. for pillion 2 yrds. ½ q^r of black 8*s.* yrd. - - -	0	17	0
" Mr. Jas. Ch. Sadle cloth a yard q^r black minikin 2*s.* yd. - - -		2	9
" Lyneing his breeches 2 yards ½ of mus. co^r bays 20*d.* - - - -		4	2
" Mr. Geo. and Mr. Ed. Child^n a yard of black bays 20*d.* - - -		1	8
" Mr. Tho. Wroe 5 yards of black cloth att 10*s.* 6*d* - - - -	2	12	6
" Mr. Ed. Cheetam 3 q^rs and d. black k. at 4*s.* - - - -		3	6

	£	s.	d.
For Mr. Jas. Cheetam 3 q[rs] bla. kers. for gamashes 4*s.* - - - -		3	0
„ Mr. G. C. coveringe 2 Sadles a yard ½ black minikin att 2*s.* - -		3	0
„ Tho. [?] 4 yards q[r] bla. do. 10*s.* 6*d.* -	2	4	7½
By Tho. Barker a yard 3 q[rs] black mi. att 2*s.*		3	6
for the hearse 19 yards ½ black bayes 2*d.* yard	1	19	0
„ Pulpit cloth 2 yards halfe q[r] bla. cost 16*s.* 2*d.*	1	14	04½
„ quishin cloth a yard and d. q[r] black cost me 12*s.* 6*d.* - - - -		14	0½
Besides the cover for corps lent the sum̄ is	223	11	9½
For a yd. 3 q[rs] of black of Mr. Croston -	1	13	3
for 3 yd. q[r] of black do. for corps 15*s.* 8*d.* -	2	10	11
Recd. 19 October 1653, 227 15 0	227	15	11½

Arthur Scolfeild.

Accompt what persons have dynned here this Wednesday October 12th 1653.

Inprimis in the garden parlor - - -	64	persons
in the litle parlor - - - -	22	„
in the house - - - - -	50	„
in the Buttery - - - -	10	„
in the Foxe parlor - - - -	11	„
in the Red Chamber - - -	46	„
in the Star Chamber - - -	16	„
in the Mullett Cham̄b - - -	19	„
in the Whit Cham̄b - - -	45	„
in the Closett - - - - -	08	„
More in the litle parlor - - -	22	„
More in the Foxe - - - -	05	„
	318	„

79 messe and 2 persons at 4[s] a messe[1] comes to 15[ll] 18 0.

Recd. the 17th of October 1653 &c. 15[ll] 18[s]

Matt. Simcock.

endorsed "Captaine Symcocks account."

[1] A messe = 4 persons or meals.

12 barrels of strong beare sent by me Joseph Werden to Cleaton at 15s ℔ barrel comes to 09li 00s 00d.

Recd. the 18th of October 1653 &c.

Joseph Werden.

October 12th

Expended at the buryall of Mr. Homfray Cheattam.

Item for beare - -	1li	9	0
Item for bred - -	0	1	0
	01	10	0

at the house of Robrt. Hoult.

Recd. 17th of October 1653 &c. Rob. Holte.

At William Holts house.

20 gallands of beear at 16 pence the galland which is - - - - - - -	1li	06s	00d
13 dousen of brade which is - - -	0	13	0
for Cheeises - - - - - - - -	0	09	0
Total - -	2	8	8

Recd. 17th Oct. 1653 &c.

William Holte.

An Account of Charges for Ordinaries and Extraordinaries att the funerall of Humphrey Cheatham Esqre.

For Mr. George Chetham—

For 100 gall. of Beere att 8*d.* ℔ gall. is - -	03	06	08
„ 26 qrts. 1 pt. of Wtt [?][1] and Claret att -	01	06	06
„ 16 qrts. 1 pt. of Sacke - - - -	01	13	00
„ Beere and tobacco more - - - -	00	09	06
„ Beere and wine more - - - -	00	05	00
„ Burnd wine and beere - - - -	00	01	06
„ 15 gall. of Canary att 7*s.* ℔ gall. is - -	05	05	00
„ 34 gall. of Wtt [?] att 3*s.* 6*d.* ℔ gall - -	05	19	00
„ Beere to the Servitors - - - -	00	02	06

[1] Is this White wine?

For diner for 113 mess 3 personnes att 5*s.* the messe is - - - - - - -	28	08	09
„ Diners for 57 Mess att 2*s.* the mess - -	05	14	00
Sume - -	52	11	05

Recd. the 17th of October 1653 &c. 52li 11s 00

Richard Halliwell.

A noate of what beere and breade was delivered out at the house of Richard Proudlove at the funerall of Humphrey Chetham Esqre October the 12th 1653.

90 dozen and 4 breades at 12*d.* a dozen -	04	10	4
134 gallon of beere at 16*d.* a gallon - -	08	18	8
	13	19	0

Recd. &c. Richard P Proudlove
his marke.

Bought of John Baguley the [1]2th of October 1653.

twoe load of malt at 23*s.* 6*d.* a load - - -	02	07	00

Recd. 18th of October 1653

John Baguley.

Expended at the Funerall of Humphrey Chetham Esqre
By Phillipp Stampe

106 Messe at 4*s.* ꝑ comes to ye some of - -	21	04	00
In Beere ye some of - - - - - -	01	07	06
All is - -	22	18	06

Recd. the 18th of October 1653 &c.

Phillipp Stampe.

An Accompt drawne forth for Ordnaryes and extraordnaryes at the funerall of Humphrey Cheatham Esqre the 11th of October 1653 as followeth—

For 28 gallons 3 qts of Whyte wyne to the house at 3*s.* 6*d.* ꝑ gallon is - - - -	5	0	8
More 17 gallons one pt of Cannary at 7*s.* ꝑ gall. is -	5	19	10

	£	s.	d.
More 2 gallons Abato one gill and ½ of Hypocrass at 2*s.* 6*d.* qt. - - - - -	0	19	1
„ for 112 Mess and ½ of meate at 5*s.* ꝑ mess -	28	2	6
„ for Sack, wyne and strong beere at dinner as may appeare ꝑ a p'ticuler Accompt - -	10	17	2
	50	19	3
More you left unpayd in the greene Chamber besydes the dish of Sturgeon my father gave - -	00	1	6
More Mr. George Cheatham Mr. Edward Cheatham and Mr. Lightbowne left unpaid in the new Exchang 3*s.* 8*d.* whereof my father payes ½ soe rests	00	1	10
Oweing unto Alexander Greene ye 17 October 1653	51	2	7

Recd. the 17th of October 1653 &c. 51ll 02s 0

Alexander Greene.

A noate of what charges that was expended at the house of Wm Moore at the funerall of Humphrey Chetham Esqre deceased October the 12, 1653.

in beere to Peeter Lingeort - - -	00	01	00
in beere to the ringers - - - -	00	07	00
Meate for 37 horses of tennants of Turton all night at 4*d.* a horse - - - -	00	12	04
36 men that came from Turton for meate and drinke - - - - - -	00	08	00
148 gallons of beere at 16*d.* a gallon - - -	09	17	04
131 dozen of bread at 12*d.* a dozen - -	06	11	00
	17	16	8

Recd. 17th of October 1653 &c.

William Moore.

Receaved the 2d Novembr 1653 by us whose names are subscribed beinge Churchwardens and overseers of the poore of the ꝑish of Manchester of the worll George Cheetham and his brother Edward Cheetham Esqre executors of the last Will and Testamt of Homfrey Cheetham late of Clayton Esqre the some of twenty pounds current mony ffor the use of the poore of our said pish of Manchester to bee distributed to the pticular poore of each division of our pish aforesaid As is underwritten, viz[t] :—

to bee distributed in Manchester Division	-	07	13	4
Salford - -	-	03	16	8
Straitford -	-	01	08	0
Blakeley -	-	03	05	00
Newton - -	-	01	07	00
Withington, &c. -	-	02	00	00
Gorton, &c. -	-	00	10	00
		20	00	00

[Signed] Alexander Greene.
Will. Page.
Arthur Bulkeley.
Samuell Harmer.
John his S C Crowther marke.
Raphe Briddock.
Thomas Fletcher
T. F
his marke.
Robert Braban.
John Thorp.
William Cowdry.
Thomas Birch.

Octob 22 1653 pish of Deane - - - 04 00 00
Joh Tilsley pastor ibi[d]

October the 22[th] 1653 - - - foure pounds.
parrish of Prestwich - - -
In witness of John ∑ Wrigley
Tho. Heape, Senior. his marke.

Received of the Executors of Mr. Humphrey Cheetham Esq[re] the sume of - - - 60 00 00
Disbursed as followeth
Imp[r]mis to Ashton - - 05 00 00

to Ouldham - -	06	13	04
to Roachdale - -	08	00	00
to Midelton - -	04	00	08
to Bury - - -	08	00	00
to Boulton - -	13	06	08
to Daine - -	04	00	00
to Radcliffe - -	02	10	00
to Prestwich - -	04	00	00
to Eckles - -	04	00	00
	59	10	00

Richard Lomax.

The receipts for the foregoing payments bear the following signatures:—

Ashton.—John Brownsword, overseer, and Richard Cooke, churchwarden.

Oldham.—Samuel Heape and George Crampton.

Rochdale.—Robert Bathe, minister.

Middleton.—Tho. Chadwick and Robt. Livesey.

Lordship of Bury (£7).—Thomas Symonds, James Hardman, and Henry Pendlebury.

Lower end of Tottington (£1).—John Lomas and John Lowe.

Bolton.—John Okey and Arthur Gardner.

Deane.—John Tilsley, minister.

Radcliffe.—Tho. Pike.

Prestwich.—John Wrigley.

Eccles.—John Valentyne.

APPENDIX IV.

THE CHARTER OF CHARLES II.

(Copied from the original Charter, by permission of the Feoffees, through Henry Taylor, Esq., their Solicitor.)

CHARLES the second, by the grace of God, King of England, Scotland, France, and Ireland, defender of the faith, &c. to all to whome these presents shall come greeting. Whereas our trusty and well beloved Humphry Chetham late of Cleyton in the County of Lancaster, Esquire, deceased, a person of eminent loyalty to his Sovereigne and of exemplary piety to God, and charity towards the poore and good affection to learning, did by his last will and testament in writing, bearing date the sixteenth day of December, which was in the yeare of our Lord God one thousand six hundred fifty and one, give and bequeath to George Chetham, sonne of his brother James Chetham, the sum of five thousand and three hundred pounds of lawful money of England, to the end hee should therewith so soone as conveniently might be purchase lands, tenements, rents, and hereditaments, of and for a good and firme estate in fee simple of the cleere yearely vallue of three hundred and eighteene pounds and did also give and bequeath unto Edward Chetham (one other of the sonnes of the said James Chetham) the sume of one thousand and seaven hundred pounds of like money to the intent, that hee should therewith, as soone as conveniently might bee purchase lands, tenements, rents, or hereditaments of and for a firme estate in fee simple, of the cleere yearely vallue of one hundred and two pounds and that the said lands soe purchased should be conveyed and assured unto Richard Holland of Denton in the said county Esquire, Alexander Barlowe of Barlowe in the said county of Lancaster Esquire, Edmund Hopwood of Hopwood in the same county Esquire, Robert Hyde of Denton in the said county Esquire, Richard Haworth of Manchester in the same county Esquire, Richard Radcliffe of the same Esquire, Henry

Wrigley of Chamber within Oldham in the said county of Lancaster Esquire, Nicholas Moseley of Ancoates in the said county of Lancaster Esquire, John Lightbowne of Salford in the same county Esquire, Robert Booth of Sawford aforesaid Esquire, Francis Moseley of Collihurst in the same county Gent., and William Radley of Oldfield within Salford in the same county Gent., Richard Johnson Clerke one of the fellowes of the Colledge of Christ in Manchester aforesaid, Richard Hollingworth of Manchester aforesaid Clerke, John Tildesley of Rumworth in the same county of Lancaster Clerke, Edward Johnson of Manchester aforesaid Gent., James Marler Thomas Minshall and James Lightbowne of the same county Gent., John Cuncliff of Hollins in the same county Gent., Ralph Worsley of Platt in the same county Gent., Alexander Norres and John Okey of Bolton in the Moores in the said county of Lancaster Gent., and Ralph Brooke of the same county Yeoman, and their heires and assignes for ever and the survivors or survivor of them, and the heires and assignes of such survivors or survivor for ever. Upon trust and confidence and to the intent and purpose that the whole profitts and revenues should bee for ever imployed for the founding of an hospitall, and the relefe education binding apprentice or other preferrement of soe many and such poore boyes or male children and in such sort manner and forme as in and by the said will is expressed and declared. And the said Humphry Chetham did in and by his said will grant severall yearely rents amounting to fower hundred and twenty pounds to bee issuing out of severall of his mannors and lands in the said will specified and expressed for supporting and maintenance of the said charitable uses untill such purchases could be had as aforesaid. And did thereby also give the further sum̄e of five hundred pounds to purchase a convenient house for the said poore boyes their governors officers and servants and desired that the great house in Manchester called ye Colledge or Colledge House might be bought for that purpose, to be conveyed to his feoffees therein menc̄oned for ever. And his will and mind was that the said hospitall might bee incorporated and made a body politique for the better ordering and governing thereof. And further gave to his executors one thousand pounds, to bee bestowed in bookes for and towards the liberary withinthe town of Manchester for the use of scholers and others well affected to resort unto and gave the further sum̄e of one hundred pounds to purchase some fitt place for the said liberary and devised all the residue of his personall estate after his debts legacyes and ffuneralls, paid to bee bestowed in bookes for the augmentation of the said liberary. Of which will he the said Humphry Chetham did ordaine and make the said George and Edward Chetham executors as thereby amongst other things may at large appear. And whereas the said Humphry Chetham about the month of December [*sic*], in the year of our Lord one thousand six hundred fifty three, departed this life sithence which the said executors have purchased the said great house or Colledge in Manchester called the Colledge house and conveyances and assureances are thereof made and executed for the use of the said hospitall and library according to the intent of the said will and the said George Chetham and Edward Chetham have for and in satisfaction of the said rest and residue of the said personal estate, granted and conveyed unto the said Edward Hopwood Robert Hyde Richard Howorth Nicholas Moseley John Lightbowne Robert Booth Francis Moseley William Radley Richard Johnson John Tildesley James Marler Thomas Minshall James Lightbowne John Cuncliff Ralph Worseley Alexander Norres John Okey and Ralph Brooke, surviving ffeoffees, and their heires, the capitall messuage or mansion house called Hamerton Hall, in the county of Yorke, and other lands, tenements, and hereditaments in Hamerton Essington Steven Moore and elsewhere in the said county of Yorke of the yearely vallue of one hundred twenty and six pounds or thereabouts to be employed to and for the said library all which howses lands and premises purchased and conveyed as aforesaid are since granted to John Guilliam of Newton Gent. Edmund Hilton of Droylsden and Edmund Johnson of Manchester Gent[lemen] and their heires, to the intent they may regrant the same unto the said governors and their successors to be respectively disposed and employed according to the purport and intent of the said will which our pleasure is shall soe remain and bee for ever. And whereas James Chetham sone and heire of the said George Chetham the said Edward Chetham Edmund Hopwood and the rest of the said surviving ffeoffees have in pursuance of the desire of the said Humphry Chetham humbly besought us to create and make them a corporac̃on and body politique and to invest them with powers and priviledges requisite for the well ordering and management of soe pious and charitable a worke.—Now know yee that wee being desireous as well upon the said humble petic̃on as out of our owne royall disposic̃on and ready inclination to incourage and promote this exemplary charity and all other works of that nature of our especial grace certaine knowledge and meere moc̃on doe by these presents for us our heires and successors, declare and ordeine that the said great house, called the Colledge or the Colledge house in Manchester aforesaid shalbee and bee called the hospital and library founded by Humphry Chetham Esquire in Manchester and incorporated by king Charles the second. And doe also create make and constitute the said Edmund Hopwood Robert Hyde Richard Howorth Nicholas Moseley John Lightbowne Robert Booth William Radley Richard Johnson John Tildesley James Marler Thomas Minshall John Cuncliff Ralph Worseley Alexander Norres John Okey and Ralph Brooke, and such other person or persons, as shalbee elected and chosen as is hereinafter expressed one body politique and corporate in deede and in name by the name of The Governors of the Hospitall and Library in Manchester founded by Humphry Chetham Esquire and incorporated by king Charles the second and that they and their successors shall, by the same name have perpetuall succession and bee able and capable in the law to have receive purchase and enjoy mannors lands tenements rents hereditaments leases goods and chattells in what nature and kind soever in fee and perpetuity or for terme of life lives years or otherwise and also to give grant assigne lease or dispose thereof or of any part or parts thereof, as to them shall seeme meete.—And also that the said governors and their successors shall and may plead and be impleaded defend and bee defended answer and be answered in whatsoever courts and places and before whatsoever judges, justices, or other officers and ministers of us our heires and successors, in all acc̃ons pleas complaints and demands whatsoever in as ample manner and form to all intents and purposes as any of our subjects able and capable in the law or any other body corporate or politique may or can and shall and may also have and use a com̃on seale for the causes and affaires of them and their successors of or relateing unto the said hospitall or library on which shall bee engraven the coat of armes of the said Humphrey Chetham with this motto *Quod tuum tene* and circumscribed, *Sigillum Hospitii Humfridi Chetham Armigeri.* And our further will and pleasure is and wee do hereby direct declare and grant that the said governors hereby constituted as aforesaid or the major part of them shall on or before the Munday in Easter weeke next elect and choose six persons to make the full number of fower and twenty, according to the purport of the said will and true intent of the said Humfry Chetham in that behalfe which persons soe to bee elected shalbe and bee reputed governors of the said hospitall to all intents and purposes together with the severall persons hereby constituted as aforesaid. And for the better management of the affaires of the hospitall and the officers and members thereof wee doe hereby for us our heires and successors declare and grant that it shall and may bee lawful to and for the said governors or the major part of them for the tyme being from tyme to tyme as occasion shall require to make ordaine and establish lawes statutes constitučons and ordinances for the good government and support of the said hospital and library and the members, officers, and other persons of in or belonging to the same or any wise relating thereunto and to impose and inflict fines and punishment for the observance and performance thereof which wee will shall bee kept and obeyed by all persons concerned, so as the same lawes ordinances constitučons fines or punishments bee not contrary or repugnant, but agreeable, to the lawes and statutes of this our realme and the last will and testament of the said Humphry Chetham and the constitučons and directions thereby made or limitted in any matter or thing touching or concerneing the said Hospitall or Library or either of them or the governeing or management thereof. And moreover wee doe by these presents for us our heires and successors give, and grant unto the Governors unto the said Hospitall for the tyme being or the major part of them full power and authority to nominate elect and appoint all officers and ministers whatsoever requisite or necessary to be imployed or intrusted in or touching the said Hospitall or Library, or the revennues or affaires thereof, and to give and administer oathes for the due and faithful executon of theire offices respectively, and that the said Governors or the major parte of them for the tyme being shall have two generall meetings in the yeare at the said Hospitall, one on the Munday in Easter weeke, and the other on the Monday after the ffeast of Saint Michael the Archangell for ever, and then and there from tyme to tyme to elect and choose one or more honest and discreet person or persons according to the directions of the said will, to be Governors or Governor of the same Hospitall and Library in the place or places of such who shalbe then dead, or shalbe removed or displaced for any just or reasonable cause which wee hereby give full power and authority to the major part of the said Governors for the tyme being to doe accordingly to the intent that the said number of fower and twenty persons may bee compleat, of which our will and pleasure is and wee doe hereby declare that the heires males of the severall and respective bodyes of the said George Chetham and Edward Chetham shall for the present and from tyme to tyme bee by vertue of these presents amongst the rest successively for ever Governors of the said Hospitall and Library. And we do hereby declare and grant that Richard Dutton now Master of the children in the said hospital, shall bee and continue in that office and employment, dureing his natural life unlesse he shall be displaced by the Governours or the major part of them for the tyme being for any just or reasonable cause. And wee doe also hereby nominate constitute and make the said Richard Johnson now one of the ffellowes of Christ Colledge in Manchester aforesaid to bee the Keeper of the said Library by himselfe or his sufficient deputy dureing his naturall life but this not to bee drawne into example in future eleccons. And knowe further that wee of our further especial grace, certaine knowledge, and meer mocon doe hereby give and grant unto the said Governors and their successors full power and authority to have take receive and enjoy the howses lands tenements and hereditaments to bee to them reconveyed as aforesaid and also the said severall yearely rents in and by the said will limitted and appointed to bee paid as aforesaid under and subject to the provisoes and condicons in that behalfe in the said will declared and expressed and also from tyme to tyme to purchase have hold and enjoy to them and their successors any other mannors lands tenements rents or hereditaments whatsoever soe as the same together with the premises already granted and conveyed as aforesaid doe not exceed the yearely value of one thousand markes, the statute of Mortmaine or any other act statute matter or thing whatsoever notwithstanding provided alwayes and our expresse will and pleasure is that the said Governor of the said Hospitall hereby constituted and named or hereafter to bee elected or chosen as aforesaid and also all and every other the officers and members of the said Corporacon before hee or they bee admitted to exercise their respective offices or places shall severally and respectively take the oathes of allegiance and supremacy before some three or more of the

Governors of the said Hospitall for the tyme being to whome wee do, hereby give full power and authority to administer the said oathes accordingly. And lastly our will and pleasure is and wee doe hereby declare and grant, that these our Letters Patent or the Inrollment thereof shall bee good and effectual in the lawe to all intents and purposes notwithstanding the not reciteing or misreciteing or mencõning of the said last Will and Testament of the said Humphry Chetham or any of the gifts limitacõns or appointments hereby made or limitted, and notwithstanding the not reciteing or mencõning or not true or certain reciteing or mencõning of the howses lands tenements or hereditaments already conveyed to and for the use and benefit of the said Hospitall and Library or either of them, or of any the conveyances or assurances thereof, or of any act statute matter or thing whatsoever to the contrary in any wise notwithstanding, although expresse mention of the true yearly value or certainty of the premises or of any of them, or of any other guifts or grants by us or by any of our progenitors or predecessors made to the said Humphry Chetham in these presents is not made or, any statute act ordinaunce provision proclamacõn or restriccõn heretofore had made enacted ordained or provided or any other matter cause or thing whatsoever to the contrary thereof in any wise notwithstanding. In witnes whereof wee have caused these our letters to bee made patent.

Witnes our selfe at Oxford the tenth day of November in ye seaventeenth yeare of our Raigne.

VYNER.

By writt of Privy Seale.

ENDORSEMENT OF CHARTER.

These Letters Patent by some omission or neglect not having been duly inrolled at the time they bear date upon a petition to the Right Honourable the Master of the Rolls by the Governors of the Hospitall and Library mentioned were by his honour ordered to be inrolled and affixed to the Patent Rolls of the year wherin they bear date

16th April 1743.

ROOKE.

Among the papers in possession of the Solicitors to the Feoffees is a certificate of inrollment of the Charter, dated 23 April, 1743, and signed "Henry Rooke, Clerk of the Rolls."

APPENDIX V.

Commemoration Sermons.

FROM the Feoffees' *Minute Book* we learn that from early days an annual sermon has been preached at the Collegiate Church in commemoration of the Founder. The duty often fell upon the librarian, who was usually rewarded with 20*s*. for his pains. In 1661 the Rev. Edward Lees, who then held the office of librarian or deputy-librarian, was voted 40*s*. for his "good Sermon, preached before the feoffees this day in Manchester Church."

So far as the editor is aware only two of these sermons, both of comparatively recent date, have been printed. One of these was preached by the Rev. John Taylor Allen, librarian, on the 4th October, 1819. On the same day the feoffees requested Mr. Allen to publish his "excellent" sermon. The resolution was passed on the motion of the Rev. John Clowes, Fellow of the Collegiate Church, who more than a dozen years afterwards met the preacher, and after reminding him of the sermon, said, "when I asked you to publish it, I did not intend to impose a fine upon you, but to pay myself for its being printed." Mr. Clowes then took Mr. Allen into a bank and gave him £20, to "pay interest as well as principal" (Raines' *Lives of the Fellows of the College of Manchester*, vol. ii. p. 324, Chetham Society, New Series, vol. 23). The other sermon was preached by Canon Raines in 1873, from the text 1 John, iv. 21, and was "published by request," with the title:—

A Sermon preached in the Cathedral and Parish Church of Manchester on Monday the 28th of July, 1873, in Commemoration of Humphrey Chetham, formerly of Clayton Hall and Turton Tower in the Palatine County of Lancaster, Esquire. By the REV. F. R. RAINES, M.A., F.S.A.[1]

The following are the biographical portions of the discourse:—

There will always be a consistency in the character of a believer. He will not be governed by self-love or by the opinions of man. He will quietly cultivate the inner life, and will seek in the due use of all the means of grace to promote in his heart an abiding sense of the Divine presence. His holy life will be a firm but silent protest "against ungodliness and worldly lusts;" and his Christian example as "a light shining in a dark place" will never be without its use. The only real social happiness to be found on earth is to be found in a communion of spirit with those who "love GOD," and who "love their brothor also."

We believe that these features of Christian character were exemplified in the life of HUMPHREY CHETHAM, whose "good works and alms-deeds which he did for the house of our GOD" and the poor members thereof, in times long gone by, we gratefully commemorate to-day. He is felicitously described, in the charter of incorporation of his feoffees granted by king Charles II., as "a person of eminent loyalty to his sovereign, of exemplary piety to GOD, of charity towards the poor, and of good affection to learning."

I hope I do not forget the solemnity of the holy place in which we are assembled, nor unduly trespass upon the indulgence of my hearers, if I attempt briefly to record a few leading passages in the life of our founder. I am aware of my inability to do justice to his various merits, although I have had an opportunity of examining his family papers and records; and as some of these means of information do not appear to have been accessible to those who have preceded me, I trust that the impressions produced by their perusal and the facts gathered from them, may not uselessly occupy our time or be "addressed to unattending ears," and that whilst we speak reverently of the servant, we shall not forget to bless his great Master and "to praise Him and magnify Him for ever."

[1] London, RIVINGTON AND HATCHARDS; Manchester, CHARLES SIMMS & Co., 1873, 8vo.

The founder was descended from a knightly family settled in this parish as early as the time of Henry III., but belonging to a prosperous branch of it, in the seventeenth century, devoted to mercantile pursuits. Of his early life we know little, but as one of his brothers had been educated at Oxford, and had afterwards become the high-master of the grammar school, it is obvious that he would receive such education as he possessed in the distinguished seminary of his native town; and he was a good son of the mother who trained him, not for herself but for the country.

He was one of six sons, all baptized in this church, and he was brought up with his two elder brothers in commercial habits. It is evident that his progress towards great wealth and high local distinction had not been gradual, as he made his two large purchases of Clayton and Turton when he had been little more than twenty years employed as a merchant. His labours were unremitting, his activity in business unsurpassed, and his punctuality and integrity recognized and appreciated both in London and Manchester. Prosperity was the result of such industry, and year after year he found, as his accounts show, that "riches and honours" increased, so that whilst comparatively a young man he was found "sitting in the gate and known among the elders of the people."

We cannot form a correct judgment of some of his proceedings without a due consideration of the turbulent times in which he lived. His lot was not cast in a tranquil season when lights and shades are blended and almost undistinguished, but when darkness brooded over the country, when the church was beset with difficulties, and when good men regarded with alarm and consternation the progress of an unnaturall rebellion. He had been carefully trained and educated as a member of the English Church, and, although a man of wide views and comprehensive charity, he stood in the ancient way and adhered to the old ritual. He reverenced the Episcopate, and wrote of the Bishops as being "our spiritual fathers," at the moment when the primate, Laud, was redressing, *at his urgent request*, the puritanical misdemeanours which prevailed in this church, and restoring the old but neglected ecclesiastical polity. He respected the learned Universities of this land, contributed to the support of a poor under-graduate at one of them, and once made a provision that certain clergymen should always be selected from their body. He loyally maintained the national creed, and, when hotly assailed, vigorously protected the church in the enjoyment of the endowments which the piety and wisdom of our forefathers had voluntarily conferred upon her for the benefit of the people. It is not too much to say that Manchester especially owes the preservation of the church in which we are assembled and its moderate endowments (notwithstanding the subsequent temporary alienation of its property), to the wise councils, the well-considered liberality, and the practical mind of Humphrey Chetham.

In civil affairs he does not appear to have been an active agent in attempting to make things better, and perhaps quietly attempted to prevent their becoming worse; but he unquestionably looked with sorrow not unmingled with indignation upon the presumption and anarchy which, under the illusion of reform and liberty, ruthlessly swept away the Church which he had once preserved, and the monarch he had always loved, and whose commissions he had executed with such exemplary care and diligence as to secure for his services the special thanks of the king.

If he afterwards worshipped with the innovating party, it may fairly be inferred that it was not because he had withdrawn his allegiance from his own communion and approved of their discipline, but from hard necessity. They had subverted the English Church and had seized her endowments. They had proscribed her service and introduced their own. A man like Humphrey Chetham must always worship God somewhere, and when, in common with all the laity of the Church, he was intolerantly refused the use of his own ritual even in his own house, under penalties, he was obliged in some sort to attend such public services as the law-givers of the day permitted to be used. His letters to Mr. Richard Johnson, one of the deprived fellows of this church and afterwards the learned preacher of the Temple in London indicate what his matured views were, and how much he personally valued the regular clergy, and also how well he understood the simple services of the reformed Anglican ritual, in its impregnable fortress of scriptural truth as interpreted by the primitive Church.

We are told by one of his personal friends, an earnest-minded and uncompromising dignitary of the Church, whom he consulted in all his charitable undertakings, that he was "a respecter of such of the clergy as he accounted truly godly, upright, sober, discreet, and sincere," who held our Nicene faith and rejected the Italian yoke; and yet he cultivated the friendship of some ministers whose religious affinities were dissimilar to his own, but who sincerely worshipped and served "JESUS CHRIST our Lord, both their's and our's."

He sympathised with the regular clergy in the straitened circumstances (notwithstanding their pastoral fidelity and provident habits) in which many of them lived, and "his spirit was" sometimes "stirred within him" as he witnessed the destitution in which their families were left at their decease. Nor may I omit to name how, on a memorable public occasion, he gave special charge to his officers that "all due respect should be paid to the persons and calling of the clergy," and that, in consideration of their slender incomes, they should be "*very friendly and favourably dealt with.*" Amongst his good works and pious aims, he had contemplated the redress and amelioration of some of these clerical hardships; but owing to the unhappy spirit of the age, the disorganized state of the Church, the spoliation and sacrilege which he had witnessed, and consequently having little confidence in the security and stability of his new endowments, he abandoned his intention of augmenting poor benefices.

He had also at another time lovingly projected a scheme for building and endowing alms-houses for the reception of poor men and women, that the wants and infirmities of age might be alleviated by a moderate provision. He had overcome, as is shown by the outline of his plan, the preliminary difficulties; but for some cause or other he abandoned his purpose. Had it been accomplished, the direct result would have been dear to GOD, and the blessed fruit of His Church.

For some years it had been his desire and the fixed purpose of his heart "to provide," like his great EXEMPLAR, "for the fatherless children and widows," and "to comfort and help" such of his brethren as were "desolate and oppressed." He seems indeed always to have been planning or doing something useful to others, and therefore useful to himself.

Our founder was unquestionably a man of unobstrusive disposition, and probably after his retirement from the active pursuits of commerce, lived a secluded life, thinking with the heathen philosopher that "the end of work is to enjoy rest." He shrank from filling high offices and ambitious dignities in the State, which were thrust upon him against his expressed wishes, and which evidently disturbed his unassuming and regular habits. He cultivated a spirit of humility, and did not "think of himself more highly than he ought to think." Although he did not live in a church-building age, he aided at least in the rebuilding of St. Paul's Cathedral and in the erection of two small chapels in his own immediate neighbourhood, one in Prestwich and the other in Salford; and the expenses incurred in obtaining a renewal of the charter of the Collegiate church of Manchester were almost entirely defrayed by his liberality. His wise discretion and disinterested proceedings in this matter have either been unknown or unrecognized, and consequently, not properly appreciated.

For several years he had gratuitously maintained, educated and apprenticed many poor boys, elected from localities where his property was situated; and there seems to be evidence that he not only benevolently employed others to instruct and to elevate these children of indigent parents in morals and religious knowledge but that he sometimes was a co-worker and taught them himself.

He certainly kept the financial accounts connected with their education, and himself methodically superintended his schools. How much should we like to know the precise system he adopted and the sort of lessons he taught in these early elementary schools! We know that the religious element was their vital principle, and that "New Testaments" and "Psalters" were provided for the daily use of his scholars, who were probably not allowed to remain under the unhappy blight of divers creeds. We may be assured that the *heart* and *conscience* were not permitted to continue fallow, or their cultivation to be deemed subsidiary, or that any indignity was allowed by him to be offered to the Divine Word, for we are told by his intimate personal friend, that "he was a diligent reader of the scriptures and of the works of sound divines." We may therefore hope that the life of many a poor scholar taught by him was as simple and pure as his own.

It will have been observed that his charities were not posthumous, nor had his intention to do good long lain dormant or long smouldered in his bosom without kindling into a genial flame; but there was a continuity of idea, a definite purpose, and a generous practice extending through a lengthened period of time only to be perpetuated after his death.

From the uniformity of his life and the consistency of his actions, as well as from his special loving loving testamentary bequests to the clergy, to friends, to servants, to his many relatives, as well as a substantial provision for the poor boys, we may reasonably infer that he would appear to advantage in the domestic and social circle, and that, surrounded by his relatives—*he* was never married—several of them generous like himself, and acquiescing in the prayerful dedication of so much of his property to God, he passed the evening of a well-spent life in tranquility and peace, and, as he himself reverently and humbly said, "hoping to be saved by God's mercy, through the merits and mediation of Jesus Christ, my blessed Saviour and Redeemer."

In addition to the foundation and endowment of an hospital and school for boys, to be, as a contemporary observed, "a seminary of religion and ingenuity," he embodied his views on popular education and mental improvement in a sensible manner, and consistent with his previous judgment on the subject. He provided that godly English books of practical piety, "such," we are told, "as he himself delighted in," and such as the generality of good men of that period approved and read, should be selected at the discretion of three of his clerical friends, and be placed in the churches of Manchester and Bolton, as well as in certain poor churches, for the edification and comfort of artisans, mechanics, and the rural sons of toil. It is worthy of being named that of these friends one of them was a clear-minded fellow of Brasenose, and of the school of Hooker and Herbert; another was a Cambridge man; and the third of the university of Glasgow: two of them, probably all three, were episcopally ordained, each of them born in Lancashire, and each well reported of for learning, piety and good works.

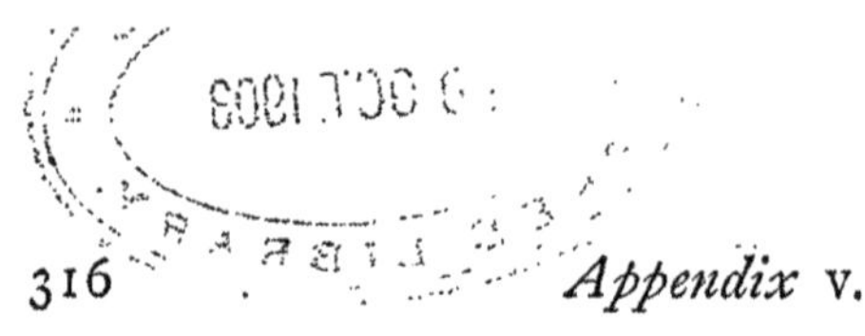

Although his own brows were not adorned with the laurels of literary fame, perhaps his noblest foundation was a library of a more learned character, to be placed, as he expressly provides, "within the town of Manchester, for the use of scholars and others well-affected to literature to resort unto." And O what a rich heritage for all time is protected and surrounded by those "studious cloisters" under the shade of this church!

These important educational institutions and charities still continue to be effectively administered according to the sound principles and clearly defined powers laid down by the founder, and have conferred large and noble benefits upon the people of this neighbourhood, and one hundred poor boys are at present carefully educated and liberally supported by his bounty. Here we have a practical illustration of the Divine commandment of the text, "that he loveth God, love his brother also."

Having long been, we trust, "wise unto salvation," and long having offered the sacrifice of prayer and praise in this majestic and sublime sanctuary amidst its lofty grandeur and silent beauty, he "fell asleep" at a good old age, after "he had served his own generation by the will of God." His dying request was, that his body might be buried in Manchester church, "surrounded by a cloud of witnesses," "within his chapel there;" and at the east end of this choir, without any memorial or sepulchral record, he still slumbers on in his resting place. But it is pleasing to name that in our day a citizen, who owed his early training and subsequent prosperity, under Divine Providence, to the school established by Humphrey Chetham, mindful of his ancient benefactor, has meritoriously brought his venerable figure prominently before us, and near his burial place may be seen a fine statue of this good man with a group of children around him. The sculptured effigy seems to unite the hopes of the dead with those of the living, and to remind us of the joyful words of the prophet, "Thy dead men shall live," for within these walls he "was made a member of Christ," and here he awaits the coming judgment day.

I would not willingly omit this opportunity of naming that the Chetham Chapel, within which the ashes of our founder repose, has unhappily been allowed to fall into decay, and the place of its

sanctuary is now defiled. Although perhaps devoid of noble conception, or high architectural genius, or elaborate decoration, it is worthy of careful study and, at least, of decent restoration. No thoughtful English Churchman can go round its hallowed walls, or mark well its crumbling bulwarks, or survey its neglected pinnacles, or regard its desolate aspect, or trace the tokens of those who once set up their banners there, without feelings of sorrow and humiliation. God has put it into the heart of the present Dean to lament the dilapidated and degraded condition of this portion of his Cathedral church, and he seeks to become, with the aid of his fellow Churchmen, "the repairer of the breach," and a reverent restorer of "the old waste place." When the building is restored to its original impressiveness—for who can doubt of its restoration?—it will be used for the sweet and peaceful *early service* on the Lord's Day, that "early morning prayer" which the devout Richard Johnson informed Archbishop Laud he had regularly "read in this choir *at six of the clock*, according to the order approved by Dr. Cosin, his grace's commissary;" and, continues Johnson, "imitating the example of my reverend diocesan" (Bishop Bridgeman), "I did then take occasion to vindicate the Common Prayer Book from unjust exceptions." By this proposed arrangement of the Dean interference with the marriages of the parishioners at the accustomed place will be avoided. But without any *utilitarian* view this interesting part of the sacred structure ought to have, without further delay, some substantial aid from the builders and be put again into comely order, that it may harmonize with the surrounding architectural beauty of a long-past century, and its present condition be no longer a reproach to our own.

Having now hastily reviewed the life of Humphrey Chetham, we find him, I think, to have been an earnest and sincere member of that branch of the Holy Catholic and Apostolic Church founded in these realms, to which it is our blessed privilege to belong; a man who was influenced "by the spirit of truth, unity and concord;" a man who, when living, "with meek heart and due reverence, heard and received God's holy word," and munificently provided for its being taught to the recipients of his bounty after his death, in order that "wickedness and vice might be discouraged," and "true religion and virtue" be maintained.

The foregoing sermon gives a high churchman's view of the Founder. The following excellent discourse is from the stand-point of a sympathetic nonconformist. It is taken from the *Christian Reformer* of November, 1853, and the author, whose name is not given in that periodical, was the Rev. Robert Brook Aspland, Minister of the Nonconformist (Unitarian) Chapel at Dukinfield from 1837 to 1856. The footnotes are Mr. Aspland's.

HUMPHREY CHETHAM.

A SERMON PREACHED AT THE OLD CHAPEL, DUKINFIED, OCT. 16, 1853, IN REFERENCE TO THE BICENTENARY ANNIVERSARY OF HIS DEATH.

Prov. x. 7: "The memory of the Just is blessed."

On this day, two centuries ago, as your ancestors returned from morning worship—whether at the domestic chapel of the estate (now a picturesque ruin), where Samuel Eaton[1] pleaded with warm zeal for what he deemed an orthodox faith and liberty of conscience, or at the church of the neighbouring parish, where John Harrison[2] with not less zeal pleaded for the same faith and for the church government of presbyters—it is not unreasonable to suppose that, as they slowly ascended the village "brow," they talked sadly of the sickness and recent death of a godly neighbour, known to all the country round, and held in high esteem for his commercial integrity and success, for the religiousness of his life, for his public spirit and his goodness to the poor. As they paused for a moment on reaching the eminence on which we are now assembled for worship, we can believe that some eyes were turned with a sorrowful expression in the direction of that picturesque moated residence Clayton Hall, where Humphrey Chetham had long lived, and whence a few days previously his body had been removed to its last resting-place in the collegiate church.

I have thought it neither improper nor undesirable to avail myself of the recent bicentenary anniversary of the death of the great

[1] Samuel Eaton was an early Independent, and a man in some matters before his age. After leaving Dukinfield, he went to Stockport, where, in connection with the Grammar School, in 1662, the Act of Uniformity found him, and whence he was ejected. He was the opponent of John Knowles, the first Unitarian in Cheshire.

[2] John Harrison was the ejected minister of Ashton-under-Lyne.

Puritan benefactor of Manchester, for the purpose of giving a brief and popular sketch of his life and times, and pointing the moral which they teach. As to the propriety of the topic to which I now ask your attention, let me say a word or two. I have been asked during the week—and the question by no means surprised me—What have we, as a particular religious society, to do with the memory of Humphrey Chetham, who professed not our faith, nor dwelt in our village, nor made it the object of any of his benefactions? In reply, I would say, we have an interest in the life and fame of every disciple of our holy Master, who has adorned by his worth our common Christian profession. Our religion teaches us to bless *the memory of the just;* and the Bible instructs us that a just man is one *that doeth justly, loveth mercy, and walketh humbly with his God.* We are to keep the eminently righteous, and especially those that from pure motives have fed and instructed the poor, in honourable remembrance. With the Gospels in our hands, which teach us the religion by recording the life of Jesus Christ, we may surely be permitted to use the biography of any one who has gone *about doing good,* as a means of moral and religious instruction. As to the local objection, let me observe, that the charities of Humphrey Chetham were not mere local benefactions. The moral light and social warmth diffused by schools, well-selected and public libraries, and other judicious charities, can no more be confined within a prescribed pale, than the light and warmth of the sun can be confined to some favoured valley or some outstanding hill. Besides, who shall say that, during the past two centuries, none of the forefathers of the hamlet were instructed or bettered in their lot through his large-minded bounties?

Again, I do not ask your attention to my present subject on the ground of any supposed doctrinal accord with the men of the seventeenth century; but I will not consent, on this account, to dissociate my sympathies from the Puritan Fathers of England. I feel that it is an honourable, though responsible, distinction, to be able to claim descent from men who, by their purity and courage, kept alive the light of spiritual religion through a dark and critical period of English history, and whose merit it is, according to the testimony of an unfriendly historian, to have fanned and saved from extinction the apparently dying flame of civil and religious liberty. It is, I firmly believe, an important thing for a religious body to be bound by historical ties to good men of a former age. Some men, I know, declaim against the folly and "cant," as they are pleased to call it, of reverencing men of a past age. I willingly admit that reverence for the past may be carried to excess. I know it will be injurious to those who fail to regard present duties; but I have yet to learn that our principles may not be strengthened, and our sense of duty may not be made more clear, by contemplating with becoming respect and honour those who, preceding us, have been faithful servants of God in their day and generation.

Humphrey Chetham was born at Crumpsall, a hamlet adjoining Cheetham Hill, in 1580. He was the fifth son of Henry Chetham, descended from an ancient and respectable family in the county of Lancaster, the head of which, in the unhappy wars of the Roses, had fought on the losing side, and been stripped of his lands soon after Henry VII. ascended the throne. In the quaint language of Fuller, in his "Worthies of England," amongst whom Humphrey Chetham is justly enrolled, "the posterity of Sir Geoffrey Chetham were unwilling to fly far from their old though destroyed nest, and got themselves a handsome habitation at Crumpsall, hard by, where James, elder brother of this Humphrey Chetham, did reside." He was baptized, July 10, at the collegiate church, of which Dr. Chadderton, Bishop of Chester, was then warden, whom a contemporary described as "a learned man and liberal, given to hospitality, and a more frequent preacher and *baptizer* than other Bishops of his time."[1]

Humphrey Chetham received (it is with every probability conjectured) his education at the Manchester Grammar School, an institution founded in the early part of the sixteenth century by Hugh Oldham, Bishop of Exeter, of whom it is recorded to his praise that he was a promoter of learning and an enemy of monkish superstition, and that, through his boldness and independence in resisting the Pope, he died in a state of excommunication. Schools of this kind were, in the early periods of our history, when knowledge was

[1] Hollinworth's *History of Manchester*.

rare, and the population and their means equally scanty, great local blessings. Had they been always conducted in the liberal spirit of their founders, they might be so still. Hollingworth, the historian of Manchester, from whom I have already quoted, says that Bishop Oldham, "out of the good mind he bare to the county of Lancaster (being, I believe, his native county), perceiving that the children thereof, having pregnant wits, were for the most part brought up rudely and idly, that knowledge might be advanced (the art of grammar being the ground and fountain of all the liberal arts and sciences), and that children might be occupied in good learning, better taught to love, honour and dread God and his laws, founded the free-school in Manchester."

The sunken fortunes of his family, happily for himself and for his native county, compelled Humphrey Chetham and his younger brothers to embark in trade. Manchester had at this early period become, indeed had been for considerably more than a century, the great seat of the manufacture of the clothing in common use by the people of the country; it was also the centre of action for merchants whose transactions had become extensive. The progress of the trade of this country may be viewed in other and more important lights than as a system of barter (serviceable on both sides) of the necessaries of life. It affected and rapidly accelerated the the progress of civilization, and it was connected with religious liberty. It served more than any other single influence to break through and destroy those feudal institutions which fostered a haughty spirit of caste, and were strong barriers against improvement and social progress of every kind. An instance of the beneficial effect of trade in sweeping away worn-out, useless and mischievous institutions, is to be seen in the history of the Sanctuary, which existed in Manchester, with all the strange privileges belonging to those institutions, till the reign of Henry VIII. Then an Act of Parliament was passed, which throws more light than any other known existing document on the character of the manufactures and trade of the town three centuries back. The preamble states that Manchester was well inhabited, and distinguished for its trade both in linens and woollens, had obtained riches and wealthy living, and employed many artificers and poor people; that by their "strict and true dealings" they had given rise to the resort of many strangers. It then recites that many of the processes of manufacture and customs of trade were endangered by the resort of light and evil-disposed persons to the town, who had fled from the consequences of their misdeeds, and found a refuge in the privileged precints of the Collegiate Church. By the salutary Act then passed, the rights of the Sanctuary were abolished in Manchester, and transferred to the Cathedral of Chester, a city in which there were no manufactures to be imperilled, and where there were municipal officers possessed of large powers for curbing and punishing evil-doers.

The connection of trade with religious liberty was also strikingly illustrated in Manchester, as well as in London and Norwich. Civil tyranny and religious persecution drove many ingenious and industrious artizans from France and the Netherlands into England, where they found quiet and protection, in return for which they enriched their adopted country by their industry and manufacturing skill. The enormities of the Duke of Alva in the Netherlands, the religious wars of France, and especially the revocation of the Edict of Nantes, drove thousands of skilled artizans into exile. Many of those from Belgium settled in Manchester, and gave a rapid impulse to the manufacturing prosperity of the town.

The branch of trade pursued by the Chethams was to purchase goods from the manufacturers of Manchester and the neighbourhood, and the sale of them to the dealers throughout England. Wealth flowed rapidly in upon the upright and energetic traders. It did not taint the character or pervert the principles of Humphrey Chetham. "He signally improved himself" (says Fuller, who derived his information from Mr. Johnson, one of the clergy of Manchester and a trustee appointed by Chetham) "in piety and outward prosperity. He was a diligent reader of the Scriptures, and of the works of the sound divines; a respecter of such ministers which (as) he accounted truly godly, upright, sober, discreet and sincere." Content with his rank and happy in the sphere of duties and simple pleasures which befitted the English merchant, he not only did not aim at, but declined some public honours. Knighthood was offered him soon after the accession of Charles I.; but as that compliment was then frequently offered to wealthy men with the sole object of extorting exhorbitant fees, the fact of his declining the honour is perhaps unimportant. He purchased large estates, and amongst them a picturesque residence at Clayton Hall, situated a mile or two on this side Manchester. In 1634, he was named by the Judges as a fit and proper person for the shrievalty of the county. He would fain have escaped the responsibility of the office, on both public and private grounds. He wished not to be brought into the King's view, feeling that the honour would be a burthen to him; and his sagacity enabled him to foresee that unsettled and calamitous times were impending. But in spite of his reluctance and disclaimers, he was appointed Sheriff in the year 1633-4.

It was characteristic of the simplicity of his habits and a sign of his indifference to the vanities of heraldry, that up to the time of his shrievalty he had not assumed the armorial bearings of his family. In consequence of his connection with trade, difficulties, real or pretended, were made respecting his right to assume arms. The gentlest natures will sometimes resent as well as resist. In the motto which he put under the crest which he in the end obtained, *Quod tuum tene*, so little descriptive of his general personal character, it was thought there might be a reference to his determination not to resign a clear right to mere prejudices or to the pride of a class.

Having the office of Sheriff forced upon him, he determined so to perform its duties that it should in his hands lose nothing of its wonted honour. Although there were some of the country gentry who resented the intrusion into knightly rank one who, though sprung from gentle ancestors, had had the sense and industry to achieve his own fortune, there were not wanting others of better mind, who willingly paid him the honour due to his character even more than his office. "He discharged," says Fuller, "the place with great honour; insomuch that very good gentlemen of birth and estate did wear his cloth at the assize, to testify their unfeigned affection to him."

In consequence of his official position, he was called upon to collect the illegal impost called Ship-money, invented by the King for the sake of dispensing with the unacceptable services of Parliament. Whatever might be his individual opinion on the conduct of the King and his advisers, the tax had received a colourable judicial sanction, and he collected it. He had none of the political enthusiasm or high bearing of a Hampden and a Pym, and he is not entitled to any share of their fame as fearless patriots, willing, if need be, to shed their blood for their country's liberties; but he quietly performed his prescribed duties, and chalked out for himself a path to usefulness and honour.

In 1640, Mr. Chetham was nominated High Collector of the Subsidies for the county of Lancaster. In 1643, he was (still greatly against his will) appointed General Treasurer of the county. When the civil war broke out, the county of Lancaster suffered more immediately and more severely than any part of the kingdom. There was not merely the presence of a hostile Scotch army, but a famine, and that followed, as is often the case, by a pestilenee. In such a state of things, it was no enviable post to be charged with the collection of the general and local taxation. When the Royal authority was superseded by that of the Parliament, Humphrey Chetham still possessed the confidence of the Government, and was still burthened with the office of Treasurer. Besides supplying the wants of the forces in his own county, and they were considerable (for we learn from a document bearing date 1644, that the army was "in great want and distress, and the county wholly spoiled and wasted by the enemy"), he had also sometimes to provide the funds required in the county of Chester, where the troops were under the command of the proprietor of this estate, Colonel Dukinfield. Copies have been preserved of urgent notes from the sturdy warrior for relief, not unaccompanied by the threat of marching his troops into Lancashire, and quartering them upon the county.

Humphrey Chetham's residence, as well as his official duties, brought him into contact, during this sad period of our history, with much anxiety, distress and misery. From the moment that the first hostile gun was fired against the citizens in the streets of Manches- by the followers of Lord Derby, until the entire cessation of the war, all the usual resources of the ten thousand people who were then resident in Manchester were cut off; trade was entirely destroyed; for confidence is the breath that animates the commercial body; and war, and above all civil war, is always destructive of that. Oh, let those who are now, with more of passion than patriotic wisdom, sounding the trumpet note of war, and needlessly urging our rulers to precipitate this country, and with it all Europe, into a state of warfare, think of all the indigence, anxiety, sufferings and horrors which that state brings in its train; and instead of manifesting impatience at the continuance of peace, let them pray that our statesmen may be enabled to protect at the same time the honour of our beloved country and the peace of Europe! So profound and varied were the sufferings and indigence of the people of South Lancashire, the district in which manufactures and commerce had previously flourished, that collections were, by order of Parliament, made on their behalf in the principal churches in London and other places.

We may feel assured that the philanthropy of Humphrey Chetham alleviated as far as possible the miseries of his neighbourhood during this painful and protracted struggle. Manchester was besieged by the Royal troops, and defended successfully on behalf of the Parliament by the inhabitants. The neighbourhood was the scene of many battles. Wigan, Stockport, Warrington, Chowbent, and various other places, witnessed the conflict of fellow-citizens. Bolton was besieged by the King's troops under Prince Rupert, and when taken, the inhabitants were exposed to the violence of troops, influenced by religious as well as political hatred, and infuriated by previous checks and defeats. The neighbouring town of Ashton-under-Lyne suffered fearfully. The following picture of the misery that prevailed in South Lancashire is taken from an appeal issued in the year 1649, and signed, amongst others, by several of the personal friends of Humphrey Chetham.

"The hand of God is evidently seen stretched out upon the county, chastening it with a three-corded scourge of sword, pestilence and famine, all at once afflicting it. They have borne the heat and burthen of a first and second war in an especial manner above other parts of the nation. Through them the two great bodies of the late *Scotch* and *English* armies passed, and in their very bowels was that great fighting, bloudshed and breaking. In this county hath the plague of pestilence been raging these three years and upwards, occasioned chiefly by the wars. There is a very great scarcity and dearth of all provisions, especially of all sorts of grain, particularly that kind by which that country is most sustained, which is full six-fold the price that of late it hath been. All trade by which they have been much supported is utterly decayed. It would melt any good heart to see the numerous swarms of begging poore, and the many families that pine away at home, not having faces to beg. Very many are craving almes at other men's dores—who were used to give other almes at their dores, to see paleness, nay death, appear in the cheeks of the poor, and often to hear of some found dead in their houses or highways for want of bread.

"But particularly the townes of *Wigan* and *Ashton*, with the neighbouring parts, lying at present under the sore stroak of God in the pestilence, in one whereof are full two thousand poor, who for three months and upwards have been restrained: no relief to be had for them in the ordinary course of law, there being none at present to act as Justices of the Peace. The collections in our congregations (there only support hitherto) being generally very slack and slender, those wanting ability to helpe who have hearts to pity them. Most men's estates being much drained by the wars, and now almost quite exhaust by the present scarcity, and many other burthens incumbent upon them, there is no bonds to keep in the infected, hunger-starved poore, whose breaking out jeapoardeth all the neighbourhood; some of them already, being at the point to perish through famine, have fetch in and eaten carion and other unwholesome food, to the destroying of themselves and increasing of the infection; and the more to provoke pity and mercy, it may be considered that this fatal contagion had its rise evidently from the wounded souldiers of our army left there for cure."[1]

These were the miserable results of war. Through scenes of this heart-sickening kind did the benevolent man of whom we are

[1] Dated May 24, 1649. This document, which is entitled "A True Representation of the Present and Lamentable Condition of the County of Lancaster, &c.," is reprinted in the "Tracts relating to the Military Proceedings in Lancashire during the Great Civil War," published by the Chetham Society, pp. 278–279.

speaking sorrowfully drag the closing years of his earthly pilgrimage. His chief personal anxiety was to make a wise disposal of the great wealth which in times of tranquility he had accumulated. It must not, however, be supposed that he did nothing in the cause of charity while alive, and that, like some founders, he attempted to atone for a life of parsimonious cruelty by devoting the wealth which he could no longer enjoy to charitable purposes. No; his last will and testament was only the completion of a scheme of benevolence of which he had tried and proved the value during a portion of his life. From this interesting document it appears (and the fact is mentioned without any ostentation) that he had "during his life taken up and maintained fourteen poor boys of the town of Manchester, six of the town of Salford, and two of the town of Droylsden; in all, twenty-two." "Having never married," says his principal biographer (the late Mr. Whatton, of Manchester), "he thus became a father of the fatherless and destitute; and doubtless many were the children of adversity that, during the life-time of this good man, successively found protection in his fostering and paternal benevolence." He did not forget, in his zeal for public charities, the claims which his nearer kindred had upon him. It incidentally appears from his will that upon two of his nephews he had settled large estates; and so entirely did the charitable appropriation of his wealth meet with their approval, that he directed his trustees to apply to them for further sums for carrying out his educational charities, should more be required than he proposed to leave. "It is observable," says Mr. Whatton, "by an examination of the numerous documents in the treasury of the college, that Mr. Chetham left behind him a great variety of wills; and it would be curious and interesting to trace the history of his intentions as they present themselves from the first of these instruments to the last. Some scheme of charity was ever uppermost in his thoughts. At one time he contemplated a suitable provision for the clergy of certain chapelries within or contiguous to which his property was situated; and at another, he had a plan for maintaining a number of aged and indigent persons in certain parishes in which he had resided. His views would seem to have varied with the extent of his acquisitions, until he was finally enabled to devise and execute one grand object, and, by concentrating his means, to render the exercise of his charity more decidedly extensive and efficient."

Amongst various minor benefactions of his, we find one which curiously illustrates the dearth of books at that period, and a curious use to which churches were put as places for the people to read in. He bequeathed the sum of £200 for the purchase of godly English books, to be chained upon desks in the churches of Manchester and Bolton, and in the chapels of Turton, Walmersley and Gorton. But the two great foundations by which his name is rendered famous, were an educational establishment for the clothing, boarding, educating, and afterwards apprenticing, the children of the poor, and a free public library. The catholic spirit in which all the details of these charities were conceived, is deserving of attention The boys were to be chosen from the poor inhabitants of certain townships in which his principal estates were situated, thus indicating his adhesion to the great principle, that property has its *duties* as well as its *rights.* There was no stipulation of creed, for all were eligible who were children of poor but honest parents, not illegitimate, nor diseased, lame or blind, when chosen. They were to be received at six years of age, and maintained and educated till they were ready to be apprenticed to some honest and useful trade.

Of charitable benefactions of this kind there were many examples in every part of England, and especially where trade had flourished. One distinguished and enlightened commercial benefactor, Sir Thomas Gresham, had preceded him (he died the very year that Chetham was born): and another scarçely less distinguished philanthropist springing out of the trading classes—Edward Colston, of Bristol—followed him. But the other great benefaction founded by Humphrey Chetham was in a direction in which he had few predecessors. Libraries were at that time rare, except in connection with the two Universities and some of the Cathedrals. A perfectly free library existed nowhere, and it is a most remarkable fact, as showing how far this good man was in advance of his times, that it was not till full two centuries after he had made provisions for founding the Library in Manchester, that the example was followed. Had Humphrey Chetham's purpose in respect to his library been out in its spirit by every successive generation of feoffees, the Chetham Library would have supplied to Manchester those urgent wants which have recently called into existence that admirable institution, one of the best ornaments of that great city, the Free Public Library now under the charge of the Corporation.

The two channels into which the stream of Humphrey Chetham's benefactions ran, different though parallel, were the result of his Puritan habits of thought. Careful attention to education was a type of this remarkable class of men, and not merely the education furnished in schools, but the after and more and more important education of the mind and heart. They were the men who carried on the work of religious reformation,—who rescued the Bible, the Book of books, from the seclusion into which, by priestcraft and Popish superstition, it had been thrust. They were lovers of books and promoters of learning. A striking proof of this is given in the history of the Pilgrim Fathers, who, when denied religious freedom at home, carried religion and freedom, and with them a high civilization, into the wilderness on the other side of the Atlantic Ocean. No sooner were they planted in peaceful society in America, though struggling with disease and the dread of famine, than they took steps for founding an institution where University learning might be taught to their children and their children's children, wisely thinking that if they once allowed the sacred, life-giving lamp of knowledge to go out, all that they most valued, all for which they had quitted their native hearths, and encountered the perils of the sea and of the untracked wilderness, would be in jeopardy of being lost.

One of this noble army of confessors, a gentleman by birth and education, whose early years had been passed in the walls of a manor house in the county of Nottingham, the archiepiscopal palace at Scrooby, did not hesitate to earn his bread at Leyden by the labour of an artizan, and with true Puritan instinct he chose the printing-press as his instrument of labour. Some of the greatest collections of books in existence in England in the time of Humphrey Chetham, owed their existence to men trained in Puritan principles. Of this number, Sir Robert Cotton was, I believe, one; and certainly another was, Sir Thomas Bodley, the great benefactor of Oxford, and the founder of its matchless Library, who in early life fled from England to escape the Marian persecution, and received a part of his education in the city of Geneva, being a pupil of the illustrious Calvin.

The Puritans were, I admit, not faultless. They were on some points narrow and fanatical; but they were always true to certain great principles. They reverenced the spiritual nature of men, and they put a high value on everything that assisted in its cultivation. They had faith in the power of religion to save and to exalt the human being, and they were wise enough to perceive that religion could not be kept pure, and could not produce its rightful effect, unless learning was upheld and education unfolded the faculties of the mind.

The will of Humphrey Chetham was signed on the 16th of December, 1651. He had then reached and passed the three-score years and ten, beyond which inspired wisdom declares that man's strength becomes *labour and sorrow.* Though oppressed with infirmities, he lived nearly two years longer; and then, in a ripe old age, full of faith and hope—above all, of the better gift of CHARITY, he surrendered his spirit to God.

I shall attempt no formal panegyric on this enlightened benefactor. If the recital of his actions have not raised your admiration, I am sure no rhetoric within my power would do it.

The portrait of him preserved in the Hospital exhibits to us the features of a wise and thoughtful man—profoundly calm, almost sad, in its expression—the brow remarkably lofty—the whole revealing a man of no common mark, capable of impressing his example and memory on a future and distant age.

It has been observed that it was somewhat a disgrace to Manchester that no monument was raised to this its great benefactor. This disgrace is now removed; and to-day the worshippers in the church where Humphrey Chetham was baptized, and where his funeral obsequies were celebrated, will enjoy the opportunity of contemplating two interesting memorials of him, a statue and a memorial window, placed there by a citizen of Manchester, who received his education in the Chetham Hospital, and who is happy in devoting a portion of the wealth which he has since obtained to an expression of his reverence and gratitude.

The times immediately succeeding Humphrey Chetham's death were not favourable to schemes having a moral or literary object. There was an unsettled government; then a violent re-action; and debauchery and tyranny, civil and ecclesiastical, ran riot in the land. Afterwards, revolution and long periods of warfare occupied the thoughts of the nation. It has been our privilege to enjoy nearly forty years of peace, during which trade and all the arts of civilization have made rapid progress. The virtues and wisdom of Humphrey Chetham have at length, in these happy times, received their due reward. Great men can afford to await the sure, though somewhat tardy, payment of time.

The further moral which I would impress upon you from this noble example is, that to do good and communicate you forget not. Let the wealthy and the powerful especially realize to themselves their privileges and consequent duties. They are stewards of God's bounties; let them be ever ready to distribute. Let them not, however, fall into the sad mistake, that charity is the mere careless, thoughtless handing over to others of that which they cannot themselves use. Without thoughtfulness and caution, their so-called charities may prove a curse rather than a blessing, by preventing self-reliance and personal exertion, by undermining honest independence, and thus increasing the destitution which they seek to relieve. Let them especially devote themselves to that best form of charity, Education, which, when perfectly carried out, elevates the mind, purifies the heart, makes the child of earth a child of God, and fits him to be an heir of Heaven.

APPENDIX VI.

FEOFFEES OR GOVERNORS OF THE CHETHAM HOSPITAL, MANCHESTER.

1.	Dec. 16, 1651.[1]		Richard Holland of Denton, Esq.
2.	,,	,,	Alexander Barlow of Barlow, Esq.
3.	,,	,,	Edmund Hopwood of Hopwood, Esq.
4.	,,	,,	Robert Hyde of Denton, Esq.
5.	,,	,,	Richard Howarth of Manchester, Esq.
6.	,,	,,	Richard Radcliffe of Manchester, Esq.
7.	,,	,,	Henry Wrigley of Chamber, Esq.
8.	,,	,,	Nicholas Mosley of Ancoats, Esq.
9.	,,	,,	John Lightbowne of Salford, Esq.
10.	,,	,,	Robert Booth of Salford, Esq.
11.	,,	,,	Francis Mosley of Collyhurst, Esq.
12.	,,	,,	Wm. Radley of Oldfield, gent.
13.	,,	,,	Richard Johnson, clerk, Fell. Coll. Ch. Manchester.
14.	,,	,,	Richard Hollinworth, clerk, Fell. Coll. Ch. Manchester.
15.	,,	,,	John Tildesley of Rumworth, clerk.
16.	,,	,,	Edward Johnson of Manchester, gent.
17.	,,	,,	James Marler of Manchester, gent.
18.	,,	,,	Thomas Mynshull of Manchester, gent.
19.	,,	,,	James Lightbowne of Manchester, gent.
20.	,,	,,	John Cunliffe of Hollins, gent.
21.	,,	,,	Rafe Worsley of Platt, gent.

[1] Date of the Founder's will.

22. Dec. 16, 1651. Alexander Norres of Bolton, gent.
23. " " John Okey of Bolton, gent.
24. " " Rafe Brooke of Turton, yeoman.
25. Apr. 16, 1666. Edward Chetham, *vice* Richard Holland, Esq.
26. " " James Chetham, Esq., *v.* Alexander Barlow, Esq.
27. " " Robert Holte of Castleton, Esq., *v.* Edmund Hopwood, Esq.
28. " " Wm. Hulton of Hulton, Esq., *v.* Robert Radcliffe, Esq.
29. " " Francis Mosley, clerk, *v.* Henry Wrigley, Esq.
30. " " Jonathan Chadwick of Chadwick, gent., *v.* Francis Mosley, Esq.
31. " " Wm. Page of Manchester, gent., *v.* Edward Johnson, gent.
32. " " Thomas Becke of Manchester, gent., *v.* Richd. Hollinworth, clerk.
33. " " Francis Worthington, of Manchester, gent., *v.* James Lightbowne, gent.
34. Mar. 23, 1667-8. Francis Lindley, Esq., *v.* John Lightbowne, Esq.
35. Oct. 5, 1668. Henry Dickenson, the elder of Manchester, Esq., *v.* Francis Worthington, gent.
36. " " Mr. Samuel Harmer, the elder of Manchester, *v.* James Marler, gent.
37. Ap. 12, 1669. Edward Mosley, Esq. [afterwards knighted], *v.* Francis Lindley, Esq.
38. " " Dr. Theophilus Howorth, *v.* Thos. Becke, Esq.
39. " " John Hartley of Strangeways, Esq., *v.* Wm. Page, gent.
40. " Humfrey Booth of Salford, Esq., *v.* Wm. Radley, gent.

41. Ap. 4, 1670. Wm. Holland of Denton, Clerk (?), *v.* Ralph Worsley, gent.
42. Ap. 24, 1671. Rev. Nicholas Stratford, Warden, *v.* Dr. Theophilus Howorth.
43. Ap. 8, 1672. Richard Fox of Manchester, Esq., *v.* Richard Howorth, Esq.
44. " " Ralph Brooke of Turton, yeoman, *v.* Ralph Brooke, yeoman.
45. Sep. 30, " Thomas Leaver of Chamber, Esq., *v.* Alex. Norris, Esq.
46. Mar. 31, 1673. Oswald Mosley of Ancoats, Esq., *v.* Nicholas Mosley, Esq.
47. Ap. 20, 1674. Major John Byrom, *v.* Humfrey Booth, Esq., resigned.
48. Ap. 5, 1675. John Sandiford of Manchester, gent., *v.* Richard Johnson, clerk.
49. " " James Lightbowne, Esq., *v.* Jonathan Chadwick, Esq.
50. Mar. 27, 1676. Thomas Holt of Castleton, Esq., *v.* Robert Holt.
51. Ap. 16, 1677. James Holt, Esq., *v.* Thomas Holt, Esq.
52. Ap. 1, 1678. James Chetham of Chetham, Esq., *v.* Major John Byrom.
53. Ap. 4, 1681. Nathaniel Bann of Salford, physician, *v.* Sir Robert Booth.
54. Oct. 3, 1681. John Hartley of Strangeways, Esq., *v.* John Hartley, Esq.
55. Oct. 2, 1682. John Hopwood of Hopwood, Esq., *v.* Wm. Holland, Esq.
56. Ap. 9, 1683. Edward Chetham, Esq., *v.* Henry Dickenson, Esq.
57. Mar. 31, 1684. Robert Wilson, gent., *v.* Richard Fox, Esq.
58. Oct. 6, 1684. Robert Lever of Darcy Lever, Esq., *v.* John Okey, gent.
59. " " Robert Hyde, Esq., *v.* Robert Hyde, Esq.

60. Oct. 6, 1684. Richard Wroe, Warden, *v.* Edward Chetham, Esq.

61. Ap. 20, 1685. William Earl of Derby, *v.* John Tyldesley, Clerk.

62. „ „ Samuel Dickenson of Blackley, gent., *v.* Samuel Harmer, Esq.

63. Ap. 5, 1686. James Grundy, Dr. of Physic, *v.* Robert Lever, Esq. [who refused to act].

64. Ap. 1, 1690. Joseph Hooper of Manchester, gent., *v.* Robert Wilson, gent.

65. Ap. 13, 1691. Sir Ralph Asheton of Middleton, Bart., v. John Hopwood, Esq.

66. Mar. 28, 1692. John Oldfield, gent., *v.* Sam. Dickenson, gent.

67. Ap. 17, 1693. Thomas Dickenson of Salford, Esq., *v.* James Chetham, Esq.

68. Oct. 1, 1694. Henry Hulton of Hulton, Esq., *v.* Wm. Hulton, Esq.

69. Sep. 30, 1965. Robert Alexander of Manchester, gent., *v.* Sir Edward Mosley.

70. Sep. 30, 1695. John Hopwood of Hopwood, Esq., *v.* John Cunliffe, gent.

71. Oct. 4, 1697. Samuel Chetham of Turton, Esq., *v.* James Chetham, Esq.

72. Apl. 10, 1699. Wm. Wood of Turton, yeoman, *v.* Ralph Brooke, yeoman.

73. „ „ Richard Percival of Manchester, gent., *v.* Thomas Mynshull, gent.

74. „ „ Alexander Davie of Salford, gent., *v.* James Lightbowne, Esq.

75. Oct. 2, 1699. Joseph Yates, Esq., *v.* Francis Mosley, clerk.

76. Ap. 1, 1700. Richard Entwisle, Esq., *v.* Robert Hyde, Esq.

77. Sep. 30. „ Joshua Horton of Chadderton, Esq., *v.* John Hopwood, Esq.

78. Mar. 29, 1703. James Earl of Derby, *v.* Wm. Richard George Earl of Derby.

79. Oct. 9, 1703. Ralph Hartley, Esq., *v.* John Hartley, Esq.

80. Ap. 9, 1705. Thomas Marsden of Bolton, Esq., *v.* Thomas Lever, Esq.

81. " " John Kay of Salford, gent., *v.* Captain Tho. Dickenson.

82. Oct. 1, 1705. John Fletcher of Salford, gent., *v.* Alex. Davie, gent.

83. " " Edward Booth of Manchester, Esq., *v.* Joseph Yates, Esq.

84. Ap. 14, 1707. Francis Davenport of Manchester, gent., *v.* Nich. Stratford, Bp. of Chester.

85. Oct. 3, 1709. Thomas Horton of Chadderton, Esq., *v.* Joshua Horton, Esq.

86. Ap. 10, 1710. Edmund Hopwood of Hopwood, Esq., *v.* Ralph Hartley, Esq.

87. Oct. 2, 1710. John Green of Manchester, apothecary, *v.* John Sandiford, gent.

88. Oct. 1, 1711. James Chetham of Smedley, gent., *v.* John Oldfield, gent.

89. " " Samuel Clowes, gent., *v.* Joseph Hooper, gent.

90. Mar. 29, 1714. Wm. Bamford, Esq., *v.* James Holt, Esq.

91. " " John Crompton of Bolton, maltman, *v.* James Grundy, Surgeon.

92. " " Sir John Bland, Bart, *v.* Robt. Alexander, gent.

93. " " Henry Dickenson of Salford, gent., *v.* Nathaniël Bann, physician.

94. Oct. 4, 1714. Edward Chetham, Esq., *v.* Edward Chetham, Esq. [No. 56.]

95. " " Rev. Peter Haddon, vicar of Bolton, *v.* Thos. Marsden, gent.

96. Ap. 18, 1715. Garvis Chetham of Turton, gent., *v.* John Crompton, gent.

97. " " John Greaves of Manchester, gent., *v.* Edward Booth, Esq.

98. Ap. 2, 1716. George Chetham, Esq., *v.* Sir John Bland, Bart.

99. Oct. 1, 1716. Sir Ralph Assheton of Middleton, Bart., *v.* Sir Ralph Assheton, Bart.

100. " " Hugh Entwistle of Bolton, gent., *v.* Henry Hulton, Esq. (displaced)

101. " " Matthew Greaves of Manchester, Esq., *v.* John Green, gent (displaced).

102. Oct. 6, 1718. John Sharples of Sharples, gent., *v.* Garvis Chetham, gent.

103. Mar. 30, 1719. John Leech of Manchester, gent., *v.* Rev. Dr. Richard Wroe, Warden.

104. Oct. 2, 1721. Rev. Thomas Morrall, Vicar of Bolton, *v.* Rev. Peter Haddon.

105. Oct. 1, 1722. Roger Neild of Salford, gent., *v.* John Fletcher, gent.

106. Ap. 11, 1726. Holland Egerton of Heaton, Esq., *v.* Richard Entwistle, Esq.

107. Ap. 3, 1727. Miles Neild of Manchester, Merchant, *v.* Oswald Mosley, Esq.

108. " " John Moss of Manchester, Woollen Draper, *v.* Richard Percival, gent.

109. Sep. 30, 1728. John Battersby of Turton, yeoman, *v.* Wm. Wood, yeoman.

110. Ap. 7, 1729. Thomas Pigot of Bowling, Esq., *v.* Samuel Clowes, gent.

111. Oct. 6, 1729. John Illingworth of Manchester, gent., *v.* John Moss, gent.

112. " " Darcey Lever, Esq., *v.* George Chetham, Esq.

113. Oct. 5, 1730. Robert Radcliffe of Foxdenton, Esq., *v.*

		Sir Holland Egerton.
114.	Ap. 10, 1732.	Gamaliel Lloyd, gent., *v.* John Illingworth, gent.
115.	Oct. 2, „	Oswald Mosley, Esq., *v.* Francis Davenport, gent.
116.	Ap. 7, 1735.	John Parker of Breightmet, Esq., *v.* John Sharples, gent.
117.	Ap. 26, 1736.	Edward, Earl of Derby, *v.* James, Earl of Derby.
118.	Oct. 4, „	Robert Booth, Esq., *v.* Roger Neild, gent.
119.	Oct. 3, 1737.	Laurence Crompton of Bolton, gent., *v.* Rev. Tho. Morrall.
120.	Ap. 3, 1738.	George Kenyon of Swinley, Esq., *v.* Miles Neild, gent.
121.	Ap. 7, 1740.	John Moss of Manchester, gent., *v.* John Greaves, Esq.
122.	Oct. 6, „	Sir Edward Egerton, *v.* John Battersby, yeoman.
123.	„ „	George Lloyd, F.R.S., Bach. in Physic, *v.* John Leech, gent.
124.	Oct. 4, 1742.	Miles Lonsdall of Bury, Esq., *v.* Sir Darcy Lever, Knt.
125.	Mar. 26, 1744.	Sir Thos. Grey Egerton, Bart., *v.* Sir Edward Egerton.
126.	May 16, 1745.	Humfrey Chetham, Esq., *v.* Samuel Chetham, Esq.
127.	Oct. 5, 1747.	Roger Sedgwick of Manchester, gent., *v.* Matthew Greaves, gent.
128.	Oct. 2, 1749.	Richard Townley of Belfield, Esq., *v.* Humfrey Chetham, Esq.
129.	„ „	Rev. Samuel Sidebotham, rector of Middleton, *v.* Robert Radcliffe, Esq.
130.	„ „	Rev. Richard Assheton, Fellow of the Coll. Ch. of Manchester, *v.* John Kay, gent.
131.	„ „	Otho Cooke of Manchester, Esq., *v.* Gamaliel Lloyd, gent.

132. Ap. 8, 1751. Rev. Samuel Lawson of Sharples, *v.* Hugh Entwistle, gent.
133. Mar. 30, 1752. Richard Assheton of Broughton, Esq., *v.* James Chetham, Esq.
134. Oct. 2, „ Wm. Starkie of Manchester, Esq., *v.* Rev. Sam. Sidebotham.
135. Ap. 19, 1756. Roger Brandwood of Bolton, gent., *v.* Rev. Sam. Lawson.
136. Ap. 11, 1757. John Pimblott of Bradshaw, Esq., *v.* Sir Tho. Grey Egerton, Bart.
137. „ „ Edward Byrom of Manchester, gent., *v.* Sir Oswald Mosley, Bart.
138. „ „ Rev. Thomas Moss, *v.* Thomas Horton, Esq.
139. Ap. 16, 1759. John Gore Booth, Esq., *v.* Robert Booth, Esq.
140. „ „ Rev. Richard Assheton, Rector of Middleton, *v.* Edmund Hopwood, Esq.
141. Ap. 12, 1762. Edward Greaves of Culcheth, Esq., *v.* Rev. Thomas Moss.
142. Ap. 12, 1762. John Houghton of Baguley, Esq., *v.* Edward, Byrom, gent.
143. „ „ Rev. Robert Oldfield, *v.* John Moss, Esq.
144. „ „ Rev. Thomas Shaw of Bolton, *v.* Roger Brandwood, gent.
145. „ „ Nathaniel Isherwood of Marple, Esq., *v.* John Pimblott, Esq.
146. „ „ John Starky of Heywood, Esq., *v.* Wm. Bamford, Esq.
147. „ „ Robert Gartside of Manchester, gent., *v.* Roger Sedgwicke, gent.
148. Oct. 4, 1762. Rev. Edmund Hulme of Rochdale, *v.* Richard Townley, Esq.
149. „ „ George Kenyon of Salford, Esq., *v.* Henry Dickenson, gent.

150. Oct. 3, 1763. Wm. Hulton, Esq., *v.* Lawrence Crompton, gent.

151. Oct. 1, 1764. Rev. John Clayton, *v.* Rev. Richard Assheton.

152. Oct. 6, 1766. Rev. John Parker, *v.* Nathaniel Isherwood, Esq.

153. " " Rev. Thomas Aynscough, *v.* Richd. Assheton, Esq.

154. " " Robert Gwillym of Atherton, Esq., *v.* Sir Ralph Assheton, Bart.

155. Ap. 20, 1767. Joseph Starky of Redivales, Esq., *v.* Rev. Edmund Hulme (resigned).

156. Oct. 3, 1768. Sir Thos. Egerton, Bart., *v.* John Parker, Esq.

157. Oct. 20, 1769. Samuel Clowes of Chaddock (Smedley), *v.* Edward Chetham, Esq.

158. Ap. 16, 1770. Henry Lonsdall of Bury, gent., *v.* Joseph Starky, Esq.

159. " " Thomas Crompton of Prestwich, gent., *v.* Thomas Pigot, Esq.

160. Ap. 1, 1771. Samuel Egerton of Tatton, Esq., *v.* George Kenyon, Esq.

161. " " Robert V. A. Gwillym of Bewsey, Esq., *v.* Rev. Robert Oldfield.

162. " " James Starky of Polefield, Esq., *v.* Wm. Starky, gent.

163. Oct. 4, 1773. John Clayton of Little Harwood, Esq., *v.* Wm. Hulton, Esq.

164. " " John Gartside of Crumpsall, Esq., *v.* Otho Cooke, Esq.

165. " " Samuel Clowes of Manchester, Esq., *v.* Samuel Clowes, Esq.

166. " " Rev. Robert Kenyon of Salford, *v.* Rev. John Clayton.

167. Oct. 3, 1774. Charles Ford, gent., *v.* Miles Lonsdall, Esq.

168. Sep. 30, 1776. Edward Earl of Derby, *v.* Edward E. of Derby.
169. " " James Cooke, Esq., *v*, Robt. Gartside, Esq.
170. " " Robert Radcliffe, Esq., Thomas Crompton, gent.
171. Mar. 27, 1780. Wm. Tatton of Withenshaw, Esq., *v.* Samuel Egerton, Esq.
172. " " Rev. Peter Haddon, *v.* James Starky, Esq.
173. " " George Walmesley, Esq., *v.* John Starky, Esq.
174. " " Wm. Bankes of Winstanley, Esq., *v.* Robert Gwillym, Esq.
175. Ap. 16, 1781. Wm. Allen of Davyhulme, Esq., *v.* James Cooke, Esq.
176. " " James Kearsley of Hulton, gent., *v.* George Kenyon, Esq.
177. " " James Bradshaw of Darcy Lever, Esq., *v.* Henry Lonsdall, Esq.
178. Ap. 21, 1783. Joseph Tipping of Manchester, gent., *v.* Edward Greaves, Esq.
179. Oct. 6, " Joseph Pickford of Royton, Esq., *v.* Robert Vernon Gwillym, Esq.
180. Ap. 12, 1784. Wm. Hulton, of Hulton, Esq., *v.* Robert Radcliffe, Esq.
181. " " Charles Lawson, M.A., *v.* George Lloyd, Esq.
182. Oct. 2, 1786. John Ridgway of Bolton, gent., *v.* Rev. Tho. Shaw.
183. Mar. 24, 1788. Thomas Barrow, Esq., *v.* Rev. Robt. Kenyon.
184. Ap. 13, 1789. Rev. Thomas Foxley, *v.* John Gore Booth, Esq.
185. " " John Arden of Ashley, Esq., *v.* Charles Ford, Esq.
186. Oct. 6, 1794. John Entwisle of Foxholes, Esq., *v.* John Houghton, Esq.

187.	Oct. 6, 1794.	Joseph Thackeray, Esq., *v.* Rev. Tho. Aynscough.
188.	„ „	John Ridings, Esq., *v.* William Allen, Esq.
189.	Oct. 6, 1800.	Rev. Thomas Bancroft, *v.* Rev. John Parker.
190.	„ „	Samuel Clowes, Esq., *v.* Lieut.-Col. Samuel Clowes [No. 165].
191.	„ „	Rev. James Lyons, *v.* Joseph Tipping, gent.
192.	„ „	John Ford, Esq., *v.* Wm. Bankes, Esq.
193.	„ „	Rev. Thos. Blackburn, Warden, *v.* Rev. R. Assheton, Warden.
194.	„ „	Wm. Fox, Esq., *v.* Wm. Hulton, Esq.
195.	Ap. 11, 1803.	Rev. Thos. Drake, *v.* John Ridgway, gent.
196.	„ „	John Ridgway, Esq., *v.* George Walmesley, Esq.
197.	„ „	Rev. Croxton Johnson, *v.* John Clayton, Esq.
198.	Oct. 3, 1803.	John Leaf, Esq., *v.* Thos. Barrow, Esq.
199.	Ap. 2, 1804.	Thomas Parker, Esq., *v.* James Bradshaw, Esq.
200.	Oct. 1, „	John Bradshaw, Esq., *v.* John Ridgway, Esq.
201.	Oct. 6, 1806.	Rev. George Heron, *v.* Wm. Tatton Egerton, Esq.
202.	Ap. 18, 1808.	Wilbraham Egerton, Esq., *v.* John Ridings, Esq.
203.	„ „	Richard Atherton Farrington, Esq., *v.* Charles Lawson, M.A.
204.	„ „	Benjamin Rawson, Esq., *v.* James Kearsley, Esq.
205.	Ap. 15, 1811.	Wm. Hulton of Hulton Park, Esq., *v.* Rev. Thos. Bancroft.
206.	Sep. 30, „	Rev. John Clowes, *v.* Samuel Clowes, Esq.
207.	Mar. 27, 1815.	Thos. Wm. Tatton, Esq., *v.* Rev. Croxton Johnson.

208. Mar. 27, 1815. Wm. Marriott, Esq., *v.* Thomas, Earl of Wilton.

209. „ „ Samuel Chetham Hilton, Esq., *v.* Rev. Peter Haddon.

210. Ap. 15, 1816. Thomas Legh of Lyme, Esq., *v.* John Bradshaw, Esq.

211. Mar. 23, 1818. George Harry Lord Grey, *v.* John Gartside, Esq.

212. „ „ Rev. Joseph Bradshaw, rector of Wilmslow, *v.* John Entwisle, Esq.

213. Ap. 12, 1819. Wm. Legh Clowes, Esq., *v.* Sir Joseph Radcliffe, Bart.

214. Oct. 4, 1819. John Entwisle of Foxholes, Esq., *v.* Rev. Thos. Drake.

215. Ap. 23, 1821. Thomas Earl of Wilton, *v.* Rev. Joseph Bradshaw.

216. Mar. 31, 1823. John Hargreaves of Ormrod House, *v.* Richd. Atherton Farrington, Esq.

217. Oct. 6, „ James Hibbert of Broughton Hall, *v.* Dr. Thos. Blackburne, Warden.

218. „ „ General Peter Heron, *v.* John Arden, Esq.

219. Ap. 4, 1825. Rev. Tho. Calvert, D.D., Warden, *v.* Joseph Thackeray, Esq.

220. Oct. 1, 1827. Rev. Tho. Blackburne of Eccles, *v.* Tho. Wm. Tatton, Esq.

221. „ „ Robert Gregge Hopwood of Hopwood, Esq, *v.* Wm. Fox, Esq.

222. Ap. 20, 1829. Rev. Wm. Fox of Statham Lodge in Lymm, *v.* James Hibbert.

223. Ap. 23, 1832. J. Wilson Patten, Esq., *v.* Rev. George Heron.

224. Mar. 31, 1834. W. Tatton Egerton, Esq., *v.* Thos. Parker, Esq.

225. Oct. 6, „ John Fred. Foster, Esq., *v.* John Hargreaves, Esq.

226. Ap. 20, 1835. Rt. Hon. Lord Francis Egerton, *v.* Earl of Derby.

227. " " Thos. Hardman of Broughton, Esq., *v.* Sam. Chetham Hilton, Esq.

228. Oct. 2, 1837. Thomas William Tatton of Wythenshawe, Esq., *v.* William Marriott, Esq., deceased.

229. " " John Entwisle of Foxholes, Esq., *v.* Rev. James Lyon, deceased.

230. " " Edward Loyd of Manchester, Esq., *v.* John Entwisle, Esq., deceased.

231. Oct. 1, 1838. Hon. Richard Bootle Wilbraham, *v.* Earl of Wilton, resigned.

232. " " Hugh Hornby Birley, Esq., *v.* Thomas Hardman, Esq., deceased.

233. Sep. 30, 1839. Right Honourable Lord Stanley, *v.* Rev. Thomas Foxley, deceased.

234. " " Richard Watson Barton of Spring Wood, Esq., *v.* John Ford, Esq., deceased.

235. Oct. 5, 1840. John Ireland Blackburne of Hale Hall, Esq., *v.* Very Rev. Dr. Calvert, deceased.

236. Oct. 4, 1841. James Collier Harter of Broughton Hall, Esq., *v.* John Leaf, Esq., deceased.

237. Ap. 17, 1843. Robert Townley Parker of Cuerden, Esq., *v.* The Rt. Hon. the Earl of Stamford and Warrington, resigned.

238. " " Robert Lomax of Harwood, Esq., *v.* General Heron, resigned.

239. Mar. 24, 1845. Rev. George Heron of Carrington, Cheshire, *v.* Honourable R. B. Wilbraham, deceased.

240. " " William Hulton the Younger of Hulton Park, Lancashire, Esq., *v.* Benjamin Rawson, Esq., deceased.

241. " " Edward Jeremiah Lloyd of Oldfield Hall,

Cheshire, Esq., *v.* Rev. William Fox, deceased.

242\. Oct. 6, 1845. Leigh Trafford of Sale, Esq., *v.* Hugh Hornby Birley, Esq., deceased.

243\. Oct. 5, 1846. Samuel William Clowes, Esq., *v.* Rev. John Clowes, deceased.

244\. Oct. 1, 1849. Very Rev. George Hull Bowers, Dean of Manchester, *v.* Rev. Thomas Blackburne, deceased.

245\. " " Sir Benjamin Heywood of Claremont, Bart., *v.* Robert Townley Parker, Esq., resigned.

246\. " " Egerton Leigh, Jun., of High Leigh, Cheshire, Esq., *v.* Rt. Hon. the Earl of Ellesmere, resigned.

247\. " " Rev. James Slade of Bolton, *v.* William Hulton, Esq., resigned.

248\. Sep. 30, 1850. Edmund Haworth, Jun., of Sale Lodge, Cheshire, Esq., *v.* Robert Gregge Hopwood, Esq., resigned.

249\. " " Peter Ainsworth of Smithills, near Bolton, Esq., *v.* Robert Lomax, Esq., deceased.

250\. " " Benjamin Dennison Naylor of Manchester, Cotton Waste Dealer, *v.* Edward Jeremiah Lloyd, Esq., deceased.

251\. Ap. 21, 1851. Edward Loyd, the Younger, of Prestwich Lodge, near Manchester, Esq., *v.* John Ireland Blackburne, Esq., resigned.

252\. Mar. 24, 1856. Robert Henry Norreys of Davyhulme Hall, Esq., *v.* Wilbraham Egerton, Esq. resigned.

253\. Oct. 6, 1856. James Crossley of Manchester, Solicitor, *v.* Edward Loyd, Esq., resigned.

254\. Oct. 14, 1857. Rev. John Shepherd Birley of Bolton, *v.* Rev. Canon Slade, resigned.

255. Oct. 14, 1857. Rev. Henry Mildred Birch, Rector of Prestwich, *v.* Sir Benjamin Heywood, Bart., resigned.

256. „ „ Daniel Maude of Manchester, Esq., *v.* Thomas Legh, Esq., deceased.

257. Oct. 4, 1858. Oliver Heywood of Manchester, Esq., *v.* William Legh Clowes, Esq., resigned.

258. „ „ John Tomlinson Hibbert of Urmston, Esq. *v.* John Frederic Foster, Esq., deceased.

259. Ap. 9, 1860. Rev. Edward J. G. Hornby, Rector of Bury, *v.* Leigh Trafford, Esq., resigned.

260. „ „ Alfred Barton of Manchester, Esq., *v.* John Wilson Patten, Esq., resigned.

261. Ap. 1, 1861. Honble. Algernon Fulke Egerton, M.P., *v.* Richard Watson Barton, Esq., resigned.

262. Oct. 6, 1862. Edward Ovens of Manchester, Esq., *v.* James Collier Harter, Esq., deceased.

263. Ap. 17, 1865. William John Legh of Lyme, Esq., *v.* Edward Loyd, Esq., resigned.

264. Oct. 4, 1865. Rev. Canon Raines of Milnrow, *v.* Daniel Maude, Esq., resigned.

265. Oct. 1, 1866. Hugh Birley of Manchester, Esq., *v.* Edmund Haworth, Esq., resigned.

266. Oct. 5, 1868. Joseph Fenton of Bamford Hall, Lancashire, Esq., *v.* John Smith Entwisle, Esq., deceased.

267. Oct. 4, 1869. John Allen of Oldfield Hall, near Altrincham, Esq., *v.* Benjamin D. Naylor, Esq. resigned.

268. „ „ Richard Milne Redhead of Springfield, Seedley, near Manchester, Esq., *v.* Edward Ovens, deceased.

269. Ap. 18, 1870. Edward Joynson, of Bowdon, Cheshire, Esq., *v.* Rt. Hon. the Earl of Derby, deceased.

270. Ap. 18, 1870. William Gray of Bolton, Lancashire, Esq., *v.* Peter Ainsworth, Esq., deceased.

271. Oct. 3, 1870. Rt. Hon. the Earl of Ellesmere of Worsley House, Lancashire, *v.* Alfred Barton, Esq., resigned.

272. Oct. 2, 1871. Hon. Wilbraham Egerton of Rostherne Manor, Knutsford, *v.* Rt. Hon. the Lord Egerton of Tatton, resigned.

273. Sept. 30, 1872. Edward Hardcastle of Headlands, Prestwich, Esq., *v.* Very Rev. the Dean of Manchester (Bowers), resigned.

274. Ap. 2, 1877. William Wilbraham Blethyn Hulton of Hulton Park, Bolton, Esq., *v.* William Ford Hulton, Esq., resigned.

275. Ap. 2, 1877. Oliver Ormerod Walker of Chesham near Bury, Esq., *v.* Colonel Egerton Leigh, deceased.

276. Ap. 14, 1879. Very Rev. Benjamin Morgan Cowie, D.D., Dean of Manchester, *v.* Canon Raines, deceased.

277. Oct. 4, 1880. Richard Henry Ainsworth of Smithills Hall, near Bolton, Esq., *v.* Edward Joynson, Esq., resigned.

278. Ap. 18, 1881. James Chadwick of High Bank, Prestwich, Esq., *v.* Colonel Gray, resigned.

279. Ap. 14, 1884. Edmund Ashworth of Egerton Hall, near Bolton, Esq., *v.* Rev. J. Shepherd Birley, deceased.

280. " " Henry Hoyle Howorth of Derby House, Ellesmere Park, Eccles, Esq., F.S.A., *v.* James Crossley, Esq., deceased.

281. " " Richard Hampson Joynson, of Richmond Hill, Bowdon, Esq., *v.* Hugh Birley, Esq., M.P., deceased.

282. Ap. 6, 1885. Rev. William Thomas Jones, Rector of Prestwich, *v.* Canon Birch, deceased.

283. Ap. 6, 1885. William Henry Houldsworth of Norbury Booths Hall, near Knutsford, Esq., M.P., *v.* Dean of Exeter (Cowie), resigned.

284. Oct. 5, 1885. Thomas Egerton Tatton of Wythenshawe, Esq., *v.* Thomas William Tatton, Esq., deceased.

285. Oct. 3, 1887. Venerable George Henry Greville Anson, Archdeacon of Manchester, *v.* Robert Henry Norreys, Esq., deceased.

286. Oct. 1, 1888. Rev. James Augustus Atkinson, of Bolton-le-Moors, *v.* Canon Hornby, deceased.

287. Oct. 6, 1890. Bulkeley Allen of West Lynn, Altrincham, Esq., *v.* John Allen, Esq., resigned.

288. May 4, 1892. Stewart Garnett of the Rookery, Eccles Old Road, Pendleton, Esq., *v.* Hon. Algernon F. Egerton, deceased.

289. " " Charles James Heywood of Chaseley, Pendleton, Esq., *v.* Oliver Heywood, Esq., deceased.

290. " " Very Rev. Edward Craig Maclure, Dean of Manchester, *v.* James Chadwick, Esq., deceased.

291. Mar. 26, 1894. Col. John James Mellor of the Woodlands, Whitefield, *v.* Joseph Fenton, Esq., deceased.

292. Oct. 1, 1894. John Hunt Grafton of Overdale, Altrincham, Esq., *v.* Rev. George Heron, deceased.

293. Ap. 15, 1895. Edward Tootal Broadhurst of Prestwich, merchant, *v.* S. W. Clowes, Esq., resigned.

294. Ap. 11, 1898. Rev. Foster Grey Blackburne of the Rectory, Bury, *v.* Archdeacon Anson, deceased.

295. Oct. 3, 1898. Rev. Edwin Hoskyns of the Vicarage, Bolton, *v.* Canon Atkinson, resigned.

296. Oct. 2, 1899, Rt. Hon. Fred. A. Stanley, Earl of Derby, K.G., G.C.B., *v.* Lord Newton, deceased.

297. Ap. 16, 1900. Sir Frank Forbes Adam of Mere Old Hall, Knutsford, Cheshire, *v.* Richard Milne Redhead, Esq., deceased.

298. " " Frederick Platt-Higgins of Holm Leigh, Bowdon, Cheshire, Esq., M.P., *v.* T. W. Jones, resigned.

299. Mar. 31, 1902. Charles Garnett of Higher Dunscar, Egerton, near Bolton, Esq., *v.* Edmund Ashworth, Esq., deceased.

APPENDIX VII.

LIBRARIANS OF CHETHAM'S LIBRARY.

1653. Rev. Richard Johnson was appointed the first Librarian, with power to appoint a deputy during his life, but not to be drawn into an example for future elections.

July 3, 1656. Rev. Robert Browne appointed deputy to Mr. Johnson.

July 22, 1658. Rev. Edmund Lees, deputy to Mr. Johnson on discharge of R. Browne.

July 4, 1666. Rev. William Harrison, B.A., deputy, on resignation of E. Lees.

Ap. 5, 1675. Rev. William Harrison, B.A., on death of R. Johnson.

Oct. 4, 1680. Rev. Humfrey Livesey, on removal of W. Harrison.

Oct. 6, 1684. Rev. Thomas Pendleton, on death of H. Livesey.

May 4, 1693. Rev. Nathaniel Banne, on death of T. Pendleton.

Aug. 24, 1712. Rev. James Leicester, M.A., on resignation of N. Banne.

Jan. 22, 1718-9. Rev. Francis Hooper, B.A., on death of J. Leicester.

May 12, 1726. Rev. Robert Oldfield, on resignation of F. Hooper.

Feb. 7, 1731-2. Robert Thyer, B.A., on resignation of R. Oldfield.

Oct. 3, 1763. Rev. Robert Kenyon, B.A., on resignation of R. Thyer.

July 24, 1787. Rev. John Radcliffe, B.A., on death of R. Kenyon.

Oct. 2, 1797. Rev. John Haddon Hindley, on resignation of J. Radcliffe.

Ap. 2, 1804. Rev. Thomas Stone, on resignation of J. H. Hindley.

Mar. 20, 1812. Rev. John Taylor Allen, on resignation of T. Stone.
Oct. 1, 1821. Rev. Peter Hordern, on resignation of J. T. Allen.
Mar. 30, 1834. Rev. George Dugard, M.A., on resignation of P. Hordern.
Oct. 2, 1837. Rev. Campbell Grey Hulton, M.A., on resignation G. Dugard.
1845. Thomas Jones, B.A., on resignation of Rev. C. G. Hulton. Mr. Jones died 27 November, 1875, when James Crossley, F.S.A., was appointed honorary librarian, on whose death, 1 May, 1883, a similar appointment was accepted by Henry Hoyle Howorth (M.P. for Salford, knighted in 1892). Since the death of Mr. Jones the general management of the library has been practically in the hands of the House Governors, Mr. Hanby and Mr. Browne, with the assistance of sub-librarians.

APPENDIX VIII.

MASTERS OR HOUSE GOVERNORS OF CHETHAM'S HOSPITAL.

Ap. 16, 1654. Richard Dutton, first overseer.
Aug. 9, 1671. Roger Harness, on dismissal of R. Dutton.
Aug. 2, 1681. John Wardle, on death of R. Harness.
June 15, 1697. Nicholas Cunliffe, on death of J. Wardle.
Mar. 11, 1706. Thomas Mercer, on death of N. Cunliffe.
July 29, 1709. Robert Benison of Manchester, on dismissal of T. Mercer.
May 16, 1735. Christopher Horrox of Castleton, on dismissal of R. Benison.
Mar. 26, 1744. Peter Antrobus of Manchester, on death of C. Horrox.
Oct. 1, 1759. Thomas Hardman of Turton, on death of Peter Antrobus.
Ap. 17, 1775. Joseph Barlow of Manchester, on death of T. Hardman.
Oct. 6, 1808. Christopher Terry of Manchester, on resignation of J. Barlow.
July 22, 1818. George Crossley of Manchester, on death of C. Terry.
Oct. 14, 1841. Luke Hadfield of Stockport, on resignation of G. Crossley.
1857. John Robinson, on death of L. Hadfield.
1868. James Bury, on death of J. Robinson.
Dec. 30, 1873. Richard Hanby (previously sub-librarian), on dismissal of J. Bury.
1886. Walter Thurlow Browne, on death of R. Hanby.

APPENDIX IX.

BIBLIOGRAPHY OF HUMPHREY CHETHAM AND HIS HOSPITAL.

AINSWORTH (William Harrison). Guy Fawkes. London, 1841.
In this novel Humphrey Chetham is introduced as in love with Viviana, daughter of Sir Alexander Radcliffe.

ASPLAND (Rev. Robert Brook). Humphrey Chetham: A Sermon preached at the Old Chapel, Dukinfield, Sunday, Oct. 16, 1853, in reference to the bi-centenary anniversary of his death [*In* the *Christian Reformer*, November, 1853]. 8vo. Reprinted in the present volume.

ASTON (Joseph). The Manchester Guide . . . Manchester, 1804. 8vo.
Pages 138–150 contain a description of the Hospital and Library as they were at the beginning of the nineteenth century.

ASTON (Joseph). Metrical Records of Manchester, in which its history is traced (Currente Calamo) from the days of the Ancient Britons to the present time. By the Editor of the *Exchange Herald.* London [Manchester], 1822, 8vo.
Some lines on Chetham's Foundations occur on pp. 10–11.

AXON (William E. A.). In Memoriam: Bibliothecarius Chethamensis (Thomas Jones, B.A., F.S.A.) [*In* Manchester Literary Club Papers, 1876, vol. ii. pp. 59–65].

AXON (William E. A.). Notabilia Bibliotheca Chethamensis. Manchester, 1877. 8vo. pp. 16.

AXON (William E. A.). Handbook of the Public Libraries of Manchester and Salford. Manchester, 1877. 4to.
Chetham Library, pp. 1–8; Church Libraries, p.p. 157–161; the latter article also in *Country Words*, February 23, 1867.

BAILEY (John Eglington). The Old "English Library" of Manchester Church. [In *Notes and Queries*, July 28 and August 4, 1877).

Referring to the formation of H. Chetham's Library at Manchester Church, with list of books purchased in 1659.

BAILEY (John Eglington). [Address on Chetham's Library, on occasion of a visit by the Manchester Literary Club.] *In* Papers of the Manchester Literary Club, vol. iv., 1878, pp. 175–178.

Also, with alterations, in Trans. of the Library Association, 1879, pp. 113–116.

BAILEY (John Eglington). The Reading Room of Chetham's Hospital (with illustration). *In* Manchester Christmas Annual, 1884, pp. 81–82.

BAILEY (John Eglington). [Abstract of a paper on an inventory of the contents of Turton Tower, 1642.] *In* Trans. of the Lancashire and Cheshire Antiquarian Society, vol. iii. pp. 197–200.

BAINES (Edward). History of the County Palatine of Lancaster. 4to.

1st ed. 1836. Chetham's Hospital and Library, with view of Hospital from River Irk, vol. ii. pp. 223–230; life by W. R. Whatton, with portrait, vol. ii. pp. 365–367.

2nd ed. by J. Harland. 1868. Hospital and Library, vol. i. pp. 299–300; life, vol. i. p. 405.

3rd ed. by J. Croston. 1889. Hospital and Library, vol. ii. pp. 78–82; life, vol. ii. pp. 250–1; pedigree, vol. ii. p. 235.

BANKS (Mrs. George Linnæus). The Manchester Man. Illustrated by Charles Green and Hedley Fitton. Manchester, 1896. 4to.

Contains several sketches of the Hospital and Library, a small one of Theed's statue in the Cathedral, and a portrait of Humphrey Chetham.

BLATCHFORD (Robert). Souvenir of a visit to Chetham College, Friday, March 29, 1901 [Manchester, 1901]. Fol. pp. 16.

Reprinted, with illustrations, from the *Clarion*, May 28, 1892.

BOOKER (Rev. John). A History of the Ancient Chapel of Blackley . . Manchester. 1854. 4to.

Notice of Crumpsall Hall and the family of the Founder, pp. 201–211.

BOOKER (Rev. John). A History of the Ancient Chapels of Didsbury and Chorlton . . . Printed for the Chetham Society, 1857. 4to.

Correspondence between H. Chetham and Mrs. and Miss Anne Mosley, pp. 147–157.

BOOKER (Rev. John). A History of the Ancient Chapel of Birch . . . Chetham Society. 1859. 4to.

Proposed purchase of the College by H. Chetham. 1649. pp. 91–3.

BOURNE (H. R. Fox). Humphrey Chetham of Manchester (chap. ix. of "The Merchant Princes of England"). In *London Society*, vol. 6, 1864, pp. 466–470. Also in "English Merchants: Memoirs in Illustration of the Progress of British Commerce." 1866.

BUTTERWORTH (James). The Antiquities of the Town, and a complete History of the Trade of Manchester . . . Manchester, 1822, 12mo.

Description of Chetham's Hospital and Library, pages 202–210.

BYROM (John). The Private Journal and Literary Remains of John Byrom. Edited by Richard Parkinson. Manchester, printed for the Chetham Society, 1854–7. 4to. 4 vols.

Incidental references to the Chetham Library occur at the following pages: i., 146, 148, 155, 439; ii., 59, 60, 85, 128, 198.

CALENDAR of State Papers, Domestic Series. London. 8vo.

1625–1649, addenda, page 664 (order to pay money to H.C.) 1635, pages 495, 549, 559, 568, 598 (Ship Money). 1637, pages 229, 230 (Ship Money).

CHARITY Commission.

16.—Further report of the Commissioners appointed in pursuance of two several Acts of Parliament . . . to inquire concerning charities in England [and Wales] for the education of the poor . . . Ordered by the House of Commons to be printed, 4 December, 1826. Fol.

Chetham's Hospital, pp. 121–138.

THE Charters of the Collegiate Church, the Free Grammar School, the Blue Coat School, and the last will and testament of the late Catherine Richards, with other ancient curiosities. Manchester, printed by T. Harper, in Smithy-door. 1791. 8vo.

Will of H. Chetham, pp. 76–142, Charter of 1665, pp. 144–155.

CHETHAM (Humphrey). The last will of Humphrey Chetham, of Clayton, in the county of Lancaster, Esq.; dated December 16, 1651; whereby he founded and endowed an hospital and library in Manchester. Also the charter of King Charles II., dated November 12, 1665, for making the trustees under Mr. Chetham's will a body-corporate. Manchester: printed by J. Harrop, opposite the Exchange [1761]. 4to. pp. [ii.] 56.

300 copies were printed by order of the Governors. Edited by Robert Thyer.

CHRISTIE (Richard Copley). The Old Church and School Libraries of Lancashire. Printed for the Chetham Society, 1885. 4to.

H. Chetham's Church Libraries, pp. 19–68.

CITY NEWS, NOTES AND QUERIES. Edited by J. H. Nodal. Manchester. 4to.

Vol. v. (1883–4): Several letters on the Chetham Library.

Vol. vi. (1885–6) contains communications on the curiosities formerly in the Library.

CLEGG (James). Extracts from the Diary and Correspondence of the Rev. James Clegg, Nonconformist Minister and Doctor of Medicine, A.D. 1679 to 1755. Edited by Henry Kirke. Buxton, 1899, 8vo.

Contains several interesting references to the use he made of the Chetham Library.

CROSSLEY (James). On the Chetham Library. In *Blackwood's Magazine*, June, 1821; also as an appendix to R. W. Procter's *Memorials of Manchester Streets.* 1874.

CROSTON (James). Humphrey Chetham and the Chetham family. *In* the *Reliquary*, vol. ix. 1868–9, pp. 107–112, 220–224; vol. x. 1869–70, pp. 17–23.

CROSTON (James). Nooks and Corners of Lancashire and Cheshire . . . Manchester: 1882. 4to.

Chap. iv. The College and the "Wizard Warden" at Manchester, pp. 157–202.

DE FOE (Daniel). Tour thro' the whole Island of Great Britain . . . 2nd ed., 1738. *See* vol. iii., p. 176–7.

EDWARDS (Edward). Manchester Worthies and their Foundations; or, Six Chapters of Local History; with an epilogue, by way of moral. Manchester, 1855, 8vo. pp. 88.

Originally published as an article in the *British Quarterly Review*, vol. 20. Chapters ii.–iv. deal with H. Chetham and his foundations; they were repeated in Mr. Edwards' *Memoirs of Libraries*, 1859, vol. i. pp. 623–679.

ENGLAND'S First Free Library. Notes on a visit to Chetham's Hospital. In *Sunday Chronicle*, Feb. 5, 1888.

ESDAILE (George). [Abstract of a paper on the parentage and the date of burial of H. Chetham.] *In* Trans. Lancashire and Cheshire Antiquarian Society, vol. iii. p. 200.

ESPINASSE (Francis). Lancashire Worthies. London, 1874, 8vo.

Life of H. C., pp. 83–95. The frontispiece to this volume is a reproduction of Heath's engraving of H. C.'s portrait.

FALKNER (Robert). Chetham's Hospital and Library. Manual and Guide, price one penny. Manchester [1902], 12mo. pp. 16 + 4. Illustrated.

FRENCH (Gilbert J.). Bibliographical Notices of the Church Libraries at Turton and Gorton, bequeathed by Humphrey Chetham. Printed for the Chetham Society, 1855, 4to.

FULLER (Thomas). The History of the Worthies of England. London, 1662, fol.

Lancashire, p. 121. Notice of H. C., from information supplied by Richard Johnson.

GORDON (Rev. Alexander). What an Old Library Did. In *Christian Life*, May 6, 1899.

Suggested by a reference in James Clegg's Diary (1679–1755) as to the influence received from reading certain books at the Chetham Library.

GREGAN (John E.). Notes on Humphrey Chetham and his Foundation. *In* Journal of the British Archæological Association, vol. vi. 1851, pp. 294–302, two plates.

[GREGSON (J. Stanley)]. Museum Chethamiense; or, a choice oratorical catalogue of the rare and valuable curiosities contained in the College Library, Manchester. Manchester, 1827, 8vo. pp. 4.

This is a report of the description given of the boys who took visitors round. The earliest reference to the curiosities is contained in *A Description of Manchester*, by a native of the town [James Ogden], 1783. They seem to have been dispersed before or about 1860. The *City News Notes and Queries*, vol. 6, has several notes on the same subject. See also Harland's *Manchester Collectanea*, vol. ii. p. 19.

HALLIWELL-[Phillipps] (James Orchard). An account of the European Manuscripts in the Chetham Library, Manchester. Manchester, 1842, 8vo. pp. vi. 26.

HALLIWELL [Phillipps–] (James Orchard). A Catalogue of Proclamations, Broadsides, Ballads, and Poems, presented to the Chetham Library, Manchester, by James O. Halliwell, Esq. London, 1851, 4to. pp. xx. 272.

HARLAND (John). Collectanea relating to Manchester and its neighbourhood, at various periods. Printed for the Chetham Society, 1866–7, 4to.

Vol. 1. Chetham Feoffees in 1788, p. 141. Barritt *MSS.*, p. 245. Vol. 2. Boy Guides, p. 194.

HENN (Rev. John). Memoir of Richard Hanby . . . House Governor of Chetham's Hospital, Manchester. Manchester, 1886, 8vo.

Chapter III. Chetham's Hospital and Library, pp. 73–115.

HURRELL (John W.). Old Oak English Furniture. Manchester, 1902, fol. Includes carved woodwork in Chetham Hospital.

JAMES (H. G.) Views in Lithography of Old Halls, &c., in Manchester and the Vicinity. 1821–5.

Includes two views of Crumpsall Hall and one of Turton Tower.

JONES (Thomas, B.A. A Catalogue of the Collection of Tracts for and against Popery (published in or about the reign of James II.) in the Manchester Library founded by Humphrey Chetham, &c. Manchester, printed for the Chetham Society, 1859–65, 4to. 2 parts.

LEIGH (Charles). The Natural History of Lancashire, Cheshire [etc.]. Oxford. 1700. fol.

Book II., page 15, contains some particulars of the benefactions of H. Chetham, who is called "that great example of industrious improvement." The Library is said to be "already furnished with a competent stock of choice and valuable books, to the number of near four thousand, and are daily increasing."

LOCAL Notes and Queries, from the *Manchester Guardian*, 1874–77, 4to.

Nos. 13, 93, and 112 refer to Kneller's painting in the Reading Room.

LOVE (Benjamin). Manchester As It Is. . . . Manchester, 1839, 12mo. (Alsosecond edition, entitled "The Handbook of Manchester," 1842.)

With description of the College (with engraving by J. Stephenson) and of the Library. In an interesting quotation from the *Manchester Guardian* of October 10, 1838, is the following curious passage: "That it is not more known may be in some measure owing to its locality, in a part of the town little frequented, of late years, except during the races at Kersal Moor. The secluded position, too, of the college or hospital, standing in a large area, apart from any buildings, and not fronting any street, tends still more to keep one of its chief treasures, its library, from the practical view of the community."

MULLIS (William). Some Account of the Blue Coat Hospital and Public Library, in the College, Manchester, founded by Humphrey Chetham, Esq., in the year 1651. Manchester, Leech and Cheetham, 1822, 12mo. pp. 18.

Anonymous, but afterwards issued, in 1826, with the name of the author, who was deputy librarian. There are subsequent editions. It also appears, *verbatim*, in *A Concise Description of Manchester and Salford*, published by Leech and Cheetham, about 1827. The editor of this Guide Book, probably William Mullis himself, states on page 143, that he was educated at Chetham's Hospital.

NEWCOME (Henry). The Diary of the Rev. Henry Newcome, from September 30, 1661, to September 29, 1663. Edited by Thomas Heywood. Printed for the Chetham Society, 1849, 4to.

—— The Autobiography of Henry Newcome, M.A. Edited by Richard Parkinson, D.D. Printed for the Chetham Society, 1852, 2 vols. 4to.

Newcome was one of the earliest readers at the Chetham Library, and the above works contain many references to it. In the first they are inadequately indexed, and in the second not at all. Some extracts from the "Diary" are quoted in Mr. Christie's "Old Libraries," but these refer to the Church Library.

NICHOLSON (Albert). The Chetham Hospital and Library. A history and description. Prepared for the meeting of the Library Association in Manchester, September, 1899. Manchester, 1899, 8vo. pp. 12.

NOOKS and Corners of Lancashire. Chetham's College and Library. *In The Shadow*, No. 24, Manchester. Feb. 27, 1869, p. 347.

PALATINE Note-Book. Manchester, 1881–4, 4to.
Vol. i. pp. 126, 218. Partnership Deed, George Chetham and George Tipping, 1609–10.
„ p. 195. Chetham Library Book Plate.
„ pp. 197, 220. Epitaph on Humphrey Chetham, by Thomas Jackson.
„ p. 212. Note on James and John Lightbown.
Vol. ii. p. 57. Clock presented to Chetham's Hospital by T. W. Freston.
„ p. 181. Article on Rev. John Prestwich, with references to the Chetham Library and the first two Librarians.
„ p. 225. Rev. J. Prestwich's bequest of books, etc., to the Library.
„ p. 232. H. Chetham's funeral certificate.
Vol. iii. p. 47. Thoresby's Visit to the Chetham Library.
„ p. 81. Edmund Chetham, M.A., died 21 Jan., 1602-3.
Vol. iv. p. 32. Hospital Boys' Gallery in Manchester Church, 1667.
„ p. 118. Autograph of H. Chetham.

PERKINS (Rev. Thomas). The Cathedral Church of Manchester, a short history and description of the church and of the collegiate buildings now known as Chetham's Hospital. London, G. Bell & Son, 1901, 12mo.

With illustrations from photographs and a plan. The view of the memorial in the Cathedral is entitled "Statue of *Sir* Humphrey Chetham."

PSALMANAZAR (George) Memoirs. 2nd edition, 1765, 8vo.

Pages 204–5 record a visit to Chetham Library, and the advice he gave as to the purchase of books.

RAINES (Rev. F. R.). A Sermon preached in the Cathedral and Parish Church of Manchester, on Monday the 28th of July, 1873, in commemoration of Humphrey Chetham, formerly of Clayton Hall and Turton Tower, in the County Palatine of Lancashire, esquire. Manchester, 1873, 8vo. pp. 18.

ROEDER (Charles). [H. Chetham's business relations with the Radcliffes of Ordsall.] *In* Trans. Lanc. and Ches. Antiq. Soc., vol. xiv. pp. 200–5, 1896.

RYLANDS (John Paul). Cheshire and Lancashire Funeral Certificates, A.D. 1600 to 1679. Record Society, 1882, 8vo.

Includes H. Chetham's funeral certificate, pp. 200–1.

SHAW (William Arthur). Manchester Old and New. With illustrations after original drawings by H. E. Tidmarsh. London, 1894, 4to.

Several references to and illustrations ot H. Chetham and the Hospital and Library.

STUKELEY (William). Itinerarium Curiosum. 2nd ed., 1776, fol.

"The college founded by Chetham, a tradesman, has a very good library, and a good salary: here are about fifty boys maintained [1725]." Centuria, vol. ii. p. 29.

SUTTON (C. W.). Humphrey Chetham [article in Dict. of National Biography, vol, x. pp. 206–7].

TAYLOR (Henry). Old Halls in Lancashire and Cheshire. Manchester, 1884, 4to.

The Chetham Hospital is described on pages 31–46, with plans, sections, and views of the Hospital; also view and plan of Turton Tower.

WAUGH (Edwin). Sketches of Lancashire Life and Localities. Manchester, 1855, 12mo.

The last sketch in this volume ("Boggart Ho Clough") contains references to Chetham's foundation, and describes a visit to the Library. Another description will be found in Mr. Waugh's *Roads out of Manchester*, in the *Manchester Weekly Times Supplement*, February 12 and 19, 1881.

WHATTON (William Robert). A History of the Chetham Hospital and Library, with a genealogical account of the Founder and the family of Chetham: to which is added an Appendix. Manchester, 1833, 4to. With portrait, views, and plans.

Forms part of the 3rd volume of Hibbert-Ware's *Foundations in Manchester.*

WORTHINGTON (Dr. John). Diary and Correspondence. Edited by James Crossley and Richard Copley Christie. Printed for the Chetham Society, vol. 2, pts. 1–2, 1855–86, 4to.

The letters from which the following passages are taken refer to his desire for the Wardenship of Manchester:—

p. 238.—"The town is now become more acceptable to me by

reason of the good library . . . . where I might have the advantage and pleasure of following my private studies" (1667). p. 326.—"As for Manchester it is my native town, which is also more acceptable to me, because there is a fair library in books (where I might pursue my studies) better than any College library in Cambridge" (1669).

WRIGHT (Rev. G. N.). Lancashire: its history, legends, and manufactures. Fisher, Sons & Co., London, &c. [1842?], Roy. 8vo.

Biog. sketch of H. Chetham, pp. 56-59. With portrait eng. by Holl.

[CATALOGUES of the Chetham Library].

Bibliotheca Chethamensis: sive Bibliothecæ Publicæ Mancuniensis ab Humfredo Chetham Armigero fundatæ Catalogus, exhibens libros in varias classes pro varietate argumenti distributos. Quanta potuit fide et diligentia edidit Joannes Radcliffe, A.M., Bibliothecæ supra dicta Custos, ac Collegii Ænei Nasos apud Oxonienses Socius. Mancunii: excudebat J. Harrop. MDCCXCI. 2 vols. 8vo.

The prelim. pages to vol. i. contain, in Latin, the rules for admission of Students, 1680 and 1789, ded. to the Feoffees, whose names are given, preface, containing acknowledgments of the work of his predecessors, Robert Thyer and Rev. Robt. Kenyon. A review appeared in the *Gentleman's Magazine*, 1792, p. 241, and this occasioned an interesting letter in a later number from Mr. Radcliffe.

Bibliothea Chethamensis [&c., as above]. Contexuit, indices adjecit, atque edidit Guilielmus Parr Greswell. Mancunii: Henricus Smith. MDCCCXXVI. 8vo.

Dedicated to Feoffees, whose names are given. Mr. Greswell was paid £250 for compiling this catalogue. He prepared a preface, but it was omitted by wish of the Governors.

Tomus IV. Edidit Thomas Jones, B.A., Oxon . . . Mancunii, Excudebat Carolus S. Simms. MDCCCLXII. 8vo.

Ded. to Feoffees, names given.

Bibliothecæ Publicæ Mancuniensis ab Humfredo Chetham Armigero fundatæ quator Catalogi Voluminum Index, sive notitia brevior unico tomo comprehensa. Edidit Thomas Jones, B.A. Oxon. Manc. MDCCCLXIII. 8vo.

Ded. to Feoffees, names given.

Catalogue of the Books and Manuscripts in the Chetham Library, Manchester, added between the years 1863 and 1881, including the collection of John Byrom, M.A., F.R.S., and all the *MSS.* Vol. vi. Manchester, printed by Charles Simms & Co., 1883, 8vo.

List of Feoffees. This catalogue was begun under direction of James Crossley, and completed under that of the Dean of Manchester (Cowie); Richard Hanby rendered material assistance; the proofs were revised by W. R. Credland.

Catalogue of the Library of the late John Byrom . . . Printed for private circulation only. London, 1848. 4to.

This library was presented to the Chetham Library by the late Miss Atherton, for whom the Catalogue was compiled by R. B. Wheatley.

INDEX.

CHETHAM GENEALOGIES:

PEDIGREES OF THE FAMILIES OF
CHETHAM OF CHEETHAM, NUTHURST, MIDDLETON, CRUMPSALL,
SMEDLEY, AND CASTLETON, IN LANCASHIRE, AND OF
GREAT LIVERMERE, IN SUFFOLK.

BY

ERNEST AXON.

(Appendix to "Life of Humphrey Chetham," by F. R. Raines and C. W. Sutton.)

PRINTED FOR THE CHETHAM SOCIETY.

1903.

JAMES STEWART
Printer.
36, South King St.
MANCHESTER

INTRODUCTION.

THE pedigrees which follow are based principally on family papers belonging to Captain CLOWES, the present representative of the Chetham family, and which he has courteously placed at the service of the Chetham Society. Most of these documents I have myself seen. When I made my notes the papers, which are very numerous, were entirely without arrangement of any kind, and it was therefore impossible to give exact references to the particular document on which my statements were based. It may however be taken that for all facts for which references are not given, or which are not obviously from other sources, the authority is a Clowes deed or paper. I must make grateful acknowledgment of the aid I have received from Mr. HENRY T. CROFTON, who kindly placed at my disposal his very extensive notes from the Clowes deeds, and has thus lightened my labours very considerably, as I did not think it necessary to go again through the papers which he had seen. I have also had access to notes made many years ago from the Clowes papers by Dr. WILLIAM FLEMING, Honorary Secretary of the Chetham Society. The authorities, other than the Clowes deeds, are all acknowledged in the footnotes. I have, as will be seen, drawn extensively, though perhaps not exhaustively, on the Raines and other *MSS.* in the Chetham Library, and on the Owen *MSS.* in the Reference Library, Manchester.

The pedigrees which follow will be found to differ in many important particulars from the Chetham pedigrees which have been printed or which remain in manuscript in the Chetham Library and elsewhere. I do not, of course, guarantee the absolute accuracy of these pedigrees. It is rarely possible in genealogy to confine oneself to the absolutely proven facts, and these Chetham pedigrees are no exception; but in all cases where I had the slightest doubt of an affiliation or an identification, I have, I think, indicated it in such a manner as not to mislead anyone.

My thanks are due to Mr. WILLIAM FARRER and Professor TAIT for valuable hints and suggestions; to Mr. GILES SHAW for the use of the proofs of his "Middleton Parish Registers"; to Mr. HERBERT C. WELCH, of the Guildhall Library, London, for the dates of the civic careers of the Chethams; to Mr. W. ASHETON TONGE, for the loan of a volume of Chetham cuttings; to Mr. WALTER T. BROWNE and Mr. H. W. KIRK, of Chetham Library, and, of course, to Mr. CHARLES W. SUTTON, M.A.

ERNEST AXON.

REFERENCE LIBRARY,
MANCHESTER.

CONTENTS.

EXPLANATORY NOTES.

1.—Dates of baptism, marriage, and burial, are as a rule from the parish registers, and if no place is stated, they are from the Manchester parish registers. Transcripts have been used throughout, either those in the Owen *MSS.* in the Reference Library, Manchester, or the printed registers issued by the Lancashire Parish Register Society.

2.—All statements for which no authority is given (other than those from parish registers) are based on the Chetham family papers, now the property of Captain Clowes.

3.—Dates of matriculation and graduation, and of admission to the Inns of Court, are from Mr. Joseph Foster's *Alumni Oxonienses*, and his *Admissions to Gray's Inn*, and from the official publications usually specified in footnotes.

4.—For all other statements the authorities are given in the footnotes.

CHETHAM GENEALOGIES.

PEDIGREE I.

CHETHAM OF CHEETHAM.

THE pedigree of the earliest family of Chetham, the family which in the thirteenth century held, under the Middletons, the lordship of Cheetham, is involved in some obscurity, both as regards the origin of the family and as to the exact relationship of the different members. It has been suggested that Henry de Chetham was a younger son of the Trafford family. This theory appears to be based on the resemblance between the coats of arms of the two families. It is not impossible that the Chethams and the Traffords were connected in the manner suggested, but the resemblance of the arms is very unsatisfactory proof of it. For one thing the griffin in the Chetham coat does not appear to be older than the 17th century, and the early coat of the Traffords had three griffins and not one as their present coat has. Another objection is that the Chethams and the Traffords must have separated at a time anterior to the use of armorial bearings by either family. The possession by Henry de Chetham of property in Chorlton is suggestive of kinship with the Traffords, but the evidence is not sufficient to theorize about. As explained in the pedigree itself there is uncertainty as to the relationship of the various persons named. It is not unlikely that the pedigree here put forward may require rearranging as further evidence becomes available.

[SIR] HENRY DE CHETHAM [knight?[1]] held in 1212 four oxgangs in Chorlton in chief of the king in thanage by the payment of 5*s*. His principal estate was at Cheetham, where he held one carve of land under Roger de Middleton, who held in chief of the king in thanage.[2] He was a witness to a grant to the monks of Kersal, *circa* 1190–1212,[3] to a grant of land in Swinton, *circa* 1205,[4] and to other local deeds. In 1223 he was sent by the Earl of Chester to Dinantpowis.[5] It appears from a deed, of apparently about 1259, that he had owned Nuthurst. By this deed, William of Eccles, clerk, granted to Geoffrey, son of Richard de Trafford, all his lands of Notehurst which the grantor's brother Thomas had of the gift of Sir Henry de Chetham, and that homage for the same was to be rendered to Sir Geoffrey de Chetham, who was one of the witnesses to the deed. In 1227 Henry de Chetham went on a pilgrimage to Jerusalem, the king's letters of protection being granted to him 3 June, 1227.[6] He was probably dead before 1235.

He is presumed[7] to be father of:—

GEOFFREY de Chetham (see next page).

ALICE [?], married to Alexander [?] Pilkington, who had a moiety of the manor of Cheetham after Sir Geoffrey's death.

CHRISTIANA [?], wife, first of Richard de Trafford, and afterwards of William del Hacking (see Chaderton pedigree).

[1] I do not find the title of knighthood in any contemporary document, but he is described as Sir in the grant of Nuthurst.

[2] *Testa de Nevill*, p. 405; Harland's *Mamcestre*, pp. 79 and 81.

[3] Farrer's *Lancashire Pipe Rolls*, p. 329.

[4] *Whalley Coucher Book*, p. 905.

[5] *Patent Rolls of Henry III.*, 1216–1225, p. 368.

[6] *Patent Rolls of Henry III.*, 1225–1232, p. 126.

[7] I have found no contemporary reference to the existence of any child or children of Henry. The presumption is based on the fact that Sir Geoffrey succeeded Henry in his estates, and that the Pilkingtons and Traffords afterwards owned lands which had

SIR GEOFFREY DE CHETHAM, knight. Sheriff of Lancashire 1259 to 1261. Knighted before 1235. His name is of very frequent occurrence as a witness to undated deeds, *circa* 1230 to 1271.[1] He granted land in Crompton, namely Gartside, to Adam of Wyndhull[2]; in Okeden, to Adam Fitz Bibbi, afterwards Adam de Okeden and Cicely his wife,[3] and *circa* 1240–50, he granted to Cockersand Abbey a yearly rent of 2*s*. to be taken in the town of Cheetham.[4] He exchanged land in Cheetham for land in Crompton and Belemoor, with Robert de Crompton, *circa* 1259, and in 1259 obtained for 10 years, at a rent of 2*s*. 6*d*., land in Crompton which Geoffrey, son of Luke de Mamecestre, held of the Abbot of Cockersand. There are three fines to which he was a party, dated 1235, 1236, and 1245.[5] He had property at Allerton in the hundred of West Derby which he probably acquired by marriage, as he and his wife Margaret occur in a fine of 1245 concerning property there.[6] In 1253 he was plaintiff in an action concerning trespass at Allerton by the monks of Stanlaw.[7] He witnessed a deed dated Pentecost, 55 Henry, son of John [1271],[8] but was dead in 2 Edward I. (20 Nov., 1273 to 20 Nov.,

belonged to Sir Henry. In some pedigrees the wives of Pilkington and Trafford are described as children of Sir Geoffrey de Chetham, but the fact that Sir Geoffrey de Chetham and Richard de Trafford were almost contemporaries suggests that the correct affiliation is that given in the text. This is corroborated by a comparison of the ages of Sir Geoffrey and of Geoffrey de Chaderton. If we assume that Sir Geoffrey was about 21 when he first occurs, *circa* 1230, he would be born about 1209. Geoffrey de Chaderton was evidently an adult, *circa* 1259, a fact we gather not only from his having a grant of Nuthurst then, but also from the dates when his children received grants of land. He was therefore born at least as early as 1238, when Sir Geoffrey de Chetham would probably be too young to be a grandfather. These presumed dates agree very well with the theory that Geoffrey de Chetham was the brother of the wives of Pilkington and Trafford.

[1] Harland's *Mamcestre; Cockersand Chartulary; Whalley Coucher Book;* Farrer's *Lanc. Pipe Rolls*, *Palatine Note Book*, vol. iv. p. 206, &c.

[2] *Whalley Coucher Book*, p. 164.

[3] Harland's *Mamcestre*, p. 350.

[4] *Cockersand Chartulary*, II., vol. ii. p. 726.

[5] Farrer's *Final Concords*, vol. i. pp. 59, 74, 91.

[6] Farrer's *Final Concords*, p. 91.

[7] *Placitorum Abbreviatio*, p. 130.

[8] *Whalley Coucher Book*, p. 886.

1274) when Guichard de Chairun and William de Northburg were appointed to take the assise of mort d'ancestor arraigned by William de Hacking, &c., against Margery, late wife of Geoffrey de Chetham, &c., touching possessions in Crompton, Manchester, and Sholver.[1]

[1] *Calendar of Patent Rolls*, 2 Ed. I., D.K., 33rd Rep., App. I., p. 425.

PEDIGREE II.

CHADERTON PEDIGREE

(To show a possible connection between Sir Geoffrey de Chetham and the Nuthurst Chethams).

RICHARD DE TRAFFORD succeeded his father Henry de Trafford *circa* 1221. His wife is presumed to have been Christiana, a daughter of Henry de Chetham and sister of Sir Geoffrey de Chetham, at whose death, *circa* 1272, she inherited a portion of his estate. She was then the wife of William del Hacking.[1]

Issue :—

HENRY de Trafford, son and heir.

GEOFFREY de Chaderton (of whom see below).

GEOFFREY DE CHADERTON. He had the lordship of the manor of Chadderton granted to him by his father. As Geoffrey, son of Richard de Trafford, he had a grant of lands in Nuthurst from William of Eccles, clerk, whose brother Thomas had the same lands of the gift of Sir Henry de Chetham. The grant is undated, but was apparently *circa* 1259, and certainly before 1273, as the land was held of Sir Geoffrey de Chetham, who was a witness to the deed. In 1278 Geoffrey de Chaderton was owner of the moiety of the manors of Cheetham and Crompton, and of lands in Sholver, Ashton, and Manchester, all of which he had apparently inherited from Sir Geoffrey de Chetham.[2] Geoffrey de Chaderton was living 1309, when he was one

[1] There is a pedigree of the Hacking amily in Abram's *Blackburn*, p. 430.

[2] Farrer's *Final Concords*, vol. i. p. 153.

of the witnesses to John de Byron's grant to Adam de Chaderton. His wife was named Jane, and he had issue :—

GEOFFREY (see below).

ADAM. As Adam, son of Geoffrey de Chaderton, he had in 1298 a grant from his father of lands in Ashworth.[1] In 1307 Roger de Pilkington granted to him lands in Crompton (including the mill) in exchange for lands in Cheetham, and by an undated deed of about the same date Alice, late wife of Alexander de Pilkington, granted to him all her rights in the lands which Adam had of the gift of her son, Roger de Pilkington.[2] In 1309–10 John de Byron granted to him four acres of land in Royton called "le Brodebente." He married Cecilia and had issue

John. In Sep., 1324, as John, son of Adam de Chaderton, he had a grant from Richard, son of William, son of Adam de Holdum of all the lands in Crompton and Royton west of Bele, which Richard had of the gift of Cecilia, mother of John.[3] Although he was evidently a landowner, he does not occur as John de Chaderton, either in the Lay Subsidy roll of 1332, nor in any of the documents quoted in Harland's *Mamecestre.* I suggest that he was identical with John de Chetham, who heads the pedigree of Chetham of Nuthurst.[4]

[1] Raines *MSS.*, vol. xxiv. p. 293.

[2] Raines *MSS.*, vol. xxiv. p. 293.

[3] Raines' *MSS.* vol. xxiv. p. 293.

[4] The evidence for this suggested identification is not conclusive, and some of the acts might be explained on the assumption that the first John de Chetham had married a Chaderton heiress. The suggestive facts are (1) that Geoffrey de Chaderton's property included a moiety of the manor of Crompton. We find in 1366 that John de Chetham was owner of a moiety of the same manor, the other moiety of which was held by the daughters of Roger de Chaderton. (2) Adam de Chaderton had property at Ashworth. So had John de Chetham. (3) Adam de Chaderton had a grant of the mill at Crompton in 1307. In 1341 John de Chetham granted one half of the mill at Crompton, and may have kept one half of the mill for himself. (4) In 1309 Adam de Chaderton had a grant of land in Royton called le Brodebent. Land of the same name belonged to the Chethams at a later date. (5) John de Chaderton had in

WILLIAM, concerned with his brother John and others in the death of Robert atte Brigge.[1]

JOHN. Witness to Roger de Pilkington's grant to Adam de Chaderton, 1306–7.

ALEXANDER de Chaderton, who, at the instance of Henry de Lacy, Earl of Lancaster, was pardoned, 16 October, 1307, for the death of Roger, son of Richard de Workesley.[2]

GEOFFREY DE CHADERTON. Occurs as a witness to several deeds as Geoffrey de Chaderton, junior, 1306-7. In ii. Edward III. he granted to his sons Alexander and Roger the homage and service and the rent of iij^{s} of Richard of Moston.[3] The Survey of 1320 states that Moston and Nuthurst were then held by Alexander and Roger de Chaderton,[4] a statement which cannot be reconciled with the grant except on the assumption that the grant is dated too late by a clerical error of the sixteenth century scribe, or that the Survey of 1320 is, in this as in some other parts, later than that year. Geoffrey de Chaderton does not occur either in the Survey of 1320 or in the Lay Subsidy roll of 1332.

1324 lands in Crompton and Royton. In 1341 John de Chetham had lands at the same places, but whether the same lands or not is not certain. (6) The absence of John de Chaderton from the Subsidy Roll of 1332 is suggestive. The only explanations that seem possible are either that John de Chetham was identical with John de Chaderton, or that John de Chetham had married the heiress of Adam de Chaderton. The name of John de Chetham is a difficulty in the way of the acceptance of this assumed identity, but there is evidence that Adam de Chaderton owned lands in Cheetham as late as 1309, and may have lived there, as may his son John de Chaderton.

[1] *Calendar of Patent Rolls.*, 5 January, 1303–4, p. 271.

[2] *Calendar of Patent Rolls*, p. 9.

[3] The original grant appears to be lost. It was however put in as evidence on behalf of the defendants in Shacklocke and others *versus* Chaderton and Chetham, Hilary term, 1575-6, as appears from a "Briefe" in the Clowes deeds. It is not quite certain whether ii. Edward III. means 2 or 11, as arabic and roman numerals are both used by the scribe. Probably, however, it is the earlier date, 1328-9, and not the later one 1337-8. It is possible that Edward III. should be Edward II., 1308-9 or 1317-8

[4] Harland's *Mamcestre*, p. 309.

Issue :—

ALEXANDER DE CHADERTON. Together with his brother Roger had a grant of Moston from their father. The two brothers occur in the Survey of 1320 as joint owners of Moston.[1] They afterwards divided the property, and the division was confirmed by an indenture dated Sunday next before the feast of St. Luke the Evangelist, 14 Edward III. (October, 1340). In July, 1356, he granted to John de Chetham and Alice his wife all his messuages, lands, &c., in the hamlet of Moston in the town of Assheton as well in demesne as lordship in fee with the homage and service of the lord of Moston. No relationship is mentioned, but the wording of the grant suggests that Alice was a Chaderton.

ROGER DE CHADERTON. Grantee with his brother Alexander of the Moston lands and a party to the confirmation of the partition between his brother and himself, in 1340. A few days later he granted his Moston lands to his son Roger.[2] His other sons were Geoffrey, John, Henry, Robert, and Richard,[3] who were all living in 1340. Apparently the later Chadertons of Nuthurst were descended from Roger, brother of Alexander de Chaderton. The family remained at Nuthurst until the early part of the 17th century.

[1] Harland's *Mamcestre*, p. 309.

[2] This is apparently the Roger whose our daughters and heirs Joan, Alice, Agnes, and Cecilia, held a portion of Crompton in 1365 (Harland's *Mamecestre*, p. 307). Possibly Alice was the wife of John de Chetham.

[3] *Raines MSS.*, vol. xxiv. p. 295.

PEDIGREE III.

CHETHAM OF NUTHURST.

JOHN DE CHETHAM. Nothing definite is known of his parentage,[1] and the suggestion already made (p. 6) as to his identity with John de Chaderton must be taken merely as a suggestion and not as an assertion. The earliest reference to John de Chetham is in the Assize Roll, Lancaster (No, 425), for 17 Edward II. [1323].

By a deed dated 25 March, 1331, Adam de Turnehaghe granted to him all his lands in Butterworth, and by a later deed in the same year William, son of Richard de Turnaghe granted to him all his messuage in "le Rodefeld" in the town of Butterworth. In the Assize Roll (No. 428) of 6 Edward III., his name occurs, and at the Subsidy of 1332 he paid 2*s*. for land in Crompton.[2]

In 1335 he granted lands in Butterworth to his son Richard, and in January, 1340-1, lands in Crompton to his son Adam, and in Crompton, Royton, Ashworth, and Manchester, to his son Robert. The last two sons granted the same lands in March, 1343-4, to their father for life. In October, 1340, he was one of the witnesses to a deed by which Roger and Alexander de Chaderton divided their lands in Moston.

He is perhaps identical with the John de Chetham named below, but if that were so the five children named below must have been by one marriage, and Thomas, the son and heir, by a

[1] The statement is made in the pedigree read before the Rosicrucians in 1868 that he was the son of Henry de Chetham, son of Sir Geoffrey de Chetham. I have no evidence that Sir Geoffrey had a son Henry, or that Henry was the father of John.

[2] *Exchequer Lay Subsidy Roll* (Record Soc.).

second marriage, and as Thomas and his descendants are found in possession of all the estates of the first John de Chetham, the issue of the first marriage must have become extinct.

John de Chetham had issue

RICHARD. In November, 1335, his father granted to him and his heirs male all his lands in Butterworth. He is mentioned as third in remainder in the grants of 1340–1. In 1348 John de Radeclif, rector of Bury, released to him all the lands in Butterworth which he had of the gift of Margery, late wife of Geoffrey, son of Richard de Tornagh, belonging to her by reason of her dower. It is possible that Margery was the wife of Richard de Chetham.

ADAM. In January, 1340–1, his father granted to him all his lands in Crompton lying on the east side of the water of Bele, together with a fourth part of the mill of Crompton. His name does not occur in the grant to Richard, 1335, but he is first in remainder in the grant to Robert, 1340–1. In 1343 he granted the same lands, &c., to his father for life.

ROBERT. His name is first in remainder in the grants to Richard and Adam, 1335–1340-1. In January, 1340–1, his father granted to him all his lands in Crompton on the west side of the water of Bele, a fourth part of the mill of Crompton, all his lands in Royton and Ashworth, and his burgages in Manchester. These he regranted to his father for life in 1343.

ROGER. Occurs second in the remainder specified by John de Chetham in the grants of 1335 and 1340–1.

MATILDA. Married Adam, son of William de Butterworth (marr. settlement dated 25 July, 1335).

* * * * * *

JOHN DE CHETHAM of Nuthurst. This John is perhaps identical with the previously mentioned John de Chetham, but the dates and other circumstances suggest that he was not the same. We know that Thomas, who follows, was the son of a John, but no Thomas occurs in the remainders to the deeds of 1335 to 1340-1. Assuming that the first mentioned John was an adult at the date of his first occurrence, 1323, he would be a considerable age in 1356, at which date Thomas was apparently not born. I assume therefore that John the grantee of Nuthurst was either a son or a grandson of the original John. The fact that no John occurs in the remainders in the grants to the sons of the first John might imply, either that there was no son of John, or that he was already provided for as son and heir.[1] It is noteworthy that none of the grantees of 1335-40 is described as son and heir.

On the day next after St. Margaret's day, 30 Edward III. [21 July, 1356], Alexander de Chaderton granted all his lands in the hamlet of Moston, in the town of Ashton, to John de Chetham, with remainder to his heirs male by Alice his wife, and in default to Joan, daughter of John de Chetham, remainder to the heirs of John and Alice, remainder for life to Alice, and after her death to the right heirs of John. In 1359 he was one of the jury in an inquisition at Preston concerning the privileges of the burgesses of Manchester.[2] In the "reasonable aid" of the second year of the regality of John, Duke of Lancaster [1365-6], he occurs as holding jointly (?) with the daughters of Roger de Chaderton one twentieth part of a knight's fee in Crompton, Deanmore [Belemoor ?][3]

Married Alice, to whom as wife of John, Adam de Polefield granted land in 1351. The wording of Alexander de Chaderton's grant of Nuthurst suggests that she was one of the Chaderton family, and she may have been Alice, one of the heiresses of Roger de Chaderton. John had issue :—

THOMAS, see below.

JOAN, named in the grant of 1356.

[1] The same argument would apply to the absence of a son Thomas from any of the remainders.

[2] Harland's *Mamcestre*, p. 454.

[3] Harland's *Mamcestre*, p. 278. The apparent date of this is 1320, but Professor Tait has kindly called my attention to the fact that this portion of the Survey is of much later date.

THOMAS DE CHETHAM, of Nuthurst, who had a lawsuit with Matilda, widow of Hugh del Holt, and tenant of lands called Storthes and Suayneshusted in Middleton, of which Chetham claimed to be the owner. In November, 1381, he seized her cattle for rent, she appealed to the sessions and lost her case. From the pleadings it appears that John de Chetham, whose son and heir Thomas was, had been seised of the property and had been paid the rents for 20 years before his death. Matilda objected to a jury which had been empanelled by Adam de Lever, bailiff of Salfordshire, because he was cousin (consanguineus) of Thomas, so a fresh jury was empanelled who decided in favour of Chetham.

Thomas de Chetham was slain by his neighbour Thomas de Chaderton. This occurred probably before Midsummer, 1386, and certainly before 21 July, 1393.[1]

An inquisition post mortem was taken 5 Henry IV. by which it appears that he held lands in Leigh [High ?] Crompton, *in capite* of the Duke of Lancaster, a messuage called the Nuthurst of the manor of Pilkington, lands, etc., called Crompton park of the Abbot of Cockersand, and a tenement called Floshhouses in Butterworth of the Prior of the Hospital of St. John of Jerusalem.[2]

He had a son, John (see below).

JOHN CHETHAM, of Nuthurst. A minor at the death of his father, as it was not until 23 August, 1404, that a precept was issued to the escheator for the county of Lancaster to give livery of his lands to John, son and heir of Thomas de Chetham.[3] He was party to several deeds concerning the two marriages of his son James, 1413 and 1439–42. From deeds it appears that he had lands in Butterworth, Castleton, Middleton, and four acres of land in "le Brodebent" in Royton. In 1428 he is described as John Chetham of Nuthurst in deeds concerning

[1] *Calendar of Patent Rolls*,, 11 Ric. II., p. 346; Towneley's *Lanc. Inquisitions*' pp. 54, 55 (Chet. Soc.).

[2] Towneley's *MSS. Evidences*, p. 306.

[3] *D.K. 33rd Rep.* App. i. p. 4; cf. *Towneley MSS. Transcripts of Deeds*, p. 201.

Crompton. In September, 1431, he granted all his lands in Crompton and Ashton to Richard de Stanley, Archdeacon of Chester, and Roger le Ward, chaplain, for his life, probably with a view to settling his estate. In 1460, John de Chetham the elder and John Milngate granted a lease of a field in Manchester.[1] He is mentioned in a release of 1 December, 1465, and probably died about that time.

Issue :—

JAMES, son and heir (see below).

CHARLES, living 1 December, 1465, when he gave a release to his brother James.

CATHERINE, wife of Ralph de Bradshaw[2] of Aspull.

[JOHN, ROBERT, and GEOFFREY. The Culcheth deed of 1460 implies the existence of a younger John, presumably a son of the grantor, while the occurrence of Robert and Geoffrey as witnesses suggest that they also were sons, or perhaps grandsons of John. Robert Chetham was witness to a grant by James Chetham dated 1470. There is, however, a possibility that the grantor of 1460 was not John Chetham of Nuthurst.]

JAMES CHETHAM of Nuthurst. His earliest occurrence in the family deeds is in connection with his first marriage in 1413, at which date he must have been very young, as his father was then presumably only about 30. One of the marriage conditions was that John, the father, was to have "gou'nñce de lez ditz James et Alianore." He was a party with his father to the deeds in connection with his second marriage. In 1451 he had a lease of Gosardhills from Roger and Katherine Chaderton. He had an exceptionally long career as heir apparent, as he

[1] Culcheth Deeds, *L. & C. Hist. and Gen. Notes*, vol. i. p. 113.

[2] *Genealogist*, N.S., vol. xvii. p. 14, where there is a pedigree of Bradshaw of Aspull, giving this marriage. There are no dates in the early part of the pedigree. In Harl. *MS.*, 1987, f. 159, the marriage is dated in the reign of Henry V. Whatton (*History of Chetham Hospital*, p. 127) quoting the same *MS.* under its old reference of 1987, f. 80, gives, in error, a marriage between John de Chetham and Catherine de Bradshaw.

probably did not succeed to the estates until about 1465. In 1468 he appears to have been again relegated to a subordinate position. In that year controversies between him and his son Thomas were referred to the arbitration of Ellis Hill and Hugh Gartside. The award was that Thomas should have Nuthurst and Sidgreaves during the life of James at an annual rent of 4*l.*, and that Thomas should surrender to James the lands at Crompton, Milncroft, and Gosardhills. The father, however, was to continue to receive from James Radcliffe and his heirs yearly 18*d.* of free ferme of Moston. He was living 25 March, 1474, when he granted a lease of land in Crompton, but died before 19 July, 1480.

Married, first (covenant dated 6 May, 1413 [1]) Eleanor, daughter of Ellis de Buckley.

Secondly (between 2 August, 1439, and 9 September, 1441) Margery, daughter of John, son of Richard de Longley. After her husband's death certain disputes between her and her sons were settled by an award of Ralph Langley, Warden of Manchester, and others, dated 10 December, 1480. She married secondly Alan Holt. On 29 June, 1486, Alan Holt and Margerie his wife, late the wife of James Chetham, acknowledged to have received from Thos. Chetham 43*s.* 4*d.* in name of dower.

Issue, probably by first wife:—

THOMAS, son and heir (see below).

MARGARET, wife of Richard Holt, of Ashworth.[2]

by second wife

EDMUND, living 10 December, 1480, when, by the award of Warden Langley, he had to pay 4*l.* to his brother.[3]

THOMAS CHETHAM of Nuthurst, gent. In 1461 he had a lease for twenty years of lands in Crompton, including Gosard-

[1] The marriage had apparently taken place on or before 8 August, 1413, when the Crompton and Ashton estates were re-settled.

[2] *Derby Household Books*, ed. by Raines, p. 198 (Chet Soc., vol. xxxi).

[3] A contemporary and probably a near relation was Adam Chetham, who, with his wife Joan and their two children, received a plenary indulgence from the Papal Nuncio, 24 August, 1477. The original document is in the Clowes papers.

hills, from Sir James Strangways, knight, and others. In 1468 the arbitrators in a dispute between him and his father awarded to the son the lands of Nuthurst and Sidgreaves at a yearly rent of 4*l.* during his father's lifetime, while the son was to surrender to his father the lands in Crompton which had been granted to him by Sir James Strangways. In 1480 Hugh Holt acknowledged that he held his lands of Storthe and Swyneshusted in Ashworth of Thomas Chetham. In the same year a dispute between Thomas and his father's widow was settled by the award of Warden Langley and others. It is probable that he was an agent or steward of the family of Byron, as in 1486 he paid money due by Sir John Byron to Robert Chetham, receiver of Sir Thomas West, Lord La Warr, of his lordship of Manchester.

In his time appears to have begun the Thealmore litigation, which in one form or another continued for a century. The Chethams and Chadertons claimed rights over Thealmore to which their neighbours objected as being an infringement of their rights of common. One of the early incidents in the contest is recorded by Thomas Chetham, in a particularly neat hand, on a paper headed "Thes bēn the nammes that sawtutt [assaulted ?] me Thomas Chetham in my howse and cast don my dyche on the frydy nēxt aftr ye epiphiny of our lord the qwech dyche was nev undychet that nomon con tell of Anno henrici septimo decimo" [January, 1501-2].

He died 20 April, 1503. His inq. p. m. is dated 22 August, 1504, and at the time of his death he had over 1200 acres in Nuthurst, Butterworth, Middleton, Castleton, and Crompton. It is probable that he was the Thomas Chetham who, by will, left a manuscript (of which he is suspected to have been the writer) of the *Gest Hystoriale* "to be an here-loome at Note-hurst."[1]

[1] *Gest Hystoriale of the Destruction of Troye*, ed. from the *MS.* in the Hunterian Museum, University of Glasgow, by G. A. Panton and D. Donaldson. Early English Text Soc., 1869–1874, p. lv. Professor Tait has called my attention to the fact that the *MS.* of Gower's *Confessio Amantis*, now in the Chetham Library, formerly belonged to the Chethams of Nuthurst. It is of about the same date as the Glasgow *MS.*

He married (covenant dated 23 August, 1466, marriage to take place before September 8 following) Elizabeth, daughter of William Heyton, Esq. She was living 22 January, 1518-9, when she is named in the marriage covenant of her grandson, Thomas.

Issue :—

JOHN, son and heir (see below).

NICHOLAS, to whom his father granted for life lands in Lenderdyne, 1 December, 1496.

[THOMAS? As Thomas Chetham describes himself in the grant to his son Nicholas as "senior" it is probable that he had a son of the same name].

[RALPH. Ralph Chetham, whose interesting will is printed in abstract below, was apparently closely connected with the main line of Chetham of Nuthurst. I have therefore ventured to assume that he was a son of Thomas, though he may have been a nephew, or still more distant relation. Little is known of him but what appears in the will. He occurs in a rent roll of Crompton as a tenant of the Chethams of Nuthurst yearly from 1520–1535. In 1521 Richard Holt, brother of Robert Holt of Stubley, granted to him lands called Ferrehouse in Cleggeswood and a meadow called Hogrode in Butterworth, late of the land of Thomas Belfield of Cleggeswode.[1] In the same year he was one of the arbitrators in a dispute between Thomas Chetham of Nuthurst and Alice Holt of Balderston concerning the Slack in Balderston.]

Prerogative Court of Canterbury 14 Crumwell.

The 12th day of September, 1537, I Rauf Chetham. My body to be buried within the Church of Our Blessed Lady of Oldham before the "quere" door. Towards the repairs of the said Church 20s. Towards the repairs of Rachedale Church 13s 4d. Towards the upholding of Our Lady service of Rachdale Church 4s. Towards the upholding of God's service at Milnerowe Chappell 3s 4d. Towards the upholding of the service that Sir Barnard Hamer occupies there 3s 4d. Towards the upholding of the Trinity service in Rachdaile Church 3s 4d. Towards the finishing of the steeple at Assheton under lyne 3s 4d. If it will please the gentlemen and other honest men of the parish of Oldham to take upon them the business to enlarge and "make more," the

[1] *L. & C. Hist. and Gen. Notes*, vol. i. p. 140.

Church of Oldham or to cover all the "Rowffe" of the said Church with lead within 5 years after my decease: then the Churchwardens shall take from my executors £4 for the same.

Forasmuch as my sons Adam, Robert, James, and Richard have willingly renounced their childs parts of goods and are content to take such bequests as I shall give to them and their children: I therefore give to them as follows: First, towards the marriage of Agnes Chetham, dau. of James my son, 4 marks. To Robert Chetham, brother of said Agnes, 10^s "in penny or penyworth." To Ellys Chetham, brother of the said Robert, 10^s in like manner. To Adam my son £5. To Robert my son £5. To every child of the said Adam and Robert 10^s. I also give to the said Adam and Robert 6 oxen, all my wains, ploughs, &c., &c., 8 blankets of the "myddelest sorte," &c., &c. To Richard my son £4 and 4 "Siffes of Otes" towards the keeping of his house; and to each of his children 10^s. To Elizabeth Chetham, daughter of Thomas Chetham 20^s. To another daughter [not named] of said Thomas 13^s 4^d. To Ellys Chetham, brother of said Thomas, 6^s 8^d; and to every child of the said Ellys 2 ewes. Legacies to servants. To Anne Chetham, daughter of William, 13^s 4^d towards her marriage. To Margery my sister 5 marks. Legacies to the wife of Robert Taylor dwelling at Oldham Church, the wife of Robert Taylor of Thorppe, Elizabeth, wife of John Taylor of Horsaige, Thomas Hill of Hollynworth (towards the marriage of his daughter), and to Rauf Hollande of Draidelseden. To Margaret, wife of Robert my son, a pair of black "Jetle bedes." To Robert my son a red cow. I will that after my decease my sons Adam and Robert shall occupy my "takke and ferme holde" which I have occupied in Riton, during all my term therein, except always such "socor" and parcel of the Morehey as I shall give to my son James. I will that the said James shall enjoy the place and farmhold which he now occupies, and after my death he shall be enlarged to his said place and farmhold "thre nottegayte" in the Morehey, he paying yearly a rent therefore. I will that James Chetham, son of Laurens my son, shall have the one half of my "takke" in Ogden as it is "mered" and Russehill in the Bendes, and that mease and land now in the holding of the wife of James Turnawe after the decease of the said wife. And Agnes, late wife of the said Laurens, shall have the other half of my said "takke" and "Jomes rondes in the byndes;" but if she marry again then Arthur Chetham, son of the said Agnes, shall enjoy the same: if the said Arthur die, then Olyver Chetham his brother to have the same. I will that James Chetham and Arthur his brother shall occupy the mease and all the lands now in the holding of the wife of Hugh Brereley and her children. I will that Richard my son shall have my "takke" in the Shawefeeld which I have taken of my cousin Adam Belfeeld during my term. I will that the rent of the house in Butterworth Hall now in the holding of John Dawson, Henry Bukkeley, and Adam Crompton, shall remain to my son Richard. Whereas Agnes late wife of Elis Mylne and her children occupies a part of a mease and lands to the yearly value of 10^s which is in my takke: I will my sons Adam and

Robert shall take the same and pay it to my master Sir John Byron, Knt. All my said sons to take the rents and profits of such takkes of freeholds as I have in writing for certain years of Mr. Thos. Radcliff of Foxedenton, Mr. Edmund Hopwood of Hopwood, my cousin Adam Belfeeld of Clegge, my cousin Thomas Chetham of Nottehurste, and Robert Butterworth of Lawe Howse, to such uses as I shall declare. Whereas there is an estate of copyhold which I have by surrender of William Ermeshoghe of certain lands lying within the town of Holme which I have fined for in the Court of Wakefield: I will that my said sons take the rents thereof to such uses as I shall declare. I give towards the upholding of Our Lady's Service at Oldham 2 "Stokkes," *i.e.* 16^{s}. To James Chetham, son of Lawrence, 2 "Segges," &c. To John Chetham, son of Laurence my son, 4 marks in "penny and pennyworth" to pray for my soul. To the 5 dau^{rs} of Adam Belfeeld 5 "Quye stirckes." To Thomas Chatterton, son of Thomas one "Twynter Quye," to be kept by John Tettlawe, his father-in-law until the said Thomas shall begin to keep house himself. To the daughter of Rauffe Holte 3^{s} 4^{d}. The rest of my goods to be disposed of for the health of my soul, by the advice of Sir William Langeley, parson of Prestwiche, and Sir Thomas Shorroke, curate of Oldham. I make my Master Sir John Byron, Knyght, Robert Langley, Esq., Sir William Langeley, Clerk, and my sons Adam and Robert, executors, and my cousin Arthur Belfeeld and Rauffe Cudwourth supervisors. Witnesses: Sir Richard Assheton, Knt., Robert Holte of Stubley, Esq., and Sir Thos. Shorrokes, curate at Oldham. Proved 10 February, 1538.

In the name of God, Amen.

I, William Cooke, Doctor of Laws, having looked into the merits and circumstances of a certain testamentary business or proving the will of Ralph Chetham, which is still pending, now declare for the validity of the said will, and that the said Sir John Byron and others are executors, and grant to them administration of the goods, &c., of the said deceased.

This diffinitive sentence was read by the said William Cook in St. Paul's Cathedral, London, on Monday, the 10th day of February, 1538.[1]

Thomas Chetham was probably also father of

[ELIZABETH.[2] Probably the Elizabeth who married John Cudworth of Werneth,[3] and was great-grandmother of Margery

[1] The reference to Shawfield makes it probable that Ralph Chetham of Shawfield, whose will, dated 21 August, 1612, and proved 15 July, 1619, has been printed in Earwaker's *Lancashire and Cheshire Wills*, vol. i. p. 163 (Chet. Soc., N.S., vol. iii.), was a descendant of the earlier Ralph Chetham.

[2] Elizabeth Chetham and Margery Chetham are both mentioned in the Inq. p.m. of Thomas Chetham, but no relationship is mentioned. Elizabeth may have been the widow.

[3] Flower's *Visitation*, 1567, p. 15 (Chet. Soc., vol. lxxxi.).

Cudworth, who became the wife of James Chetham of Nuthurst, gent., after 1572.]

[MARGERY.[1] Ralph Chetham mentions his sister Margery, 1537.]

JOHN CHETHAM of Nuthurst, gent. Born about 1470, being found to be 34 and more at the date of his father's inq. post mortem. On 22 June 1 Henry VIII. [1509], he received a general pardon for a long list of offences. From the pardon it appears that he had at various times lived at Nuthurst, at Hulme, and at Crompton, that he was variously described as esquire and as gentleman, and that he was executor of his father's will. His inq. p.m. was taken 7 Henry VIII. [1515-6], and it was found that he had lands, &c., in Nuthurst, Butterworth, Middleton, Castleton, and Crompton, and that Thomas was his son and heir.[2]

Married (between 10 January and 1 February, 1486-7) Margery, daughter of Ellis Prestwich of Hulme, esq. She was the mother of his two sons.

He married secondly Clemence, who is described in the marriage covenant of Thomas Chetham, 1518-9, as "late wief of John Chethm̃ fader of Thome." She was the daughter of William Radcliffe of Ordsal, esq., and presumably widow of James Hulme of Davyhulme.[3] As "syster Clemens Cheetam" she was named in the will of Eleanor Langley of Agecroft, 1532,[4] which lady was also a daughter of Wm. Radcliffe of Ordsal.

Issue by the first wife :—

THOMAS, son and heir (see below).

ELLIS (see the pedigree of CHETHAM OF MIDDLETON).

by the second wife

ELINOR, JANE } Received legacies under the will of Eleanor Langley of Agecroft, 1532. No relationship is stated, but it seems probable that they were children of John by his second wife.

[1] See note a on previous page.

[2] Towneley's *MS. Evidences*, p. 321.

[3] Foster's *Lancashire Pedigrees*.

[4] Piccope's *L. & C. Wills*, vol. ii. p. 17 (Chet. Soc., vol. li.)

THOMAS CHETHAM of Nuthurst, gent. Born about 1490, being aged 26 at the date of his father's inquisition post mortem, 1515-6. In June, 1519, he visited London during legal proceedings concerning a chief rent in Moston, and a document headed "Costs of Thos. Chetham to London from Nuthurst and the lying v dayes and home agayne in June A° R[s] 11 H. VIII." shows his total expenses to have been *22s.* 1½*d.* The same litigation took him to London on several later occasions. He and Edmund Chaderton were plaintiffs in an action, 1537-8, concerning tithe corn at Manchester, Moston, and Blackley.[1] He was bailiff of the Earl of Derby's manors of Bury and Pilkington. He is named in the will of Ralph Chetham, 1537, and paid the subsidy of 1541.[2] He died 25 November, 1546, being seised of mesuages in Notehurst, Butterworth, Middleton, Castleton. Crompton, &c.[3]

Married first (between 22 January and 9 March, 1518-9) Elizabeth, daughter of John Hopwood, esq. She appears to have been the mother of his children.

Married secondly (after 20 April, 1539, the date of Alexander Lever's will[4] Elizabeth, widow of Alexander Lever of Bolton, and daughter of Robert Bolton of Little Bolton, esq. There is a draft of a jointure deed in the family papers, but it is undated. In 1542-3 Thomas Chetham and his wife Elizabeth were defendants in an action in the Duchy Court concerning claims to tithe corn and to the goods and chattels of Alexander Lever, deceased.[5] In the year following Chetham's death she, as widow of Thomas Chetham, and executrix of her former husband Alexander Lever, brought an action against John Chetham and others for detention of title deeds to lands and tortious possession of goods and chattels.[6]

[1] Fishwick's *Duchy Pleadings* (Rec. Soc., vol. xxxv. p. 112).

[2] *Rec. Soc. Misc. I.*.

[3] *D.K. 39th Rep.*, App. No. 3, p. 552.

[4] Earwaker's *Lancashire and Cheshire Wills*, vol. i. p. 221 (Chet. Soc., N.S., vol. 3).

[5] *Ducatus Lanc. Pars. III.*, vol. ii. p. 69.

[6] *Ibid.*, Pars. II., vol. i. p. 223.

Issue:—

JOHN, son and heir (see below).

RALPH.[1] Possibly the "uncle Chetham" named in the accounts of Henry Chetham, 1574.

ELIZABETH, named in the will of Ralph Chetham, 1537. Married at Middleton, 30 April, 1548, to Thomas Birch of Birch, gent. The marriage covenant is dated 16 April, 1548.[2]

Another DAUGHTER is mentioned in the will of Ralph Chetham, 1537.

JOHN CHETHAM of Nuthurst, gent. Born about 1522, being aged 26 at the date of his father's inquisition post mortem.[3] On 4 February, 1547-8, he and Edmund Chaderton made a partition of Thealmore. Like several of his predecessors he had litigation with the commoners concerning his rights over Thealmore, and was also defendant in an action brought by a Chaderton.[4] On 10 February, 1555-6, he released to Sir John Byron his lands called Tunshill Haye and the following day received from Sir John Byron a grant of a rent charge of 2*s*. out of the same lands. In 1567 John Byron, esq. of Newstead, appointed, him to keep for him all his courts in the county of Lancaster. The wording of the document suggests that Chetham had previously acted in the same capacity.

He died 5 December, 1573, and was buried 7 December. His inquisition post mortem was taken at Preston, 9 March, 1573-4. His will, dated 4 August, 1557, has been printed.[5] A will dated 5 December, 1573, is referred to in a schedule annexed to the grant of the wardship of his son James. An inventory was taken 8 December, 1573. At the date of the will of 1557 he was seised in fee simple of over 580 acres in Nuthurst, Crompton, Floshhouses, Balderston, Butterworth, and Moston.

1 Hunter's *Familiæ Minorum Gentium* (Harl. Soc.), p. 583, quoting Harl. *MS.*, 1549, f. 42.

2 Raines *MSS.*, vol. xxii. p. 507, vol. xiv. p. 81.

3 *D.K. 39th Rep.*, App. No. 3, p. 552.

4 *Duc. Lanc.* Pars. III., vol. 2, p. 278.

5 Earwaker's *Lancashire and Cheshire Wills*, p. 57 (Chet. Soc. N. S. 3).

Married [1] Isabel, who is named in her husband's will in 1557. In the marriage covenant of her son Henry she is called Elizabeth. Her maiden name has not been found in the family papers, but she may be the Elizabeth Heaton whom a John Chetham married at Middleton, 21 January, 1549-50. She was buried 5 January, 1596-7. Her will dated 3 January in the same year is given below.[2]

> In the name of god amen I Isabell Chetham of Nutthurst in the countie of Lanc̃ widowe sicke in bodie but wolle in mynde and of good pfect remembrance wth my sellfe thankę be unto Allmightie god therefor doe make and expresse this my laste will and testament in maner and forme following fyrst I comende my solle to Jesus Christe my Savioure and my bodie to be buried in my pishe church at Manchester where my frendę thinke best Itm I geve and bequethe unto my daughter [Anne] all my goodę movable and unmovable after my debptę [debets] beinge payde and my funerall expencę dischardged Exceptinge one great Garner and one maullt arke wch I geve unto my sonne James Chetham and allso I geve unto him [my soone] foure great Channdlers and also I doe geve unto Cateran Ja[cc]kson my servaunte one cuborde standinge in the deyhouse and for the better execucon herof I doe make constitute and ordayn my sonne James Chetham and my daughter Anne Chetham my true and lawefull Executors of this my last will and testament declared the thirde day of Januarye in the xxxix^th^ yeare of the Reigne of our Soverayne ladie Queene Elezabeth by the grace of god of Englande Frannce and Irelande deffendrix [*sic*] of the fayth, &c.
>
> Wittneses hrof Margerye Chetham
> Thomas Mello^r^ &
> Rauffe Jackeson.

[1] According to Ormerod (*History of Cheshire*, Ed. by Helsby, vol. ii. pp. 320, 322) John Chetham married Anne, daughter of John Bruen of Bruen Stapelford, and Canon Raines (*Assheton's Journal*, p. xviii. Chet. Soc. vol. xiv.) assumes that this John Chetham was of Nuthurst. As Anne was a widow in 1531, she was presumably much older than John Chetham of Nuthurst, whose wife is called either Isabel or Elizabeth in all the family papers which mention her. The identification seems therefore to be a mistake, or else John Chetham of Nuthurst had been twice married.

[2] This will is not now in the Probate Registry, Chester. There are two copies of it in Captain Clowes's papers with slight differences which are indicated by the brackets.

Proved 21 January, 1596, before Zacharia Saunders, clk., vicar of Bolton, by virtue of a commission from the Consistory Court, Chester.

Inv. dated 11 January, 39 Eliz.
(ordinary household furniture and dress),
total 69 16 4.

Issue of John and Isabel :—

HENRY CHETHAM, of Nuthurst, gent., son and heir to his father John, at the date of whose inquisition post mortem (9 March, 1573–4) he was aged 22 years and more. In connection with the Thealmore litigation he was in London in 1574–5, an account of this expenditure being amongst the family papers, as also notes of expenditure at Lancaster, also in connection with Thealmore.[1] He was accidentally drowned at Middleton while riding through a brook called Middleton water at about 8 o'clock in the morning, 5 January, 1576–7. Buried at Middleton on the day following. A coroner's jury was held at Middleton on 9 January, 1576–7. Administration was granted 13 September, 1589, to his brother James.[2] By inq. p.m. taken at Bolton 25 April, 1579, it was found that James Chetham was his brother and heir. A previous inquisition had, in error, found that James was brother to John, instead of to Henry.

On 18 October, 1574, he covenanted to marry before the Christmas following Jane, widow of Ralph Cudworth of Werneth, gent., and daughter of Arthur Asheton of Rochdale, gent. It does not appear whether the marriage took place. Her first husband died in 1572, leaving several children, one of whom married James Chetham, brother of Henry. In the Visitation pedigree of 1664–5 Henry is stated to have married a daughter of Sherburne, and to have been father of his successor. The latter statement is certainly inaccurate, and probably also the former.

[1] These accounts name several unidentified relations, *i.e.* "my cosen Hurleston," a barrister; "my aunts house at Fishwick, my uncle, my sister."

[2] Earwaker's *L. & C. Wills*, p. 207 (Chet. Soc. N. S. 3).

ELIZABETH, living 1557.[1]

MARTHA, living 1557.[1]

ANNE, living 1557,[1] and in 1613, when named in the will of her brother and then unmarried.

JAMES, heir to his brother (see below).

JOHN, living 1582.[2]

GEOFFREY, living 1582.[2]

THOMAS, living 1582.[2] Probably the Thomas Chetham of London, gent., who was executor of the will of John Chetham, citizen and fishmonger, 1591. The phrase in the will of his brother James, "the heyrs male of Tho. Chetham my brother," suggests that he had died before 31 January, 1613–4, leaving male issue.

GEORGE, living 1582.[2]

JAMES CHETHAM, of Nuthurst, gent. Succeeded his brother when a minor, his wardship and marriage being granted to his mother. On 19 April, 1582, he made a settlement of his estate on himself and his wife for life, with remainder, failing male heirs, to his four brothers. On 3 October, 1601, he made a settlement for the maintenance of his children, should he die during their minority.

By his will, in which he desires to be buried in the parish church of Manchester, "where my auncestors are buryed," he settled Nuthurst on his son Thomas, and his heirs, with remainder to his son-in-law George Chetham and his issue by his wife Isabel, and then to the heirs male of Thomas Chetham "my brother." The will[3] is dated 31 January, 1613-4, and was proved at Chester, 19 January, 1614–5. The inventory is dated 11 January, 1614–5. Is stated in his inq. p.m (dated 28 March, 1615) to have died 27 December, 1614, which is given by the Collegiate Church registers for his burial.

[1] Named in father's will.

[2] In the remainder under a settlement made 19 April, 1582, by their brother James Chetham.

[3] Earwaker's *L. & C. Wills*, p. 156 (Chet. Soc. N. S. 3).

He married before 19 April, 1582, Margery, daughter of Ralph Cudworth of Werneth, gent. She is named in the Visitation, 1567, and in her father's will, 1572, being then unmarried. Administration of the goods of Margery Chetham of Nuthurst, widow, was granted 1620 (Chester Diocesan Registry).

Issue :—

THOMAS, son and heir (see below).

ISABEL,[1] married before 1613, to George Chetham, of London, afterwards of Clayton, brother of Humphrey Chetham, the Founder. Died 19 November, 1650. Buried 26 November, 1650. M.I. in Cathedral.

ALICE,[2] married (by licence dated 23 May, 1610)[3] to Adam Holland of Hulme Hall, yeoman. Both living 1626.[4]

MARY,[2] married before 1613 William Bowker the younger.

SUSAN,[2] baptised 17 August, 1593. Dead before 31 Jan., 1613–4.

SARAH,[2] living unmarried 1613. Married . . . Chapman before 1626.[4]

MARTHA,[2] baptised 14 March, 1595–6, living unmarried 1613. Married . . . . . Prestwich, before 1626.[4]

ANNE.[2] Married (by licence dated 2 August, 1615) to Richard Tonge of Tonge, gent. She (?) was buried at Middleton, 24 December, 1637.

ELIZABETH, is mentioned in the will of George Chetham of Clayton, 1626, and was then unmarried and dwelling in London.

JOHN, baptised 9 October, 1597. Probably the infant buried 7 February, 1597–8.

THOMAS CHETHAM of Nuthurst, gent. Baptised at Middleton, 15 April, 1599, and was aged 15 years 11 months 2 weeks and no more at the date of his father's inquisition post mortem, 28 March, 1615. His custody and marriage were granted by the King to his mother 10 July, 1615. On 2 July,

1 Raines *MSS.*, vol. xvi. p. 358.

2 Mentioned amongst the minor children in the settlement of 1601.

3 Raines *MSS.*, vol. xvi. p. 358.

4 Named in the will of George Chetham of Clayton, 1626.

1623, he was found by inquisition to have arrived at the age of 21, and received seisin of his father's lands. High Constable of the Hundred of Salford, 1623.[1] Compounded for knighthood 1631,[2] and in 1635 certified that Humphrey Chetham was a member of his family, and was entitled to the same arms.

During the Civil Wars [3] he took the side of the Parliament, and occurs in Raines and Sutton's *Humphrey Chetham* (p. 146) as a captain of foot soldiers, and he assisted in the relief of Manchester. In 1644 his name occurs first in the petition for provision to be made out of sequestered estates for preaching ministers at chapels in the parish of Manchester.[4]

He was buried 7 November, 1657.

A draft will made in June, 1625, is in existence. His last will was dated 2 November, 1657. He does not mention his son and heir Francis. His executors, his son-in-law Jonathan Chadwick of Chadwick, gent., and James Holland of Hulme Hall within Moston, gent., were to sell Flashhouses in Butterworth for the equal benefit of his daughters Mary, Dorothy, Margaret, and Susan, and each of his younger sons George, John, and William were to have a life annuity from the Nuthurst and other property, out of which 300*l.* was also to be raised for the benefit of the daughters. Of the personal property one-third was left to the wife Susan, one-third to the children George, John, and William Chetham, Mary Chadwick, Dorothy, Margaret, and Susan Chetham equally, and the remaining third between the wife and children equally. He ratified his wife's jointure, and in case the yearly sum of 10*l.* was not paid to her he devised to her after default the closes of his demesne of Nuthurst called Newfield and Coptonhill for her life.

[1] Kenyon *MSS.* (*Hist. MSS. Comm.*, p. 29).

[2] Rec. Soc., vol. xii.

[3] In the *Civil War in Lancashire* (Chet. Soc.) it is surmised that Captain Chetham was of the Nuthurst family. The identity seems settled by a witness in one of the lawsuits in 1698, who remembered "old Captain Chetham of Nuthurst."

[4] *Cal. Dom. S.P. Add.*, 1625–1649, p. 669.

He married first (covenant dated 27 October, 1617) Mary, daughter of Francis Forester, of Watling Street, co. Salop, esq., She was buried 29 March, 1625.

Married secondly at Bramhall, 29 April, 1634,[1] Susanna Walker, widow. She was the daughter of Sir William Davenport of Bramhall, and was married (1st) at Stockport 26 January, 1630-1, to Sampson Walker of Stafford, gent. He was drowned, and was buried at Stockport 9 November, 1631. She was living at Butterworth in 1660. Buried 25 February, 1679–80.[2]

Issue :—

by first wife

MARY, baptised at Newton Chapel 30 November, 1618 (*Cath. Registers*). Married 20 November, 1648, to Jonathan Chadwick of Chadwick, gent. She died 17 July, 1668. M.I. in Cathedral.[3] Jonathan Chadwick was the executor of the wills of his father-in-law and of his brother-in-law George.

JAMES, described as son and heir in will of 1625. Buried 26 September, 1639.

FRANCIS CHETHAM of Nuthurst, esq. Born September, 1621, baptised 21 October, 1621, his godfather being Humphrey Chetham the Founder, in whose will of 1642 he is mentioned. Succeeded his father, 1657. In 1659 he mortgaged Nuthurst Hall and its closes, and property in Crompton and the Flashhouses in Butterworth to Edward Chetham of Chetham, gent., for 1,100*l.* to be repaid in three years together with 6 per cent interest. In 1662 the mortgage appears to have been renewed for 1000*l.* In 1669 the mortgage was held by Joseph Duerden of Rochdale, gent. Little is known of the life of Francis Chetham, he took part in no public work, and it is probable that he was a chronic invalid. In

[1] Stockport Registers.

[2] A deed quoted in *Reliquary*, vol. xviii. p. 88, mentions a Mrs. Cheetham, daughter of William Davenport of Henbury. This lady, who does not appear in the pedigrees of the Henbury Davenports, is perhaps the Margaret Davenport who was married at Stockport 2 July, 1639, to John Cheetham.

[3] Owen *MSS.*, vol. xxiii.

1659 he was "so infirme that without great danger of his body he is not able to traell to Lancaster," and at the Visitation of 1664–5 the family pedigree was entered on his behalf by his brother George. He does not appear to have been married,[1] and he certainly had no surviving son as he was succeeded by his brother John. His administration bond is at Chester, and being amongst the "infra" wills he must have been very poor at his death. He was buried 22 January, 1677–8.

THOMAS, baptised 15 December, 1622. Perhaps the Thomas Chetham *Anglus* who graduated at Edinburgh, 15 April, 1645.[2] Buried 18 February, 1655–6, as "Thomas Chetham the younger of Nuthurst, gent."

GEORGE CHETHAM of Salford, gent. Was a godson of George Chetham of Clayton, and is named in his will, 1626. Perhaps the George Chetham *Anglus* who graduated at Edinburgh 15 April, 1645.[3] He was a party to a mortgage deed in 1669 as next in entail to his brother Francis. Buried 31 March, 1670. His will is dated 18 February, 1669–70, and was proved at Chester, 1670, but is not now to be found there, having been destroyed by damp. The abstract below is from a "true coppie" examined by Edw. Sandiford, now amongst the Clowes papers.

George Chetham of Salford, gentleman, Sicke of body, &c. Whereas I am seised of an estate of inheritance in fee simple, to me and mine heirs and assigns for ever of and in three closes or parcels of land with their appurtenances called the Sidgreaves lying in Nuthurst which are defeazable and redemptable upon 100*l.* by my brother Francis Chetham esq. at a day yet to come. If Francis redeem the said lands by paying 100*l.* that sum is to be part of personal estate and if said brother shall not redeem the said lands they are to be sold and the sum realized and the profits before the sale to be disposed of with the rest of my personal estate as follows. Debts and funeral expences out

[1] In several pedigrees he is said to have married Mary, daughter of John Hopwood of Hopwood, Esq. The marriage is not mentioned in the Chetham pedigree in the Visitation of 1664; while in the Hopwood pedigree the lady is stated to have married Francis Chadwick of Nackbank.

[2] *Catalogue of Edinburgh Graduates*, p. 63.

[3] *Catalogue of Edinburgh Graduates*, p. 62.

of whole personal estate. 20*s.* to "my brother in law Jonathan Chadwick gent. to bye him a ringe withall." The rest of personal estate equally amongst John, Jonathan, Thomas, William, Mary, and Sarah Chadwick sons and daughters of said Jonathan Chadwick.

Sole executor brother in law Jonathan Chadwick.

Dated 18 Feb. 22 Charles 2 1669.

[signed] George Chetham.

Witnesses

Thomas Minshull jun^r

Nathan Leech.

JOHN, heir to his brother (see below).

by second wife

WILLIAM CHETHAM of Moston, gent. Baptised at Bramhall, 26 March, 1635.[1] Under his father's will he had an annuity of £6 13*s.* 4*d.* arising out of Nuthurst. He appears to have borrowed money from Alexander Davie, and on 8 April, 1682, executed a deed assigning his annuity to pay the interest. He then described himself as "of Moston, mercer." He is probably the William buried 17 March 1687–8.

He had issue

Susannah, baptised at Manchester, 9 July, 1667. A Susannah C. was married 30 September, 1690, to John Lowe.

Alice, baptised at Blackley, 29 August, 1669.[2]

DOROTHY, baptised at Bramhall 16 March, 1635–6,[3] and in 1659 was living unmarried.[4]

MARGARET, living 2 November, 1657, unmarried. Married to John Gucson before 20 July, 1659, when she and her husband gave a release to Francis Chetham.

SUSAN, living 1657. Under age and unmarried, 1659.

AN INFANT, buried 28 July, 1640.

[1] Stockport Registers.

[2] Booker's *Blackley*, p. 84.

[3] Stockport Registers.

[4] On 16 April, 1700, Nathaniel Kelsall of the parish of St. Peter's, Chester, and Dorothy Chetham of Manchester, were married at the Collegiate Church, but it is not likely that this refers to the Dorothy of the text.

JOHN CHETHAM of Nuthurst, esq., was born before June, 1625, when he is named in his father's draft will. In 1664 he was living at Linton, Cambridgeshire.[1] On the death of his brother George in 1670 he became heir to his brother Francis, and, as such, in 1673, he was party to a lease. He was then "of Manchester." On the death of Francis in January, 1677-8, he inherited Nuthurst. In June, 1678, he mortgaged portion of the estate to Humphrey Chetham of Newton, and seven months later appears to have obtained a mortgage on the whole of his estates to John Waite and Cornelius Nedham. During the next few years his mortgage transactions were numerous. In 1682 he sold portion of the property to Alexander Davie of Salford, who was a mortgagee of another portion of the estate. In 1688 the estate was mortgaged to Matthew Hallowes, and in 1692 John and his son of the same name agreed to sell Nuthurst to Edward Chetham of Manchester, the price being £1650, the bulk of which was to pay off the Hallowes mortgage. The purchase was not completed until 2 March, 1697–8, and John and his son appear as "of Nuthurst" to their deaths.

He was buried 11 December, 1694, as "John Chetham of Nuthurst, esq." His will, in which he describes himself as "of Linton," was dated 16 March, 1681–2. He left all Nuthurst to his son John, £150 to his daughter Grace, and £30 to his son Thomas.

He married Grace or Mary,[1] daughter of Thomas Flack of West Wickham, co. Cambridge, and widow of John Mead, of Linton, co. Cambridge.

Issue:—

JOHN CHETHAM of Nuthurst, esq. He occurs 1678 to 1688 as son and heir apparent to John in several of the Nuthurst mortgage deeds and in 1692 was a party to an agreement for the sale of Nuthurst to Edward Chetham. He succeeded his father, and he was still "of Nuthurst" at the time of his death, his burial on 4 January, 1697–8, being recorded as that of "Mr.

[1] *Cambridgeshire Visitation*, 1684; *Genealogist*, vol. iii., p. 297.

John Chetham of Nuthurst." He probably died unmarried. It appears from a receipt dated 2 March, 1697 [-8] that he made a will, and that his sole executor was Richard Tonge of Tonge, gent. On the death of John Chetham, Nuthurst passed into the possession of Edward Chetham of Manchester, barrister-at-law, who, as we have seen, had agreed to purchase the property in 1692.

GRACE, is mentioned in her father's will, and in one of the Nuthurst deeds, 1681-2. Died unmarried. Buried 26 September, 1688.

THOMAS. Is named in the Visitation 10 September, 1664, and in his father's will, 1682. Nothing further is known of him.

GEORGE. Is named in the Visitation, 10 September, 1664, but as he does not occur in his father's will, he, it may be presumed, died unmarried before 1682.

PEDIGREE IV.

CHETHAM OF MIDDLETON AND OF COUNTY SUFFOLK.

ELLIS CHETHAM of Middleton, gent. (younger son of John Chetham of Nuthurst, gent., by Margery, daughter of Ellis Prestwich of Hulme, esq., *see* p. 19). Named in the marriage covenant of his brother Thomas, January, 1518–9. Had a grant for life, from his brother, of the Slack in Castleton, 26 October, 1524, and was a witness to one of the Thealmore deeds, 3 February, 1526–7. Mentioned in the will of Ralph Chetham of Oldham, 12 September, 1537.

Married Jone, daughter and heir of Richard Jakes of Middleton, gent.

Issue:—

THOMAS (see below).

JOHN CHETHAM, of Great Livermere and Bury St. Edmunds, co. Suffolk, gent., who entered his pedigree and arms at the Suffolk Visitation of 1561.[1] In 1572 he presented to Queen's College, Cambridge, of which William Chaderton, of the Nuthurst family, was then president, the advowson of Little Eversden, Cambridgeshire, in consideration of which benefaction he and his heirs were to have the privilege of nominating to one of the smaller scholarships in the college, a privilege now long obsolete.[2] It is possible that he was the same man as John Chittam of London, citizen and fishmonger, to whose executors "James Chetam of Nuthurst, gent.," and "Thomas Chittam of London, gent.," one George

[1] *Suffolk Visitation*, 1561, ed. by Howard, vol. ii. p. 59. Dr. Howard's notes to the pedigree have supplied much information relating to this branch of the family.

[2] Lysons' *Magna Britannia*, vol. ii. part 1. p. 193; Searle's *History of Queen's College*, pp. 319–320.

Gipps of London, gent., fishmonger, gave a release dated 13 May, 1591, now amongst the Clowes deeds. Married Katharine, daughter of . . . Richmond of Hedenham, co. Norfolk. She was buried in the chancel of Great Livermere Church, 2 January, 1577.

Issue :—

John Chetham, of Great Livermere, gent., who had an only child, *Frances*, married at Newgate, 21 September, 1587, to Roger Mounteney, of Shipdam, co Norfolk, gent.[1]

Frances.

Katharine., married Francis Bircham, of Norfolk.

MARGERY. One of this name was married at Middleton, 24 June, 1554, to Robert Wild.

ELIZABETH, was living and apparently unmarried in 1575 when Henry Chetham of Nuthurst made a memorandum for his visit to London, "To talk wth my cosyn Chethm̃ of Suff. concernyne ten pounds he promysed to pay his sister Eliz. towards preferment of her marriage." She may however be the Elizabeth marrried at Middleton 28 October, 1565, to Thomas Ratclift.

THOMAS CHETHAM, of Middleton, gent., was living in 1575, when he intrusted a letter for his brother to the care of Henry Chetham of Nuthurst, then about to go to London.

Married at Middleton 28 April, 1545, Agnes Ireland, probably a neighbour, as the name was then common in Middleton.

His children are unknown, the Middleton registers not giving any details of parentage. The name occurs sparingly in the registers. Probably one of his grandsons was John Chetham of Middleton, gent., whose inq. p.m., dated 22 September, 1635, states that he held of Ralph Assheton of Middleton, one messuage, four cottages, and twenty acres of land, meadow, and pasture in free and common socage by fealty and 28*s.* 2*d.* rent. The

[1] *Harleian Society Registers*, vol. xxi. p. 208., cf. *Marriage Licences, Bishop of London*, p. 15 Harl. Soc., vol. xxv.).

inq. p.m. states that John died 29 June, 1634, and that Thomas Chetham was his brother and heir, and was aged 50.[1] The burial of John is in the registers under the date given by the inquisition for his death.[2]

[1] *Towneley MSS. Evidences*, p. 249.

[2] Apparently belonging to this branch of the family, as he used the arms of Chetham quartering Jakes, was Thomas Chetham, Keeper of the Records in Birmingham Tower, Dublin, 1595, Chief Examinator in Chancery, 1601, and Clerk of the House of Lords (Ireland), 1607. Died 6 December, 1624, having married Mary, daughter of John Forster, Lord Mayor of Dublin. He had an only daughter Margaret, born 21 April, 1604, married 28 May, 1623, Nicholas Loftus, esq., and died October, 1666, cf. *Notes and Queries*, 1st Ser. vol. xi. p. 182-3, *Calendar of State Papers, Ireland*, 1603–1614, *Calendar of Carew MSS.*, 1603–1624. In Burke's *Armory*, apparently quoting from a funeral certificate, he is described as of Nuthurst, co. Lancashire, and Hacketstown, co. Dublin.

PEDIGREE V.

CHETHAM OF CRUMPSALL, TURTON, AND CASTLETON.

The Chethams of Crumpsall were probably descended from the Chethams of Nuthurst, but the precise connection, if any, is unknown. When Humphrey Chetham was satisfying the Heralds as to his right to use the same arms as the Nuthurst family, he put in a certificate from Thomas Chetham of Nuthurst to the effect that Humphrey was of a younger branch of the Nuthurst family, but Thomas Chetham did not venture to give the details of the relationship. In a pedigree printed in the *Lancashire Visitation*, 1613, but obviously not a visitation pedigree, the connection is placed a few generations before the time of the FOUNDER. The pedigree is there traced from one Edward Chetham, stated to be a younger brother of John Chetham of Nuthurst. There is, however, no evidence for this connection, and the fact that there were Chethams living in Crumpsall at a much earlier date than this is some evidence that the affiliation at this period is an error. The recollection of James Chetham, the elder brother of the FOUNDER, went only to his great grandfather, and he evidently did not know of the connection with the Nuthurst family. The connection, if it existed at all, was probably much earlier than the 16th century. It may be pointed out that there were younger sons in several of the early generations of the Nuthurst Chethams, and probably there were others of whom no record remains, so that there would be no inherent impossibility of the Crumpsall family being descended from the Nuthurst family.

The first Chetham of Crumpsall of whom I have any note is Thomas, son of Hugh de Chetham of Cormesale, who occurs in the calendar of Duchy Chancery Rolls in 1417–1418.[1] Canon Raines[2] mentions an Edward Chetham and his son Ralph Chetham, both living 1479, and tenants in Crumpsall of the Prestwich family, and a son of the latter, named Edward, living 1520, who died 1537. I have been unable to verify the references given by Canon Raines. I find, however, in the settlement on marriage of Nicholas Prestwich and Margaret Trafford (3 September, 1478), Edward and Hugh Chetham of Crumpsall, but no relationship is stated.[3] There are numerous references to various Chethams whose place in the pedigrees is uncertain, and for that reason I begin this pedigree of Chetham of Crumpsall with Edward Chetham, great-grandfather of the FOUNDER. Contemporary with him were Robert Chetham of Manchester, whose will, dated 1573 and proved 1578, mentions his wife Isabel and his sons Edward and Robert;[4] Edmund Chetham of Crumpsall, whose estate was administered by Alice, his relict, 1584;[5] and many others, the name having become a common one, with representatives in every grade of society, from gentlemen down to labourers. All these Chethams doubtless considered themselves members of the family of Chetham of Nuthurst.

EDWARD CHETHAM of Crumpsall. His name is the first on the pedigree given by James Chetham (his great grandson) to the Heralds, 20 June, 1635.[6] In 1541, when he styled himself merchant, he settled on his eldest son James the residue of his lease of the Crumpsall property,[7] and in 1545 he, or a namesake, farmed the tithe corn of Crumpsall at the will of the Warden and Fellows of the Collegiate Church, paying annually

[1] *D.K. 33rd Rep.*, App. I., p. 15.

[2] Raines and Sutton's *Life of Chetham*, p. 3.

[3] Raines *MSS.*, vol. xxv. p. 142.

[4] Earwaker's *Lancashire and Cheshire Wills*, p. 207 (Chet. Soc. N.S. vol. 3).

[5] *Ibid.*

[6] Howard's *Suffolk Visitation*, vol. ii. p. 62, quoting Harleian *MSS.* 1987.

[7] Raines and Sutton's *Chetham*, p. 4.

101*s.* 6*d.*[1] He is stated in the Visitation pedigrees to have been a younger brother of a Chetham of Nuthurst, but no Edward occurs as a relation in the numerous Nuthurst documents of the early part of the 16th century.

He had issue :—

JAMES (see below).

ANOTHER son whose name James Chetham could not remember in 1635. It seems possible that his name was Ralph, and that he was identical with the "servant" of that name mentioned in the wills of James Chetham, 1571, and Henry Chetham, 1602. Whether this servant of 1571 and 1602 was a relation of his employers is not certain, but the will, abstracted below, of a Ralph Chetham of Crumpsall, 1616, presumably the same person, shows that a person of that name was a very near relative.

Ralph Chetham the elder of Crumsall husbandman, 21 November, 1616. To be bur. in parish church of Manchester.

To right hon[ble] Edmund Prestwich of Hulme esq[re] (my good landlord and master) a crowne in gold and to my Mistress his wife another crowne in gold. Mine ould Mistress his mother a crowne in gold. Mr. Raphe Prestwich 30*s.* Mr. Ellis Prestwich Mr. John Prestwich and Mr. Thos. Prestwich 2*s.* each. My nephew Edmund Chetham of Crumpsall 3*s.* 4*d.* Alice wife of Adam Chetham of Blakeley 12[d]. Anne now wife of Danyell Travis of Blakeley 30*s.* Cozen George Chetham of London 40*s.* Cozen Humfrey Chetham of Manchester £4. Godson Raphe Chetham the younger, bro. of Geo. and Humfrey £8. "I do not owe anything to any person or persons whatsoever." After legacies and funeral expenses residue in two parts one to said Cozen Humfrey Chetham and the other to godson Raphe Chetham, over and above the legacies. Cozen Humfrey C. sole ex[r]. Henry Rollynson of Broughton and Jas. Wroe of Heaton Gate overseers.

Signed by mark.

JAMES CHETHAM of Crumpsall, yeoman. In the 1541 subsidy he was assessed in Cheetham township at £20 in goods.[2] In September, 1548, he purchased (jointly with Ralph Siddall of Withington) two parts of the manor and demesne lands of Kersal.[3]

[1] *Lancashire Chantries* (Chet. Soc.), p. 18.

[2] *Rec. Soc. Misc.*, vol. i.

[3] *Chetham MSS.*, B. 45 (Chetham Library).

In 1567 he was owner of three burgages and three closes of land in Manchester. Though described as a "yeoman" in the Kersal deeds and in his will, he occurs in a number of deeds as a "merchant," and he appears from his will to have been in business to the end of his life. He and his wife Katharine were defendants in an action concerning a burgage in the Milnegate, Manchester, in 1565.[1] His death occurred between 16 September, 1571, the date of his will, and 3 October, 1571, when his death was returned by the jury of the Court Leet.[2] His will, which was proved 20 November, 1571, is interesting, and is therefore given at length from a contemporary copy in the family papers.

In nomine Domine Amen the xvij^th^ daye off September Anno dñi 1571 I James Chetam of Crumsall wythin the County of Lancaster yoman sicke in body but of good and perfecte remēbrāce Laude and praise be unto almightie God Ordayne and make this my present testament Hearein Contayninge my holl wyll and mynde in fourme and manner folowinge that ys to wytt firste and principally I geve and bequeath my soule unto Almighty god the father trustinge that by the merits of Christs death and passion to be One of the number of his Elected childrenn and my mortall bodye to Christyann buriall wythin the Colliage Church of Manchester In ꝑmis I do gyve and bequeathe unto my sonne Henry Chetam all my landes tenementę tackes and burgagees lyeinge and beinge in Kersall Manchester and Cromsall or els whearesoever they be And also it ys my wyll that my saide sonn Henry Chetam shall have the fourte parte of all my goodes and Cattallę whatsoever the[y] be And also all my cartes wheles wenes [=wains?] ploughes axes mattockes spades wythall other instrumentę partayninge to husbandry. It̃ I do gyve and bequeath unto Alis Travis doughter of James Travis the yonger fourty pooundes and then it ys my will and mynde that the saide James Travis shall have the tuission of the saide Alis and of hir goodes tyll shee come to leafull age or mariage beinge bounden for the paiment thereof wyth sufficient suerties. It̃ I do give and bequeath unto An Travis wiffe of the

[1] *Ducatus Lanc. Pars. III.*, vol. 2, p. 311.
[2] *Manchester Court Leet Records*, vol. i. p. 142.

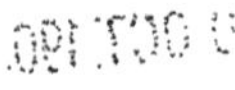

saide James Travis my doughter twenty poundes and also unto John Travis Henry Travis and Ann Travis children of the saide James Travis nyne poundes nyne shillingę eighte pence which the saide James Travis their father ough unto me. It̃ I do give unto Katrin Keneon and Ann Keneon doughters off George Keneon twenty markes to be equally devided betwixte them And then yt is my will that Henry Chetam my sonn shall have the Custodie of the said twenty markes till the saide Katrin and Ann Keneon come to leafull age or mariage. It̃ I do give unto Rauffe Chetam my servande ten poundes. It̃ unto Elin Chetam doughter of Rauffe Chetam twenty shillingę. It̃ unto everi Childe that I am godfather unto twoo shillingę a pece. It̃ unto the reparasions of Manchester Church six shillingę eighte pence. It̃ unto Alis Brocke six shillingę eighte pence. It̃ unto An Brocke six shillingę eight pence. It̃ unto Katrin Brocke vj[s] viiij[d]. It̃ I do give unto the mendinge of Chetam Lawen [Lane] fourty shillingę. It̃ unto Edward Dawsonn vj[s] viij[d]. It̃ unto John Ham̃ [Hamer] my servande man three shillingę foure pence. It̃ to Hugh Oliṽ [Oliver] ij[s]. It̃ unto An Barre [?] ij[s]. It̃ unto Margaret Huitę [Hewitts?] ij[s] It̃ Nycolas Ridingę of Blakelow ij[s]. It̃ unto the wyf of Edmund Houlme xx[d]. It̃ it is my will and mynde that One busshell of good barly shalbe delte yearely to the poore howshoulders wythin this parrissh of Manchester for the space of ten yeares at or before the feaste of Easter. It̃ I do give and bequeth all the reste of my goodes after that my fourthbringinge detę legasies and funeralls be discharged and paiede unto James Chetam sonn of Henrie Chetam to perfourme and fulfill this my laste wyll or testament I do constitute ordayne and make my trew and leafull executors Henry Chetam my sonn and James Chetham sonn of the saide Henry. Supervisors S[r] Rodger Wrigley and Nycolas Brocke. Afore these recordes S[r] Rodger Wrigley clerke Edwarde Briddocke and Nycolas Gyllyam. Edwarde Bryddocke Nycolas Gilliam.

These be the dettę owinge unto me the said James Chetam. Inp̃mis Edwarde Taylear de Ouldum for wyne vj[li]. It̃ Alexander Lowe of Stoppart lij[s] iiij[d] suerty for Edward Warren. It̃ Willyam Hardye of Manchester for suertyshipp for his sonn Henry Hardye v[li] x[s]. It̃ the same Henry Hardy lix[s] and his brother Robart Hardy suerty for the same. It̃ George Smyth of Hull for Cottens xj^{li} xx^{d} [*sic*]. It̃ Rauffe Costerdine of Blakeley mylne for wines [?] ix^{li}. It̃ Ambrose Jacsun of Alkrentum for suertyeshipp for his father Francis Jacsun iiij^{li} v^{s}. It̃ Mr. John Chetam of Nutterst for iiij trees as yett standinge the p^{r}ce of eṽy tree ix^{s} vj^{d}. It̃ for a pece off a boole of a tree which was posted v^{s}. It̃ the saide John [Chetham] ough to me for iiij busshellę of barly eṽy hoope ij^{s} viij^{d}. It̃ George Batersby of Bury for yrne iiij^{s}. It̃ Edward Disun of Manchester ix^{s} iiij^{d}. It̃ the saide Edwarde vj^{s} for one pece of golde which he had to chaunge. It̃ the saide Edwarde att another tyme iij^{s} iiij^{d}. It̃ the saide Edwarde at another tyme iij^{s}. It̃ the saide Edwarde xij^{d} for hallffe a stone of talow and yt not delyvered. It̃ Lawrence Burye of Gooden for suertyshippe iij^{s}. It̃ Stephane Hill for a hope of whete iij^{s} x^{d} to paye. It̃ Robart Chadertonn of Alcrenton for suertyshippe for yrne to Alexander Smyth vij^{s}. It̃ Rauffe Costerdine for one oxe iij^{li} vj^{s} viij^{d}. It̃ the same Rauffe for xxth trees which I have payde fore and not as yet taken away iiij^{li} viij^{s} iiij^{d}. It̃ the same Rauffe for iij hoopes of wheate xiiij^{s}. It̃ the same Rauffe for one siffe of otes. It̃ payde for the saide Rauffe at Weschester for his sune iij^{s}. M^{d} that there is one bill of dett off Mr. Hawke off Chester xiiij^{li} xiij^{s} iiij^{d} in the handes of Rauffe Barlowe of Chester the Sum̃e. It̃ the saide Rauffe Barlowe hathe one oblygation of myne in his kepinge. It̃ Wyllyam Ravellde for ij siffę of otę and a hallffe xx^{s}. It̃ the same Wyllyam of lente money vj^{s} viij^{d}. It̃ Willyam Reede of Manchester of lent money xl^{s}. It̃ the same Wylliam x^{s} which he receyved in Rachedale. It̃ John Wolsencrofte of Bury parrishe for xx pecę xxij^{li} viij^{s} iiij^{d}. It̃ the saide John for hallffe a pece v^{s}. It̃ Mris. Prestwich of Hulme for yrne xx^{s}. It̃ Thomas Boultonn of Sallforde of lent money xx^{s}. It̃ ux̃ Wyllyam Ravellde for xxxviij ponds of flax iiij^{d} ob̃ eṽy pound. It̃ Lawrance Walwerke for xxx poundes of flax iiij^{d} ob̃ the pounde. It̃ Rauffe Smyth of Chester ough unto me viij^{li}. It̃ John Kirkes of Chester marchande ough unto me viij^{li} xij^{s}. And Rauffe Barlowe hath receyved and hathe my byll for the same It̃ Adam̃ Hyll (?) vij^{s}.

These be the dettę which I the saide Jam̃s Chetam do oughe as foloweth. In p̃mis unto Raufe Costerdine for iiij trees xiij^{s} iiij^{d}

Itm to the saide Rauff more for iiij toppes ij^{s} viij^{d}. Itm to the saide Rauffe for a paire of hosse iij^{s}. Itm to the saide Rauffe and hys wiff for a pigge ij^{s}. And for one busshell of barlye. Itm to Rauffe Chetam my servande iij^{li} vi^{s} viij^{d}.

Whereas one Rauffe Sekersun of Lyrpull merchande hath suwed me for lxxx^{li} I do take it of my death and as my sowle shalbe saved at the laste daye when god shall judge the quicke and the deade that I do ough none such det unto him either less or more but contrary wise I do take ytt of my charge that the saide Rauffe Sekersun ough unto me the sum̃ of vj^{li} or above.

M^{d} that after the will of the saide James Chetam was made finisshed and ended and also openly red to him in the ꝑsence of the recordes contayned in the same will and others the prieste asked the sayde James whether he did owe or was behinde wythe any mariage goodes to his sonnes in lawe James Travis or to George Keneon or to awther of them or whether he did promise unto them any thinge at his laste end or no the saide James affirmed and saide that as he woulde answere att the dreadefull daye of judgement and as he shoulde then be saved he did owe nothing unto them nor to awther off them but th^{t} the weare in his det and not he in theires. Proved 20 November, 1571.

At his inq. p.m. 13 Eliz. it was found that he had properties at Kersal, Ashton, and Manchester, and that his son Henry was his heir, and was 28 years of age.[1]

James Chetham married, apparently about 1541, Katherine . . . . . who was living in 1567, but presumably died before her husband.

Issue:—

Edward, died without issue, presumably in his father's lifetime.[2]

Henry (see below).

Anne, married James Travis the younger. She was living and had four children, 1571, when she is named in her father's will.

[1] Towneley *MSS. Evidences*, p. 305.

[2] Howard's *Suffolk Visitation*, vol. ii. p. 62, quoting Harleian *MSS.*

ANOTHER dauhgter married George Kenyon of Kersal, and had issue *Katherine* and *Ann*, who, with their father, are named in the will of James, 1571.

HENRY CHETHAM of Crumpsall, gent. Inherited his father's holding at Crumpsall and his property at Kersal and Manchester, and in 1578 and 1586 was one of the complainants in actions against the burgesses of Salford for trespass on Kersal wood or moor.

Died 29 April, 1603. Buried 1 May, 1603, as "of Cromsall, householder." An inquisition post mortem was taken at Newton, 25 August, 1603, when James was found to be his son and heir.[1] His will, dated 6 March, 1602-3, was proved 4 May, 1603, and has been printed.[2]

Henry Chetham married (post nuptial settlement dated 15 July, 1567), Jane, daughter of Robert Wroe of Heaton, yeoman. The date of the marriage is unknown, but the eldest son was born 7 April, 1565, and in his will, dated 7 December, 1565, Robert Wroe [3] mentions "Jane my daughter now wyff of Henry Chetham." She was executrix of her husband's will, made her own will 19 August, 1616, and was buried 27 October, 1616.

Issue :—

JAMES (see below).

EDWARD is named as second son in the marriage settlement of James, 1588, and also in the pedigree of 1635 given by James to the Heralds. His name does not occur in the will of Henry, 1602. It is probable that he was identical with Edmond, following.

EDMOND, High Master of the Manchester Grammar School. Said to have been M.A. of Corpus Christi College, Oxford, but his name is not in Foster's *Alumni Oxon.*, nor in Clark's *Register*. His will, dated 28 December, 1602, and proved

[1] Rylands' *Lanc. Inquisitions*, vol. i. p. 2 (Rec. Soc., vol. 3).

[2] Piccope's *Lanc. and Ches. Wills*, vol. iii. p. 164 (Chet. Soc.).

[3] *L. & C. Wills*, p. 232 (Chet. Soc. N.S. vol. 3).

9 January, 1602-3, is printed by Earwaker.[1] He was buried 21 January, 1602-3, the register describing him as "Edward Cheetam M^r^ of Arts and Scohlem^r^ of the free schole." In a posthumous reference to him in his father's will he is called Edmond, but no brother of that name is given by James Chetham in the 1635 pedigree.

ANNE, married (1) 16 March, 1594–5, by licence, to Daniel Travis, of Blackley, gent. He died 26 May, 1617. Inq. p.m. taken 15 January, 1619–20.[2] (2) . . . Roger Key of Blackley.

GEORGE CHETHAM of London, merchant, and afterwards of Clayton, gent. Baptised 12 May, 1576. Apprenticed 27 June, 1592, to George Tipping of Manchester, linen draper. On 4 Jan., 1609-10,[3] he became a partner with Tipping. By the terms of partnership Chetham, who is described as "of Manchester, clothier," was to manage the London business of the firm, which dealt in "Stopport clothe, frizes, white, ruggs, and bayes." This partnership was to last for one year only. Chetham remained in business in London for a dozen years or more, being partner with his brother Humphrey. In 1611 he is described as "citizen and grocer of London," he being a member of the Grocer's Company. He was elected Alderman of Aldersgate ward, 22 April, 1625, and was discharged 28 April, 1625, having been in office only six days.[4] He had on 20 February, 1620–1, jointly with his brother Humphrey, purchased Clayton from the Byrons.[5] He died at Clayton Hall, and was buried at the Collegiate Church, 5 Jan., 1626–7. He had no children. His will is dated 29 June, 1626. He describes himself as George Chetham of Clayton, gent. After payment of his debts and of the funeral expences (which are not to exceed £150)

[1] *Lanc. & Ches. Wills*, vol. i. p. 20 (Chetham Society, N.S., vol. 3).

[2] Towneley's *MSS. Evidences*, p. 1177; Rylands' *Lancashire Inquisitions*, Part p. 157.

[3] *Palatine Note Book*, vol. i. p. 126.

[4] Information of Mr. H. C. Welch, Guildhall Library.

[5] Raines *MSS.*, vol. vi. p. 211.

he leaves half his goods and chattels to his wife Isabel. The other half he reserves to himself and directs that from it legacies should be paid. He mentions his brother James, his brother-in-law Roger Key, his sister Ann, wife of Roger Key, and her children by her first husband Daniel Travis, his sister Alice Chetham, his sisters in law Isabel, wife of his brother James, Margaret, wife of his brother Ralph, Alice, wife of his brother in law Adam Holland, Martha Prestwich, Ann Tonge, Sarah Chapman and Elizabeth Chetham, the last "dwelling in London," his godsons Samuel, son of George Tipping, George, son of his brother in law Mr. Thomas Chetham of Nuthurst, and George, son of his brother in law Adam Holland, and several servants and friends, all of whom received legacies. The residue of the lease of the house in London in which he had lately lived was left to his brother Humphrey. Jane and Isabel, daughters of his brother James, were left £40 each, and Edward their brother £20, his "cozen and now servant George Chetham," eldest son of his brother James, had £300. To the poor of Manchester 50*s.*, and to the poor of Salford 50*s.* Fifty poor old men were each to receive a "black Frize coat" (15 of Manchester, 15 of Salford, 10 of Crumpsall, "where I was born," 5 of Droylsden, and 5 of Failsworth). Mr. Doctor Giffords of St. Michaels in Bassishawe in London 5l., and the poor people of that parish 5l. He directed that the yearly exhibition or sum of money paid by him to the "two preaching curates in Manchester Church" should have continuance for ever, and likewise for the "candles to furnish the large candlestick withall in the Church, according as is specified in my book for three months in the deep winter yearly." The residue to his wife whom he appointed sole executrix, with, as overseers to assist her in London, Ralph Hough and his nephew George Chetham, and, as overseers in Lancashire, Adam Holland and John Gyllyam of Newton, each overseer to receive 6*l.* 13*s.* 4*d.*

George Chetham married (before 31 January, 1613) Isabel, daughter of James Chetham of Nuthurst, gent. She survived her husband, was mentioned in the 1642 will of Humphrey Chetham, and died 19 November, 1650. On her M.I.[1] and in the register she is described as "of Chorlton Row." Buried 26 November, 1650.

SYMON, baptised 9 April, 1579. It is stated in his father's will, 6 March, 1602–3, that he had already been paid his portion, and he is mentioned in an indenture dated 16 May, 1603, but does not occur in his mother's will, 1616. He probably died young and without issue.

HUMPHREY CHETHAM of Clayton, esquire. Baptised 10 July, 1580. Apprenticed 2 October, 1598, to Samuel Tipping of Manchester, linen draper. Was a merchant in Manchester, and purchased Clayton, 1620, Turton, 1627, and other estates. High Sheriff of Lancashire, 1635. Founded the Hospital and Library in Manchester by his last will, dated 16 December, 1651, and proved at London (P.C.C.).[2] He died unmarried on 20 September, 1653, and was buried in the Collegiate Church 12 October, 1653. As Humphrey Chetham is dealt with in detail in the work to which this is an Appendix, it is unnecessary to give here any more than is necessary to show the precise position in his family of Manchester's great benefactor.

RALPH, buried 3 February, 1583–4.

ALICE, baptised 26 September, 1585. Named in father's will. Living at Aspull, 1654. Died unmarried, being the last of the immediate family circle of the Founder, and was buried at Bolton 26 May, 1658, as "Ould Mris Alice Cheetham de Little Bolton, in Mr. Cheetham's chancell."

RALPH CHETHAM, linen draper. Baptised 20 February, 1591–2. Was probably a partner with his brother Humphrey, and for some years his home appears to have been at Clayton. He is said to have died while on a journey to London, and to have been buried at St. Alban's, Herts. His will, dated 11 May, 1629, was proved 1630.[3]

[1] Raines *MSS.*, vol. xi. p. 180.
[2] Several previous wills are in existence
[3] Raines *MSS.* vol. xxvii. p. 178.

He married (by lic. dated 24 August, 1618,[1]) Margaret, daughter of Adam Smyth of Manchester (boroughreeve, 1610). She was baptised 8 December, 1594. Her will, in which she describes herself as Margaret Chetham of Turton, widow, is dated 20 May, 1638,[2] and was proved in the same year. Issue :—

Mary, baptised 16 April, 1620, Married, before 20 May, 1638, John Cunliffe of Hollins, gent., from which marriage descend, in the male line, Lord Masham and the Cunliffes, baronets.

Margaret, baptised 30 March, 1621. Married 4 January, 1642–3, to the Rev. John Tildesley, M.A., Vicar of Deane, and was buried at Deane 29 April, 1663. M.I. there.[3]

Martha and *Ellen*, baptised at Clayton (entered in Collegiate Church register 4 April, 1622). Buried 24 April, 1622.

George Chetham of Elton, gent. Baptised 1 May, 1623. He is said to have been an idiot. In the several settlements made of his estates by his uncle Humphrey in 1650 and 1651 he is placed last in the remainder. In 1650 he was living at Clayton, in 1654 at Elton. Under his uncle Humphrey's will he received a legacy of 200*l.* The reference to him in the will of his brother-in-law John Tildesley, 1684,[4] suggests that he was then in the care of John Cunliffe, another brother-in-law. It is possible that he was the "Mr. George Chetham of Darcie Lever" who was buried at Bolton 1 May, 1709. According to the pedigree compiled by Ralph Cooper, a kinsman, he died a bachelor at "Leer near Turton."[5]

[1] Raines *MSS.*, vol. xvi. p. 365. The marriage is not in the Collegiate Church Register.

[2] Raines *MSS.*, vol. xxvii. p. 178.

[3] Owen *MSS.*, vol. xiii. p. 113.

[4] Raines *MSS.*, vol. xxvii. p. 210.

[5] Ralph Cooper's *Chetham Registers MS.* (Chetham Library).

Samuel, baptised 28 October, 1624; buried 15 March, 1625–6.

Ralph, baptised 30 April, 1626; buried 5 February, 1628–9.

Elizabeth, baptised 15 July, 1627. On 1 July, 1648, as Elizabeth Chetham of Clayton, she signed an acquittance of her uncle Humphrey, executor of her father's will. On the 24th of the same month she is described as the wife of Edward Croston. She must therefore have been married between these dates. Her husband was Edward Croston of Accrington, gent. They both received legacies from Humphrey Chetham, 1654, and she is named in the will of John Tildesley, 1684.

Humphrey, baptised 3 March, 1628–9. He is named in his father's will, but nothing further is known of him, and he is not named in his mother's will. Possibly he is the "infant son of Mr. Raphe Chetham late of Manchester linen draper," who was buried 18 January, 1630–1. If this infant was not Humphrey he must have been a posthumous child.

JAMES CHETHAM, of Crumpsall, gent. Born 7 April, 1565. He occurs 1595 to 1602 as "of Salford, clothier." In 1603 he was "of Salford, gent.," and in 1606 he was living in Deansgate, and was then described as "gent." In 1599 he obtained a renewal of the lease of the Crumpsall tenement, and in 1622 purchased the property (one messuage and fourteen closes of land) from Edmund Prestwich of Hulme, esq., for £350. He added to the family estates at Kersal. In 1620 he was high constable of the hundred of Salford,[1] and in 1631 compounded for knighthood.[2] In a bill in legal proceedings in 1674 he is stated to have been "in the late civil wars . . imprisoned and sequestered," but of this there is no other evidence. He had by indenture dated 29 September, 1640, transferred to his eldest

[1] Axon's *Manchester Sessions*, vol. i. pp. 112, 114 (Rec. Soc.). [2] Rec. Soc. vol. xii.

son all his landed estates in Crumpsall, Kersal, and Audenshaw (with a trifling exception) in return for an annuity; and a few months later he sold to the same son his household goods to the value of 304*l.* When he sold his property to his son he reserved the use of one chamber at the west end of his house at Crumpsall "wherein hee nowe usuallie lyeth and one litle roome behinde the same chamber," and it is probable that he spent most of the remainder of his life there, though in a receipt dated 6 June, 1651, we find him described as "of Thornham," the residence of his daughter.

He was buried 1 July, 1654. His will was dated 8 June, 1654.

He married first, 29 October, 1588 (covenant dated 25 October, 1588),[1] Elizabeth, daughter of George Holland, of Salford, gent. She was buried 12 January, 1605-6.

Second, 22 September, 1606, Isabel Kendall, widow. She was daughter of Edmund Goldsmith of Salford, and sister of Mrs. Margaret Nugent, founder of the charity bearing her name. She married first, 14 January, 1588-9, John Tipping, of Salford, clothier, who was buried 16 July, 1592, having had three children, one of whom was the wife of Francis Mosley of Collyhurst. Second, 27 July, 1595, William Kendall, citizen and grocer of London, who died May, 1601, leaving one daughter. Mrs. Isabel Chetham was buried 22 November, 1635.

Issue of James by his first wife :—

EDWARD, living 1598, when he is named in the will of his grandmother Isabel Holland.[2] Buried 9 November, 1604.

ISABEL, baptised 30 November, 1590, buried 8 July, 1603.

JANE, buried 5 July, 1591.

JAMES, buried 23 January, 1591–2.

GEORGE, baptised 1 July, 1593 (see below).

HENRY, baptised 25 May, 1595. Apprenticed 13 December, 1611, for nine years, to William Taylor of London, citizen and haberdasher. Probably died before 1626, as he is not named in the will of his uncle George Chetham.

[1] Parchment Book, Chetham Library.

[2] Piccope's *Wills*, vol. ii. p. 147 (Chet. Soc., vol. 51).

JAMES, baptised 16 June, 1601, buried 21 August, 1614.

JANE, baptised 10 April, 1603. License, to be married at Rochdale or Eccles, dated 20 March, 1626–7, to John Kay of Thornham, in Middleton, yeoman (post nuptial settlement dated 28 January, 1644). She was a widow in 1651. Died at Salford, and was buried 17 August, 1675.

ISABEL, baptised 4 December, 1604. Married at Rochdale, 28 August, 1639, to Richard Lomax (or Lomas), of Redivales, Bury. She is named in the will of Humphrey Chet-Chetham, 1651.

Issue of James Chetham by his second wife:—

ALICE, baptised 16 July, 1607, buried 26 August, 1607.

EDWARD, baptised 9 October, 1608, buried 21 May, 1610.

ELIZABETH, baptised 12 November, 1609, buried 9 December, 1609.

HUMPHREY, baptised 11 August, 1611, buried 26 November, 1611.

EDWARD, baptised 31 January, 1612–3 (see pedigree of CHETHAM OF SMEDLEY).

GEORGE CHETHAM, of Clayton and Turton, esq. (eldest surviving son of James Chetham). Baptised 1 July, 1593. Apprenticed to his uncle George Chetham, of London, citizen and grocer, 1 October, 1611, for 8 years, and was admitted to the freedom of the city 22 October, 1619. In 1626 he was "servant" to his uncle George, and probably succeeded him in business. In February, 1636-7, he was living in Bassishaw, London, but soon afterwards he appears to have returned to Lancashire, though he must have retained some connection with London, as he was on 25 September, 1656, elected Alderman of Candlewick ward. From this office he was discharged 4 December, 1656.[1] In September, 1640, he acquired the family estates from his father, and was then "of Crumpsall." In 1642 and 1648 he was also of Crumpsall, in 1643 "of Cheetham," and in 1648 of Cheetham Hill, no doubt all three names referring to the

[1] Information of Mr. H. C. Welch, Guildhall Library.

same place. From 1648 to 1653 he was living at Turton as a tenant of his uncle Humphrey, from whom, in 1653, he inherited Turton and Clayton and other lands in Harwood, West Leigh, Horwich, Manchester, Droylsden, Gorton, and Newton, all in Lancashire, and at Bolton by Bolland in Yorkshire. He was High Sheriff of the county of Lancaster in 1660. On 9 July, 1662, he settled his Turton estate on himself, with remainder to James, his eldest son, subject to a charge for the benefit of Henry, Abigail, and Ann Chetham, his children.

He died at Clayton Hall, 13 December, 1664, aged 70, and was buried in the Collegiate Church 21 December. Amongst the Clowes papers are two of his wills (neither of them proved) dated 1 September, 1643, and 30 November, 1652, and in both he directed that he was to be buried in the Clayton chapel within the parish church of Manchester.

George Chetham married :—

(1) On 10 July, 1632 (marriage settlement dated 12 July, 1632) Elizabeth, daughter of Henry Johnson, of Manchester, mercer. She was buried 17 November, 1636.

(2) On 11 June, 1639,[1] Abigail, daughter of William Gelsthorpe, of Northampton. She died 3 July, 1649, and was buried 6 July, 1649.

(3) (Pre-nuptial settlement dated 2 September, 1651. Occurs in a fine 11 March, 1651-2, as then married). Katherine, daughter of the Rev. Edward Assheton, M.A., rector of Middleton. Baptised at Middleton, 8 December, 1605. She is named in the will of 1652, was living at Turton, 1665-8, at "the Wood," 1669-70, and at Cheetham Hill in 1673–9. Her will, dated 29 April, 1680,[2] was proved at Chester, 1683.

Issue by first marriage :—

HUMPHREY, baptised in London on or shortly before 1 July, 1634, Mr. R. Johnson being proxy for his godfather, the Founder.

[1] Dates of marriages from Diary of G. Chetham, quoted by Canon Raines in *Manchester Courier*, March 20, 1877. Neither marriage took place at Manchester.

[2] Raines *MSS.*, vol. xxvii. p. 178.

His first schoolmaster was Robert Symonds. Matric. Corpus Christi College, Oxford, 1 April, 1656.[1] In the wills of 1643 and 1652 his father mentions that the family estates were settled on him, but he did not live to enjoy them, as he died at Turton Tower 13 February, 1658–9, aged 23 years and 7 months, and was buried 18 February, 1658–9. A funeral sermon preached by his brother-in-law Livesey was printed in 1660.

ELIZABETH, educated at the school of Mrs. Amisse. Mentioned in her father's 1643 will as entitled with her brother Humphrey to receive a legacy under the will of her grandfather Johnson, and again in that of 1652, the latter stating that she had married without her father's consent. Her portion was therefore not to be paid until her husband had made a settlement upon her of equal value. She married the Rev. James Livesey, M.A. Cambridge, who was minister of Turton 1650–2, and Atherton 1652–6, and rector of Great Budworth 1657 to his death 7 February, 1681–2 (cf. Shaw's *Bury Classis*, p, 248, Chet. Soc., N. S., vol. 41).

by second marriage :—

ABIGAIL, mentioned in her father's wills of 1643 and 1652. Went to "Ned Byrom's" school at Rodegreene 17 June, 1647, with her brother James and sister Anne. She died unmarried and was buried at Prestwich "from Hardman's Fold" 25 March, 1714.

JAMES, born 24, baptised 31 August, 1641 (see below).

ANNE, baptised 1 December, 1642, and died unmarried. Buried 10 March, 1664–5.

GEORGE, baptised 28 December, 1643, at Manchester, as "George, son of George Chetham, of Chetham, gent.;" buried at Bolton 3 February 1648–9, the entry in the register being "George Cheetam, son of George de Turton, inter Cappellam." The diary of George, the father, under date 3 February, 1648, says "for necessary charges same day my son George Chetham was buried att Boulton in my Uncle's

[1] Foster's *Alumni Oxon.*

Chapell [died] first of February, 1648, the some of £17 2*s.* 0*d.*" From this George the "Chetham claimants" in the 18th and 19th centuries deduced their pedigree. See "The Chetham Claimants," *post* p. 70.

HENRY, baptised 14 June, 1648. Mentioned in his father's 1652 will. Matriculated Oxford University (Brasenose College) 14 July, 1665, aged 18. Of Gray's Inn, student 2 May, 1668, barrister-at-law, 1675, bencher 1701, Serjeant-at-law, 1705.[1]

Buried 2 January, 1711–2, at Prestwich, being described as "Henry Chetham, Serjeant at law, from Hardman's Fold." A marriage licence[2] dated 10 July, 1685, was issued for his marriage with Mrs. Mary Osborne of Derby, spinster, but whether the marriage ever took place is not known. No mention of the wife or of any children has been found in the Clowes papers.

JAMES CHETHAM, of Turton, esq. Born 24, baptised 31 August, 1641. Matriculated, Oxford University (Gloucester Hall), 10 December, 1658. Student of the Middle Temple, 1662.[3] Through his wife he was a large landowner in Derbyshire, and was high sheriff of that county in 1692.[4] He was a deputy lieutenant for the county of Lancaster.

He died suddenly 20 May, 1697, and was buried in the Collegiate Church. M.I.

James Chetham marr. (licence dated 29 April, 1672) Margaret, daughter of Sir Samuel Sleigh of Etwall, co. Derby, knight. She died at Salford, 22 January, 1709-10, aged 64, and was buried in the Collegiate Church. M.I.

Issue :—

MARGARET, born 17 March, 1672–3, baptised at Bolton 6 April 1673, buried there 17 October, 1673.

[1] Foster's *Alumni Oxon.*

[2] *Marriage Licences, Vicar General,* 1679-87 (Harl. Soc., vol. 30, p. 206).

[3] Foster's *Alumni Oxon.*

[4] Leave was given him to reside out of the county, 29 December, 1692. *Cal. Dom S.P.*, 1691-2, p. 538.

ABIGAIL, born 1 November, baptised at Bolton 17 November, 1674. Died unmarried 27 December, 1714. Buried 31 December, 1714, in the Chetham Chapel, Collegiate Church. By will, dated 24 December, 1714, in which she describes herself as "of Manchester spinster," she left 5*l.* to the poor of Manchester, 5*l.* to the poor of Turton, and 100*l.* to be invested and the interest bestowed by her executor "upon such pious use or uses either for the minister of Turton Chappell . . or upon any other pious use" as he shall think fit. She mentions her late father and mother James and Margaret, her brothers Samuel, Humphrey, Gervase and James, and other relations. Amongst the Clowes papers is a document, dated 27 December, 1714, by which she distributes her clothing amongst specified relations, and a receipt for a legacy under her will dated 28 April, 1715.

SAMUEL CHETHAM, esq., of Turton, and afterwards of Castleton, co. Lancaster. Born 2 August, baptised at Bolton, 19 August, 1676. Matric. Oxford University (Corpus Christi College) 21 April, 1694, aged 17. Succeeded his father in the Turton and Clayton estates, and from his mother or her family he had extensive estates in the county of Derby, some of which he sold in or about 1700. He was also (with his brothers) in the remainder to the entailed estates of Sir Edward Coke of Langford, co. Derby, baronet (will dated 15 November, 1726), but the remainder was remote, and never took effect. He obtained, with his wife, Castleton, and built the new part of the hall in 1719.[1] J.P. county Lancaster; Deputy Lieutenant 9 September, 1714;[2] High Sheriff, co. Lancaster (Patent dated 13 January, 11 Geo. II. [1737-8]). Honorary freeman of Liverpool, 7 Sept., 1713.

Died, "after about two hours' sickness,"[3] without issue, 20 March, 1744-5, and was buried at the Collegiate Church 27 March, 1745.

He married[4] at Rochdale, 21 July, 1714, Mary, daughter of

[1] Raines *MSS.*, vol. ii. p. 175.

[2] Raines *MSS.*, vol. vi. p. 230.

[3] Raines *MSS.*, vol. iv. p, 183.

[4] Raines *MSS.*, vol. i. p. 16.

James Holt, of Castleton, esq. She was baptised at Rochdale, 4 November, 1691. Living at Birthwait, co. York, in 1747. She was buried at the Collegiate Church, 25 May, 1749.

GEORGE, born 11,[1] baptised 17 December, 1678, at Bolton. His accounts have been preserved,[2] and from them it appears that he was apprenticed to Mr. Samuel Winder of London, 25 March, 1698, for five years, a premium of £300 being paid.[3] On 9 July, 1698, he left London for Saphia[4] in Barbary, arriving there on 21 August, 1698. Two years later, on 20 October, 1700, he left Saphia, and arrived at Leghorn, 8 December, 1700. He died there, unmarried, 17 April, 1701, and was buried in the Old Protestant Cemetery.[5]

HUMPHREY CHETHAM of Castleton, esq. Born 10, and baptised at Bolton 23 April, 1680. From his accounts[6] it appears that, like his brother George, he was apprenticed for five years to Samuel Winder of London, his bonds being dated August, 1700, and a premium of £300 being paid. On 17 August, 1700, he left London for Saphia in Barbary, and arrived there 8 October. On August 30, 1701, he sailed for Leghorn, arriving there 15 November, and was there for many years as a merchant, making visits to England in 1706 and 1717. He was one of eighteen English merchants in Leghorn to whom Henry Plenus dedicated his Italian grammar.[7] Afterwards he was a merchant in Great St. Helens, Bishopsgate Street, London, until he succeeded to the family estates on the death of his brother Samuel in 1745. J.P. co. Derby 10 January, 1748.[8] His books were

[1] The date given on his tombstone is 9th.

[2] Raines *MSS.*, vol. xi. p. 408.

[3] The age of the two brothers at the time they entered Winder's service suggests that they were rather bound servants than merely learners of the trade, but George uses the term "to bind me prentice".

[4] Probably Saffi in Morocco.

[5] *Misc. Gen. et Her.*, 3rd Ser., vol. ii. p. 184.

[6] Raines *MSS.*, vol. xi.

[7] *N. & Q.*, Feb., 1875, p. 156.

[8] Cox's *Derbyshire Annals*,

sold in 1773.[1] Died unmarried 9 July, 1749.[2] Buried 17 July, 1749. By his will, dated 1 December, 1746, he left his Lancashire estates to his cousin Edward Chetham.

REV. JAMES CHETHAM, D.D. Born 22 October, baptised at Bolton 8 November, 1681. Matriculated at Oxford University (Balliol College) 1 February, 1700–1, aged 19. B.A. 1704, M.A. 1707, B.D. and D.D. 1720. Vicar of Etwall, co. Derby, 1714, and of Hanbury, co. Stafford, 1723. Master of the Hospital and Free School of Sir John Port, knight, in Etwall and Repton. Canon 1716, and Chancellor of Lichfield 1726. J.P. co. Derby, 3 October, 1710.[3] Died 22 October, 1740, without issue, buried at Etwall. Will dated 14 October, 1740. His wife was Frances, daughter of Sir Humphrey Briggs of Haughton, co. Salop, baronet. She survived him. Her will, in which she is described as of the Close in Lichfield, was dated 13 May, 1754, and proved 24 January, 1758, directs that she shall be buried at Etwall in the same vault in which her husband was buried. She bequeathed her husband's portrait to her brother Hugh Briggs.

HENRY, baptised at Bolton 2 May, 1683. Died at Turton of consumption[4] 27 May, 1703, aged 20. Buried at Bolton May 30. M.I.[5]

GERVASE, of Liverpool, merchant, being admitted to his freedom 10 Oct., 1708.[6] Amongst the Clowes papers there is a letter from him dated "Leverp. June 10th 1704" referring to the consecration of "our church." Died aged 34, and was buried 23 May, 1718, in the Chetham Chapel, Collegiate Church. M.I.[7]

JUDITH. Died unmarried 2 January, 1710–11, aged 24. Buried

[1] Nichols' *Anecdotes*, vol. iii. p. 638.
[2] Raines *MSS.*, vol. iv. p. 183.
[3] Cox's *Derbyshire Annals.*
[4] Raines *MSS.* vol. xi.
[5] Owen *MSS*, vol. x. p. 176.
[6] Liverpool Corporation Book of Record, vol. vi. p. 310.
[7] Owen *MSS.*, vol. xxiii. p. 332

5 January, 1710–11, in the Chetham Chapel, Collegiate Church. M.I.[1]

EDWARD. Died 15 February, 1705–6, in his 19th year. Buried at Bolton 17 February. M.I.[2]

[1] Owen *MSS.*, vol. xxiii. p. 322.
[2] Owen *MSS.*, vol. x. p. 176.

PEDIGREE VI.

CHETHAM OF SMEDLEY, NUTHURST, AND CASTLETON.

EDWARD CHETHAM of Smedley, in Cheetham, gent. (eldest son of James Chetham of Crumpsall, by his second wife. *See* p. 49). Born 10 September, 1612; baptised 31 January, 1612–3. Was apprenticed in London, but never followed any trade or employment on his own account, although, writing from London, 10 May, 1637, to his father, he states that his "time is almost expired," gives reasons why he cannot stay with his master, and proposes to mortgage his lands and borrow money from his friends to enable him to start business for himself.

On 17 March, 1639-40, he obtained a renewal of the lease which his father-in-law had had of Smedley. He benefited considerably under the will of his uncle Humphrey Chetham, 1653, the Ordsall and Pendleton estates being settled on him, and he also had a legacy of £2000 to be laid out on lands to be settled on him and his issue. In 1659 he purchased a portion of the estates of the Chethams of Nuthurst, and at about the same time was the mortgagee of Nuthurst itself.

He was an invalid for many years prior to his death, and received in 1672 a licence excusing him from serving on juries. The depositions in the family lawsuits show that for many of his later years his business had been transacted by his eldest son. He died 27 August, 1684, and was buried on the 28 August, 1684, at the Collegiate Church.

His will was dated 6 August, 1682. He describes himself as Edward Chetham of Chetham, gent. He leaves to his son George £100, and to Mr. Thomas Minshull the younger £5. £5 apiece to each of his sons and son-in-law Lever, and to each of his daughters and daughters-in-law to buy mourning. To his son James all his law books at Smedley and twenty of his best books, and household goods to the value of £20. To his cozen George Tipping he leaves his "best suite of wollen apparrell." His son Edward having been given £800 during his lifetime to have no other part of his personal estate than is left him by will. Remainder of personal estate to be divided into five equal parts. One part to his daughter Alice wife of Rawsthorne Lever gent. (who is to give security that the money will be at her disposal). One part to son Edward if he will give a sufficient release for his filial portion "which he had of me in my life." If he refuses his part to be divided equally between the younger children, George, Alice, Isabel and Mary equally. The other three parts to his children George, Isabel, and Mary equally. James Chetham, eldest son, and Thomas Minshull the younger of Manchester to be executors.

He married, after 17 July, 1639, and before 17 March, 1639–40, Alice Massey, *alias* Wilson, illegitimate daughter and testamentary heir of Robert Wilson of Smedley, yeoman. She was born about 1621, and was buried at the Collegiate Church, 7 July, 1681. M.I.[1]

Issue:—

JAMES CHETHAM, of Smedley in Cheetham, esq. Baptised 29 December, 1640. Entered Gray's Inn 13 July, 1659. Matric. Oxford (St. Edmund Hall) 11 April, 1660. Author of the *Angler's Vade Mecum*. Died unmarried. Buried 14 December, 1692. J.P. co. Lancaster.[2] Will dated 27 November, 1691. He left all his estates in the county of Lancaster to his brother "George Chetham of Manchester, woollen draper," and his heirs, thus ignoring his next surviving brother and next of kin Edward Chetham, of Nuthurst. The reason he gives is "because hee [Edward] hath severall times made attempts to take away my life and swore hee would bee my death either by stabb or poyson." This will led to a lawsuit, as Edward Chetham claimed that the estate

[1] Owen *MSS.* vol.xxii. p. 185.

[2] *Calendar Dom. S. P.*, 1690–1, p. 378.

was entailed, that James Chetham had not the power to bequeath the lands, and that George Chetham had prevented access to the testator, and had otherwise unlawfully influenced him. Evidently from the subsequent history of the estates the will was upheld.

HUMPHREY CHETHAM, of Whitworths in Newton, gent., baptised 3 January, 1643-4. In 1664 he is described as "of Cheetham, gent.," and in 1668, when he purchased lands in Moston, as "of Smedley, merchant." After his marriage he appears to have resided at Whitworths in Newton, which he had with his wife. He died without issue, and was buried 30 August, 1680. His will was dated 25 August, 1680, and was proved at Chester, 14 September, 1680, by Edward Chetham, sole executor. The testator left his real estate to his brother Edward and his heirs male, with remainder to his brother James and his heirs. His plate was divided between his wife and his brother Edward. He left legacies to his brother George and his sisters Mary and Isabel.

Humphrey Chetham married at Eccles, 28 January, 1668-9 (the marriage is recorded in the Collegiate Registers), Mary, daughter and heiress of John Whitworth, of Newton. She brought an action against her brother-in-law Edward Chetham (as trustee under her husband's will), for a portion of the personalty which she claimed under an agreement. In the pleadings in this case she mentions that before her marriage she was seised of lands in the parish of Manchester of a value of £140 yearly, which lands she conveyed to her husband who settled them to the use of himself for life with remainder to his wife for life and jointure and afterwards to his heirs. Curiously enough she did not remember the date of her marriage, for in 1683 she stated that the proposals of marriage were made "about 8 or 9 years since." In his reply the defendant gave the correct date, "15 years ago." From one of the depositions in the suit it appears that she had re-married, her husband being Ralph Worsley of Platt, gent. She was buried at Platt 8 August, 1701.

EDWARD CHETHAM (*see* below).

ALICE, baptised 19 August, 1652. Married at Prestwich, 11 September, 1677, to Rawsthorne Lever, of Kersal, gent. and died before 22 October, 1687.

GEORGE CHETHAM, of Smedley, esq. Baptised 17 August, 1654. Prior to succeeding to the family estate he was in business as a woollen draper in Manchester, and apparently lived at Broughton. In 1692, under the will of his eldest brother, James, he inherited Smedley and other lands, his elder brother, Edward Chetham of Nuthurst, being passed over, with resulting legal proceedings. J.P. county of Lancaster.

He was buried 28 May, 1729. His will, dated 9 July, 1724, was proved 2 May, 1730.

Married at Church Kirk, 21 April, 1679 (recorded in Collegiate Church Registers), Elizabeth, widow of . . . . Gawthorne, of Manchester, and sister of Jonathan Greene of Manchester, chapman.

She was buried 27 October, 1710.

Issue:—

Elizabeth, baptised 23 January, 1679–80. Buried 3 October, 1680.

Mary, baptised 8 May, 1681.

James Chetham, of Smedley, esq. Baptised 9 November, 1682. Matric. Oxford University (Wadham College) 18 April, 1700, aged 17, and in the same year was entered at the Inner Temple.[1] On his father's death he inherited his lands in Broughton, Salford, Moston, Failsworth, Cheetham, Pendlebury, and Rochdale. Amongst the Clowes papers is a memorandum apparently by Mr. Clowes of Chaddock, that on 22 June, 1750, Mr. James Chetham had told him that the value of his estate was at that time £2,760 yearly rent, and £700 a year in lease. J.P. co. Lancaster. High Sheriff co. Lancaster, 1730. Contributed £200 towards the raising of troops in 1745.[2] He died unmarried. Buried 10 Febru-

[1] Foster's *Alumni Oxon.*

[2] *Palatine Note Book*, vol. iii. pp. 235–6.

ary, 1752. Admon. granted 12 March, 1752, to Ann Chetham, sister and next of kin.

Alice, baptised 16 December, 1684. Buried 11 February, 1749–50.

Margaret, baptised 18 February, 1685–6. Buried 12 November, 1690.

George, baptised 26, May, 1687. Buried 21 July, 1701.

Martha, baptised 30 January, 1688–9. Buried 23 September, 1749.

Elizabeth, born and baptised 26 August, 1690. Buried 23 March, 1694–5.

Lydia, baptised 2 January, 1691–2. Buried 20 August, 1699.

Ann Chetham, of Smedley. In 1752, on the death of her brother, she became possessed of his Smedley, Broughton, and other estates. She died unmarried, and was buried 24 February, 1762. Her will is dated 7 April, 1761, and by it she left the residue of her personal and the whole of her real estate to her "cousin Edward Chetham."

ISABEL, baptised 21 March, 1656–7, of Manchester, spinster. Buried 2 April, 1708. Will proved 1708.

MARY, baptised 22 May, 1659 (Collegiate Church registers), and June 2 (Blackley registers), buried 15 September, 1659.

MARY, born 23 August, 1661, baptised at Smedley, 5 September, 1661 (Collegiate Church registers). Married 5 October, 1693, Alexander Davie, of Salford, merchant. Died at Ouster [?], and buried at Manchester, 17 August, 1698. He was buried 3 July, 1705.

EDWARD CHETHAM, of Nuthurst, esq. Baptised at Collegiate Church, 22 September, 1647. Matriculated [Christ Church], Oxford, 14 December, 1666, aged 18. Entered Gray's Inn 14 April, 1670. Barrister-at-law 1678, Bencher[1] 1706. On 21 October, 1684, he acknowledged (to the executors of his

[1] Foster's *Alumni Oxon.*

father's will) to have received of Edward Chetham, of Smedley, gent., his father, £800 at least bestowed upon him in his education during the time of his "abode for sixteene years at Oxford and att the Inns of Court," and he therefore released the executors from all claim to any filial portion. In February, 1686–7, he and his wife won an action against the executors and others claiming the fifth part of the residue of his father's estate to which he was entitled on relinquishing his claim to a filial portion. He was defendant in an action brought by his sister-in-law, the widow of Humphrey Chetham, and he contested the legality of his brother James' will, claiming that the estate was, or ought to have been, entailed. He denied the charge made against him by James, and produced evidence as to his honourable character.

On 2 June, 1698, he is mentioned in a Nuthurst deed as having the entire right in Nuthurst. His will as "of Manch^{r}, esq." is dated 30 March, 1710.

Died 8 May, 1714. Buried 11 May at Collegiate Church. M.I.[1]

Married at Collegiate Church, 12 May, 1683 (marriage agreement dated 26 April, 1683), Mary, daughter of John Abraham, of Manchester, grocer (John Abraham's will, dated 10 May, 1681, contains a bequest of £1,000 to his daughter Mary, with the proviso that it is to be void if she "shall marry cohabitt or dwell with Thomas Haworth sonne of Laurence Haworth late of Berdwood neare Blackburn yeoman . . . . as her husband"). She died 27 February, 1706–7. Buried at Collegiate Church. M.I.[2]

Issue:—

Alice, baptised 16 July, 1685. Married at Chapel-en-le-Frith 28 February, 1714, to Adam Bland, of Manchester (first cousin of Sir John Bland, of Kippax and Hulme[3]). He was buried at St. Anne's, 8 August, 1723.[4] She was

[1] Owen *MSS.* vol xxii.p. 180.

[2] Owen *MSS.*, vol. xxii. p. 180.

[3] *Genealogist*, N.S., vol. xviii. p. 257.

[4] Owen *MSS.*, vol. xxix. pp. 21, 22, vol. lxx. p. 156.

living at Mortlake, a widow, in 1769, when, on the death of her brother, Edward Chetham, esq., she became one of his coheiresses, her share in the estate being half the personalty, and the Turton, Droylsden, Failsworth, Manchester, Newton, Spotland, and Salford estates. She died at Kingston-on-Thames in 1774,[1] and is now represented by the Freres and Hoares.

MARY, buried 16 June, 1686.

MARY, baptised 4 October, 1688, buried 16 November, 1688.

MARY, born *circa* 1694. Married 22 November, 1716, to Samuel Clowes the younger, of Manchester, gentleman. On the death of her brother she became one of his coheiresses, receiving half his personalty and the Broughton, Pendlebury, Kersal, Crumpsall, Moston, and Cheetham estates. The Salford estate was purchased from her sister, the other co-heiress. Mrs. Clowes died 5 January, 1775, aged 81, and was buried in the Collegiate Church. From her descend the Clowes family of Broughton, now represented by Captain Henry Arthur Clowes, of Norbury Hall, Ashborne, the present owner of the Broughton and other estates of his ancestors the Chethams.

MALE CHILD, buried 12 May, 1687.

EDWARD CHETHAM, of Nuthurst, afterwards of Smedley and Castleton, esq. Born 25 December, baptised 27 December, 1689. Barrister-at-Law, of Gray's Inn. Admitted 7 May, 1709; called to the bar 16 June, 1718, and became a bencher 10 November, 1736.[2]

Recorder of Macclesfield, 1740–50,[3] and Deputy Steward of Macclesfield Courts (resigned 1750).

On the death of Humphrey Chetham of Castleton in 1749, Edward Chetham inherited by will the bulk of the estates of that branch of the family. On the death of his cousin Anne Chetham of Smedley in 1762, he inherited, by her will, the whole of her estates in Broughton, Smedley, and elsewhere.

[1] Lysons' *Environs of London*, vol. i. p. 246.

[2] Foster's *Gray's Inn Admissions.*

[3] Earwaker's *East Cheshire*, vol. ii. p. 468.

He thus united for the first and last time the properties of all the branches of his family. His character has been aspersed by the Chetham "claimants" of the 19th century, who charged him with having fraudulently kept their ancestor from his "rights," and who imagined that he "stept into" his various estates as next of kin. His right to the properties he owned was in no case as heir-at-law, but invariably by will, and the "heir" whom he is alleged to have defrauded was, though a namesake, no relation of the family whose estates his descendants desired. Edward Chetham was a methodical man of business, and the family archives contain a very large number of his letters, with drafts of the replies. After a perusal of many of these letters, I concur with Dr. William Fleming, who wrote: "I am satisfied that he was a man of strong mind, sound judgment, great intelligence, quick in his profession, and truly charitable and benevolent, yet withal very prudent." An amiable weakness ot the last of the Chethams was the desire to find a male heir of the family, and amongst the letters are several from various families of Chetham setting forth their claims. Amongst them were relatives of the family which at a much later date produced the plaintiff in the action of Chetham *v.* Hoare. Edward Chetham died 19 February, 1769, having been more or less of an invalid for many years. He was buried in the Collegiate Church, where there is a M.I. to his memory. He was the last male representative of the family.

Male Child, buried 26 July, 1684.

THE ARMS OF THE CHETHAMS.

ALTHOUGH the Chethams were obviously of gentle rank for many centuries, I have found no very early use of arms by them. This may be due to the fact that the seals of many of the documents have been lost, and I may have omitted to note all the seals existing. There are, however, existing several seals of the 14th and 15th century, and in no case are these armorial. Of the Chethams of Chetham I have found no seals of any kind. The earlier Chethams of the Nuthurst family used seals with initials.

The first John de Chetham of the Nuthurst family sealed several documents, *circa* 1340, with a seal bearing what appear to be the initials I. C. In 1413 a later John de Chetham was using a seal bearing the letter I (?) with a star. In 1441–2 his seal has the initials I. C. with a crown above, and other ornaments. In 1474 an armorial seal occurs attached to a deed. It is apparently *a chev. between three* [ ]? possibly the coat with the three fleams mentioned later.

The first official confirmation of arms to the Chethams appears to have been at the Suffolk Visitation of 1561, when the following were recorded as the arms of Chetham of Livermere, a junior branch of the Nuthurst Chethams:—

ARMS. *Arg. a chev. gules between 3 fleams sable* (CHETHAM) impaling *vert a mermaid or* (PRESTWICH).

CREST. *A griffin passant regardant gules wings endorsed and membered or.*

Both arms and crest were charged with a crescent on a crescent for difference.

The arms of Chetham being impaled with Prestwich suggests that Mr. Chetham of Livermere had produced for the satisfaction of the Herald a seal originally engraved for his grandfather, John Chetham of Nuthurst (d. 1515), who married a daughter of Ellis Prestwich of Hulme, and if so this would take the use of the arms back to the end of the 15th century.

In 1588, John Chetham of Livermere, was using a coat of arms—

> *Quarterly* 1 *and* 4 *Arg. a chev. gules between three fleams sa.* (CHETHAM) 2 *and* 3 *Arg. on a fess engrailed sa. three escallop shells or* (JAKES) impaling PRESTWICH.

In 1582, James Chetham of Nuthurst, sealed a document with a *demi-griffin.* In 1601 James Chetham was using the motto *Quod tuum tene,* and a quartered coat of arms 1 *and* 4 *a chev. between three fleams* (? they look rather like herons' heads), 2 *and* 3 *a fess engrailed.* The figures are not very distinct, but probably the arms are those of Chetham and Jakes, though the user had no descent from the latter family. In 1611, James Chetham of Nuthurst, used a diamond shaped seal with the letters I. C. and some ornament. The funeral certificate of Thomas Chetham of Hacketstown, co. Dublin, gives, as quoted by Burke's *Armory,* his arms as *Az. a chev. between three fleams or.* He was apparently one of the Nuthurst Chethams. The arms are identical with the arms of the Suffolk Visitation, but the tinctures differ. Several members of the later generations of the Nuthurst Chethams used borrowed seals, thus in 1659 Francis Chetham used on a deed a seal with the Chadwick arms, in 1682 William Chetham used a seal with the arms of Assheton, and in the same year John Chetham used a seal with the crest of the same family.

Of the four Visitations of Lancashire three, those of 1533, 1567, and 1613,[1] had taken place without the Heralds discovering the existence of the Chetham family. At the fourth Visitation, 1664-5, three families of the name entered their arms and pedigrees. The pedigree of the Nuthurst Chethams was entered for

[1] The pedigree of Humphrey Chetham, included in the printed edition of this Visitation, is a later addition.

Francis Chetham by his brother, and the following arms[1] were allowed.

Quarterly 1 *and* 4 *argent, a griffin segreant gules, within a bordure, sable, bezantée.* 2 *Argent a chevron between three cramp-irons, gules.* 3 *Gules a cross doubled-crossed, or.*

CREST.

A demi-griffin, gules.

The coat was, so far as I have evidence, quite fresh for this family of Chetham, and was not in agreement with the prior decision of the Heralds at the Suffolk Visitation of 1561. The reason for this coat of arms having been recognized is probably to be found in the history of the arms of Humphrey Chetham.

[1] The first and fourth quarters have the arms of Chaderton, being the arms of Trafford with a bordure for difference, the second quarter has the arms of Chetham as found at the Suffolk Visitation, the difference between "fleams" and cramp-irons being only nominal. The tinctures are however different. The third quarter contains another version of the arms of Chaderton. The griffin segreant was a favourite charge in Lancashire heraldry, as it is, according to Papworth, the principal charge in the coats of Culcheth, Chaderton, Trafford, Caterall, Grimshaw, and Bold. The coat charged with the three fleams or cramp-irons is supposed by some antiquaries to be the coat of the family of Nuthurst of Nuthurst, and the charges are described as "nuthooks." I do not know what evidence there is for assuming that the Nuthursts bore these arms, or indeed that there ever was a family of Nuthurst of Nuthurst.

The Crumpsall Chethams to which he belonged do not seem to have used arms. They had not appeared at a Lancashire Visitation, and though a London Visitation began in 1633 George Chetham of London did not enter his pedigree and take out arms until after his uncle's arms were settled. In 1635, however, Humphrey Chetham became high sheriff, and displayed a coat of arms, which Randle Holme of Chester had found for him, and which Holme erroneously supposed to be that of Chetham of Nuthurst, with a crescent for the difference of a younger branch of that family. Objection was taken to this coat, and it required some tact and money before the authorities were satisfied. Some of the correspondence is printed in the *Life of Humphrey Chetham* (vol. ii. p. 101), from which it appears that Mr. Chetham's representatives and the Heralds were satisfied that the arms were in fact those of Chaderton, and had been improperly used by the Sheriff. Nevertheless, in order to save his credit, the Heralds granted to Humphrey Chetham the arms which he had borne at the Assizes with the minute difference of a cross doubled-crossed or upon the shoulder of the griffin in the crest.

Randle Holme's blunder in "finding" for Mr. Chetham these arms resulted in his being the first recorded arms for a Chetham residing in Lancashire, and logic demanded that if Mr. Chetham, the sheriff, was allowed certain arms, with a difference as a younger branch of Nuthurst, the senior line of the family should bear the same arms without the difference. Hence at the 1664 Visitation the Nuthurst Chethams were allowed the arms without difference, the Turton Chethams were allowed the arms as used by Humphrey Chetham, and the Chethams of Chetham were allowed the same arms with a trefoil for difference instead of the crescent. The later members of the Chetham family generally used the arms allowed to Humphrey Chetham. Burke's *Armory*, however, gives as the arms of Chetham of Ash, co. Derby (that is the last two generations of the Turton Chethams, *Ar. a chev. gules between three fleams or.* I have not found this coat used separately on any of the family deeds. Mary Chetham (afterwards Mrs. Clowes) used in 1714 a seal with the arms of Chaderton (the cross) only, and in the same year the same lady and her sister Alice, afterwards Mrs. Bland, used a seal with a *griffin segreant* but without bordure.

THE CHETHAM CLAIMANTS.

A NOTICE of the Chetham families of Manchester would be very incomplete without some reference to the Chetham "claimants" who some thirty years or so ago contested the right of the co-heirs of Edward Chetham of Castleton to estates they had inherited through him. The case was decided against the claimant, but unfortunately on a technical point which left many worthy people with the feeling that justice had not been done to the "male representative" of Humphrey Chetham. Although the claimant laid great stress on a mutilated marriage register of 1724, the legality or otherwise of the marriage in 1724 had really no important bearing on the case. The claimant's case, if the matter had been decided on any other than technical grounds, turned on the identity of a certain George Chetham, gentleman trumpeter, from whom the claimant could prove his pedigree, with George, son of George Chetham, esq., of Turton. This assumed identity can be shown to be an error, for the facts of the life of George, the son of George Chetham, esq., are well known. He was, as the claimant agreed, baptised at the Collegiate Church, 28 December, 1643. He was buried, as the claimant denied, at Bolton, 3 February, 1648–9. The fact is proved by the Bolton parish register, which records the burial of "George Cheetam son of George de Turton, inter Cappellam." It is confirmed by an entry in the father's diary (quoted by Canon Raines in the *Manchester Courier* of March 20, 1877). The proof, quite strong enough in itself, is supported by the absence of a son George from (1) the will of George Chetham, esq., 1652 (2) the settlement of his estates made by George Chetham, 1662 (3) the Visitation pedigree, 1664–5, and

(4) the will of Katherine, widow of George Chetham, 1680. It should also be noted that Henry Chetham, next younger brother of George, and fourth son of George Chetham of Turton, was described as second son on his admission as a student of Gray's Inn. He was, of course, second surviving son, two of his elder brothers, Humphrey and George being dead.

This very strong case is further confirmed by the few definite facts in the career of George Chetham, trumpeter, the undoubted ancestor of the claimant.

The facts of the life of George Chetham the trumpeter, as given by the claimant, are that he was the son of George Chetham, esq., was baptised in Manchester 28 December, 1643, and that he became a "gentleman Trumpeter in Sir John Byron's troop of gentlemen yeomanry." I do not know if Sir John Byron ever commanded a troop of "gentlemen yeomanry," but if he did it must have been before 24 October, 1643, when he became Lord Byron. His trumpeter must therefore have been an adult two months before George son of George Chetham, was baptised. In 1653 we find that the trumpeter at the funeral of Humphrey Chetham was George Chetham. The claimant's pedigree requires this distinguished functionary to have been only ten years old at the time. The herald who drew up the account of the funeral was very careful to prefix "Mr." to the names of all Humphrey's relations and all other people of family who were present, but there is no "Mr." to the trumpeter's name, although according to the claimant's pedigree the trumpeter was the son of Humphrey's principal heir. George Chetham the trumpeter appears to have been indentical with an innkeeper whose name occurs frequenty in the Court Leet Records from 1648 (when according to the claimant he was only five years old), for breaking the assize of ale. This innkeeper (or another of the name) purchased a burgage in Hanging Ditch in 1665. He appears to have married late in life, and became a man of some substance. In 1680 he is described as "Mr. George Chetham trumpeter," but the Mr. does not occur in later entries. His burial in January, 1687–8, is entered as that of "George Chetham of Manchester, trumpeter." The claimant of the 19th century did not invent his claim. The first devisers of it appear to have been two brothers, who about 1757 endeavoured to obtain assistance from Edward Chetham, esq., of Castleton, by claiming to be, not the rightful heirs of his property, but poor relations. They succeeded in their immediate object. The pedigrees they submitted to their patron are false in several particulars. They assumed that George Chetham of Turton was the son of a George Chetham born in 1615, whereas he was the son of James Chetham. But the pedigree, false as it is, suggests that George Chetham, trumpeter, was identical with George Chetham, son of John, who was baptised in 1615, a date that would agree very well with the known facts of the trumpeter's career. It is possible to excuse the 19th century claimant, a poor man who had inherited traditions of a pedigree which made him rightful heir to great estates, but it is impossible to excuse Mr. James Croston for perpetuating the false pedigree by inserting it in his edition of Baines's *Lancashire* many years after its falsity had been shown by the facts adduced publicly by Canon Raines.

INDEX.

KEY PEDIGREE.

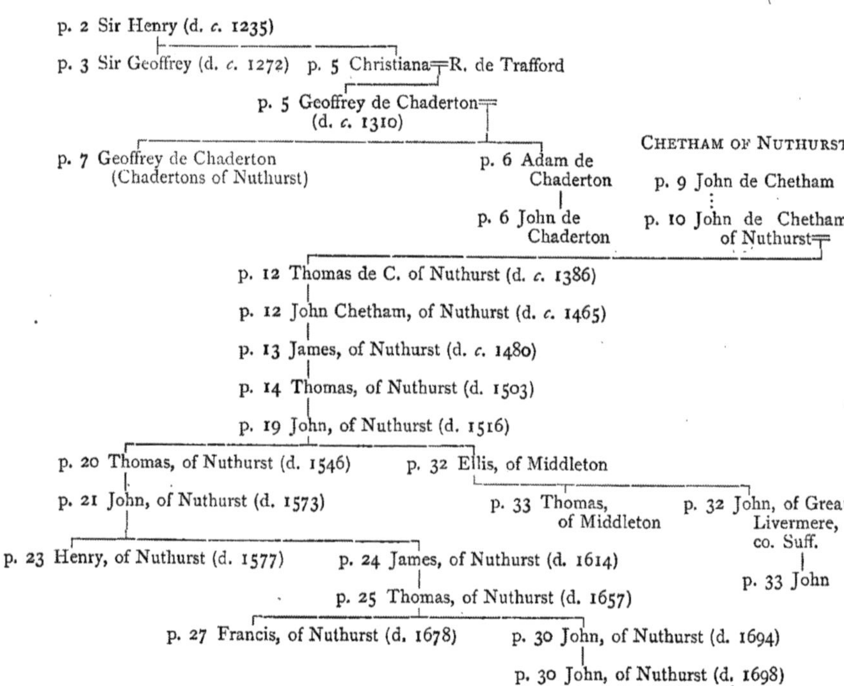

CHETHAM OF CRUMPSALL.

p. 36 Edward, of Crumpsall

p. 37 James, of Crumpsall (d. 1571)

p. 42 Henry, of Crumpsall (d. 1603)

- p. 47 James, of Crumpsall (d. 1654)
    - p. 49 George, of Turton (d. 1664)
        - p. 52 James, of Turton (d. 1697)
            - p. 53 Samuel, of Castleton (d. 1745)
            - p. 54 Humphrey, of Castleton (d. 1749)
    - p. 57 Edward, of Smedley (d. 1684)
        - p. 58 James, of Smedley (d. 1692)
            - p. 62 Alice, Mrs. Bland coheiress.
            - p. 63 Mary, Mrs. Clowes coheiress.
        - p. 61 Edward, of Nuthurst (d. 1714)
            - p. 63 Edward, of Castleton &c.
        - p. 60 George, of Smedley (d. 1729)
            - p. 60 James, of Smedley (d. 1752)
            - p. 61 Anne, of Smedley (d. 1762)
- p. 42 Edward, Highmaster (d. 1603)
- p. 43 George, of London and Clayton (d. 1627)
- p. 45 Humphrey The FOUNDER
- p. 45 Ralph

The Fifty-ninth Report

(20th of the NEW SERIES)

OF THE

COUNCIL OF THE CHETHAM SOCIETY,

Read at the Annual Meeting, held by permission of the Feoffees, in the Audit Room of Chetham's Hospital, Manchester, on Wednesday, the 23rd of July 1902, by adjournment from the 1st of March.

SINCE the last report four volumes have been issued to the members, namely, the *Act Book of the Ecclesiastical Court of Whalley*, edited by Miss ALICE M. COOKE, M.A.; and *A History of the Ancient Chapel of Stretford*, Vol. II., by Mr. H. T. CROFTON, being the second and third volumes for 1899–1900, and the 44th and 45th vols. of the New Series; *The Portmote or Court Leet Records of Salford, 1597–1669*, Vol. I., edited by Mr. J. G. DE T. MANDLEY, and *Chetham Miscellanies*, Vol.. I. forming the first and second volumes for 1900–1, and the 46th and 47th of the New Series.

The *Act Book* comprises a record of the proceedings of the Court held by a Commissary of the Cistercian Abbey of Whalley, for the period of twenty-eight years (1510–1538), the causes being those reserved for ecclesiastical jurisdiction within the royal forests of Pendle, Trawden, Rossendale, Bowland, and Blackburnshire. It presents a curious picture of social life in certain Lancashire villages during the period immediately preceding the Reformation, and besides being an important contribution to local annals, is a welcome addition to the somewhat scanty memorials of the procedure of the Pre-Reformation

Church courts. The Society is much indebted to the learned editor for the pains taken in her arduous task. She acknowledges the assistance of Mr. Joseph Hall, M.A., in collating the proofs with the text of the original manuscript and in giving other help. For this the thanks of the Society are due, as they are also to Miss Ethel Elliott for her help with the index to the volume.

The second volume of Mr. CROFTON's *History of the Ancient Chapel of Stretford* contains much hitherto unpublished material, namely, a survey of the Churchwardens' Accounts during the eighteenth century; an account of the Manorial and other like early records relating to Stretford, with full details of the proceedings of the Court Baron from 1700 to 1733, and 1782 to 1872; lists of Trafford Tenancies for 1782; and Vestry Minutes and Poor Law Records of the Nineteenth Century. The volume is furnished with a remarkably full index and glossary, and with a dozen maps of the Trafford estates in the Stretford township in 1782. The illustrations, like those in the first volume, are provided at the expense of the editor.

The first volume of the *Salford Portmote Records* contains the proceedings of that Court from 1597 to 1632, and is a valuable supplement to the Manchester Court Leet Records, to which it bears many resemblances. The genealogical and topographical information which it embodies will be welcomed by local antiquaries. The value of the records as throwing light upon the government of the town in the seventeenth century is well brought out by Alderman Mandley in his interesting preface.

The volume of *Chetham Miscellanies* contains (1) The Inventories of Church Goods in the Amounderness and Lonsdale Hundreds in the year 1552, edited by Colonel FISHWICK, and completing the Inventories for the other Hundreds of Lancashire, edited by the late Mr. J. E. BAILEY, and printed in the first series of the Society's publications. (2) A reprint of George Walker's rare pamphlet, published about 1641, on behalf of preaching lecturers in Lancashire. It is a useful representation of the spiritual needs of the county of the days of Charles I. The editor, Mr. C. W. SUTTON, has added some biographical and bibliographical information about Walker, who was born at Hawkshead in 1582, and suffered imprisonment for his puritanical teachings. (3) Reprints of several exceedingly scarce tracts, originally published in 1679, relating to

Charles Bennett, the so-called "Wonderful Child," of Manchester. These have been edited by Mr. WILLIAM E. A. AXON. (4) Memoranda concerning the estates and tenants of the Mosley family in Manchester and neighbourhood in the seventeenth century. Mr. ERNEST AXON, the editor, has prefixed to these family jottings an elaborate genealogy of the Mosleys of Manchester and Hough, of Ancoats, Rolleston and Collyhurst, and of Garrett and York.

With regard to the works in progress it may be reported that the *Life of Humphrey Chetham* is in the press and will be issued during the present year. The same may be said of the second and concluding volume of the *Salford Portmote Records.* The third and final volume of Mr. CROFTON'S *History of Stretford Chapel* is also in the press. Mr. FARRER has begun work on the third volume of his *Cockersand Chartulary* which will be ready next year. It will be in two parts, as was the case with the previous volumes. Mr. C. T. BOOTHMAN hopes to finish his *Account Book of Sir Nicholas Shireburn* sometime next year.

Another volume of *Chetham Miscellanies* will probably include a life of Ambrose Barlow, O.S.B., from an unpublished manuscript, edited by Mr. W. E. RHODES, M.A.; a Series of Latin poems composed and recited by Scholars of the Manchester Grammar School in 1640, and some pieces by John Byrom, which have been found since the collected edition of his poems was issued. The two last contributions will be edited by the PRESIDENT.

The Council has under consideration the printing of the lists of "Protestors" of 1641–2, complete transcripts of which were obtained from the original returns in the House of Lords by the late Mr J. E. Bailey, who published the Manchester and Salford names in the *Palatine Note Book.* These returns are perhaps the most complete of the early lists of the inhabitants of the county that could be found, and, as Mr. Bailey remarked, "form an excellent basis for the calculation of the population and for the study of nomenclature, while they are invaluable for historic and genealogical purposes."

Among other suggested works which have not yet been decided upon, are a new edition of the early documents relating to Manchester, which were edited many years ago by the late Mr. John Harland, and a new edition of Hollinworth's *Mancuniensis.* It is hoped, also, that some Cheshire documents may be put in hand before long.

During the past year the Society has lost five members by death, namely, Mr. J. Ridgway Bridson, of Bridge House, Bolton; Mr. William Law of Littleborough; Mr. George H. Swindells of Heaton Moor; Mr. G. H. L. Tootell of Preston; and Mr. J. Holme Nicholson, M.A., of Wilmslow. The last named member acted for many years as one of the Society's auditors.

The projected works include the following:—

Life of Humphrey Chetham. By CHARLES W. SUTTON, Esq.

Materials for the History of the Church of Lancaster. Part III. By W. O. ROPER, Esq., F.S.A.

Account Book of Sir Nicholas Shireburn. By C. T. BOOTHMAN, Esq.

History of the Chapelry of Newton.

History of the Parish of Lytham. By HENRY FISHWICK, Esq., F.S.A.

Chetham Society Miscellanies, New Series, Vol. II.

Dr. *The Treasurer in Account with the Chetham Society for the year ending February 28th, 1902.* **Cr.**

	£	s.	d.	£	s.	d.
By 174 Subscriptions for current year	174	0	0			
,, 16 do. Arrears collected	16	0	0			
,, 22 do. paid in advance........	22	0	0			
				212	0	0
,, Books sold to Members				4	5	0
,, Dividends on £200 Lancashire and Yorkshire Railway 3°/o Preference Stock.....				5	13	3
,, Bank interest				5	7	7
				227	5	10
Balance from March 1st, 1901				319	17	1
				£547	2	11

				£	s.	d.	£	s.	d.
To C. Simms & Co. :—									
Vol. 44, Act Book of Whalley...........				136	19	5			
Vol. 45, History of Stretford Chapel Vol. II..........................				119	18	1			
				256	17	6			
Reported at last meeting	138	2	6						
Less now appropriated...	45	0	0	45	0	0			
							211	17	6
Total advanced for printing in progress	£ 93	2	6						
Sundry printing							6	15	7
,, Honorary Secretary—Postage, &c........................							2	19	0
,, Treasurer—Postage, &c.							2	6	3
,, Sutton & Co., Carriage of Vols. 43 & 44							6	8	0
,, Guardian Fire Assurance Co.								10	0
,, Lancashire & Yorkshire Railway, registering Mr. Christie's death							0	5	0
,, Bank charges.....							0	17	5
							231	18	9
Balance, 28th February, 1902							315	4	2
							£547	2	11

Audited and found correct, February 23rd, 1903,

JOSEPH THOMPSON, } Auditors.
T. R. WILKINSON, }

J. JOSEPH JORDAN, Treasurer.

UNIVERSITY OF FLORIDA
3 1262 07830 161 0

Milton Keynes UK
Ingram Content Group UK Ltd.
UKHW021128231023
431175UK00007B/652